Completely Perfect

By the same author

Perfect
Perfect Host
Perfect Too
The A–Z of Eating

Completely Perfect

120 Essential Recipes for Every Cook

Felicity Cloake

PENGUIN BOOKS

PENGUIN BOOKS

UK I USA I Canada I Ireland I Australia
India I New Zealand I South Africa

Penguin Books is part of the Penguin Random House group of companies
whose addresses can be found at global.penguinrandomhouse.com.

Text in this edition first appeared in *Perfect*, published in
Fig Tree 2011 and *Perfect Too*, published in Fig Tree 2014
This updated selection published in Penguin Books 2018

001

Copyright © Felicity Cloake, 2011, 2014, 2018

The moral right of the author has been asserted

Set in 12.5/14.75 pt Mrs Eaves
Typeset by Jouve (UK), Milton Keynes
Printed and bound in Great Britain by Clays Ltd, Elcograf S.p.A.

A CIP catalogue record for this book is available from the British Library

ISBN: 978-0-241-36787-2

www.greenpenguin.co.uk

For Suse, without whom none of this would have happened

Contents

Introduction

*P*erfect is a bold claim for anything, let alone something as personal as food – taste is gloriously individual, and frankly, all the more wonderful for it. To call a recipe perfect, let alone eight years' and two books' worth of them, feels like the height of hubris; unless the raw ingredients happen to be the collected wisdom of the world's finest cooks.

Let me take you back to the chilly winter of 2010, when I began writing a new column for the *Guardian* website, pitting Delia Smith and Gordon Ramsay against Heston Blumenthal and his mentor Harold McGee on the best way to prep mushrooms, trying out Michelin-star mash and making cheap jokes about pricks with forks during a hard-hitting investigation into sausage cookery. It soon became clear that mining the experts for tips was fertile ground: who better to tell you how to make chilli con carne than the good folks of the International Chili Society, or to deliver a primer on tarte au citron than the Roux brothers themselves?

Though, after almost a decade of cooking up dozens of recipes every month, I'd class myself as a fairly competent home cook, the perfection within these pages has very little to do with me; it comes from the hundreds of chefs, cooks, food writers and helpful *Guardian* readers who have contributed to the feast that follows. These are the 'perfect recipes' that I've found the most useful over the years – the Saturday lunch soups and Sunday night dals, the roast chickens shared with friends and the chocolate cakes baked in celebration (and even scaled up for a couple of weddings too).

The premise of the column is to test out as many different versions of a particular dish as possible, in order to establish, once and for all, what really works. It's surprising how often seemingly trustworthy sources disagree over the vital details — whether to blind bake pastry, or put cream in carbonara — which can be confusing, and often downright enraging when all you want is dinner. You may not have time to try out six different ways of making meatballs, or meringues, but I do, and believe me, after eight years, I'm pretty damn critical.

Thankfully, after making a particular dish six or seven times, you get a good idea of where the potential for disaster lies, so I can promise you that every recipe in these pages works: I'd stake my best knife on them. Where something seems like more a matter of personal preference than culinary life and death — which vegetables to put in a minestrone, or whether cheese has any place in a gratin dauphinoise, for example — I've tried to flag this up so you can make your own choice according to taste.

These dishes aren't cutting-edge food (you'll search in vain for spherified kimchi juice or daikon dust) but they deliver. Few things in life are more certain than the fact that, when sous vide machines have gone the way of the melon baller, and spiralizers are two for a quid at car boot sales, we'll all still be enjoying crumble and custard.

A FEW TIPS

I have to admit, without wanting to do myself out of a single ounce of respect, that there's no great magic to cookery: as long as you've got that rare thing, a reliable recipe, and follow it fairly faithfully (a little more or less oil, or a generous hand with the chilli, is unlikely to kill a dish), very little can go wrong.

You can, however, make life easier for yourself in the kitchen: those happy souls who seem to find it all a breeze are usually just organized.

1. Check you've got all the ingredients, and equipment, before starting. I cannot stress this enough – thinking vaguely that you've seen some ground almonds in the cupboard somewhere is not good enough if you're considering embarking upon macarons. (That said, confident cooks can usually find a decent substitute for most things; it's all a matter of practice.)

2. Read the recipe carefully all the way through before starting, too: just in case, while the stew's simmering on the hob, you should be making dumplings, rather than reading the paper.

3. Get all the ingredients out, measured in the correct quantities if possible, and put them close by where you'll be working. The art of mise en place, or 'putting in place', before embarking on a recipe, is practised in professional kitchens for good reason; it's all too easy for the garlic to burn while you're ferreting around for the bay leaves or tinned tomatoes.

4. Taste early and often (where practical), and always, always before serving something up (unless it's a cake or a tart where a sneaky sliver is going to be obvious). Remember that seasoning can alter during the cooking process, so what tastes right when you add it might seem bland on the plate. Keep a load of teaspoons handy by the hob for this purpose. (Or use your fingers, it's what they do in many professional kitchens. Sorry.)

5. Most disasters can be salvaged by a bit of lateral thinking. With sweet dishes, as long as it's cooked, there's very little that can't be turned into a delicious dessert by mixing it with ice cream or crème fraîche. Savoury — well, a generous sprinkle of herbs or grated Parmesan, or a jaunty fried egg garnish will hide a multitude of sins. And if all else fails, check out the quick fixes on page xxvi.

LAYOUT AND EQUIPMENT

You really need very little to be a decent cook: an oven or a hob (although some people swear by microwaves for melting butter, steaming vegetables and so on, they're really not essential; I don't own one), and a few basics, so it's better to spend money on good-quality items like knives, pans, et cetera, rather than buying a lot of stuff you'll use once in a blue moon.

Think practically: I'm not one of those food writers who gets sniffy about garlic presses (I use mine regularly), but if you've got a knife, you don't need one. The same, strictly speaking, goes for a colander: a large sieve will do the job just as well.

Always go for sturdy-looking cookware, the duller the better, rather than flashy celebrity-chef endorsed ranges — professional catering suppliers are an excellent place to start, because their stuff is designed to work, and work hard, rather than looking pretty on a shelf. Rarely cheap, it is usually good value.

If you're building up a kitchen from scratch (lucky you!), here are the basics that'll come in useful; you can acquire everything else as you go along.

- BASIC Heavy-duty chef's knife and sharpener: sharp knives will not only make your life easier, but are actually safer because they're less likely to slip into your tender flesh

  Also Useful Smaller paring knife, kitchen scissors, bread knife, cleaver (a recent discovery on my part, but already indispensable for stuff like pumpkins and squashes, as well as for jointing meat), knife roll or block (keeping them in drawers is both dangerous and counterproductive, because they'll blunt)

- BASIC Wooden chopping board (kinder on knives), and scourer to clean

  Also Useful More chopping boards, so you can keep onions away from strawberries. A couple of smart ones (i.e. not pock-marked by use, or charred by carelessness) are handy for serving stuff like cheese and bread on

- BASIC Silicone spatula: a great multi-tasker, will stir, flip and scrape out the pan or bowl

  Also Useful Wooden spoon, fish slice, tongs (my favourite), slotted spoon, ladle, palette knife, metal skewer for testing doneness

- BASIC Grater (preferably a super-sharp Microplane or similar box grater with multiple sides for zesting citrus, finely grating Parmesan, etc.), vegetable peeler

Also Useful Mandoline for thinly slicing vegetables for dauphinoise, salads and the like, apple corer

- BASIC Balloon whisk

Also Useful Hand-held electric beaters, stand mixer, pan whisk

- BASIC Pestle and mortar and potato masher

Also Useful Stick blender, food processor

- BASIC Large, heavy-based frying pan, with lid

Also Useful Griddle pan, omelette pan (small frying pan), wok

- BASIC Heavy-based small, medium and large saucepans, with lids

Also Useful Stockpot for cooking stocks, jams, and stuff in quantity

- BASIC Ovenproof casserole dish, roasting tin

Also Useful Cast-iron dishes to go from hob to oven, baking dishes smart enough to go straight on to the table (Falcon Enamelware is sturdy and good value for money)

- BASIC Baking tray

Also Useful Grill pan, cake tins (a 23cm round springform tin, plus two 20cm sandwich tins, would be a good start), muffin and fairy cake tins, tart tin, loaf tin, cooling rack

- BASIC Scales, preferably electronic, measuring jug, reliable timer (your phone will do)

  Also Useful Measuring spoons, food thermometer, oven thermometer, ruler

- BASIC Fine sieve

  Also Useful Colander, coarse sieve, steamer

- BASIC Large mixing bowl (Pyrex, stainless steel or ceramic rather than plastic, which tends to scratch), smaller heatproof bowl to fit over a saucepan and act as a bain-marie

  Also Useful More bowls of various sizes! One is never enough

- BASIC Tin opener, corkscrew, pastry brush, greaseproof paper

  Also Useful Baking beans (you can use dry rice or pulses otherwise), rolling pin (a clean, empty wine bottle is an acceptable substitute at a pinch), biscuit cutters, clingfilm and foil, freezer bags

- BASIC Dark-coloured apron (unless you want to wash it every day), kitchen roll for blotting fried food and mopping up spills, thick tea towels to do everything from drying your hands to getting hot things out of the oven (hang a clean one from your apron when you start cooking, so it's always handy)

  Also Useful Sturdy oven gloves and more tea towels (like the bowls, they're endlessly useful)

A word on non-stick

For some people, non-stick technology is the enemy: although it's
safe when used properly, if over-heated, that magic coating emits
what Bee Wilson describes in her fascinating history of culinary
technology, *Consider the Fork*, as 'several gaseous by-products', which
can be harmful if ingested. Also, because food doesn't stick if your
pan is working efficiently, you miss out on the lovely little crusty
brown bits which make things like fry-ups so tasty.

You can achieve a non-stick effect without chemicals by seasoning a
cast-iron pan, but it takes dedication: wash the pan in hot soapy
water, then rub it with fat or oil, and heat it very gently for several
hours. Eventually it will develop a coating as slick as the newest
Teflon number, which every meal cooked in it thereafter will add to.
Don't scour it, and avoid anything too acidic, and you won't even
need to re-season it as often as you ought to replace a non-stick pan.

That said, I still own non-stick cookware too. It's
useful for scrambled eggs and the like, and I'm a
short-termist.

GETTING THE MOST FROM YOUR OVEN

Beyond occasionally sweeping out the crumbs from the bottom,
most of us pay very little attention to this workhorse of the kitchen,
but a little meditation on how limited cooks were before the advent
of the domestic oven should set you straight. Anyone can turn an
oven on, but to get the best from yours, you need to get to know it.

For a start, is it conventional or fan-assisted? In other words, does it have a great big fan in it? My oven does, but if yours doesn't, then you should use the higher temperatures indicated in the recipes that follow (though, to be honest, after a spell in a professional kitchen recently, I realized that unless you're baking, the oven temperature makes surprisingly little difference, save for time: when food looks done and feels done, it generally is).

Unless you want to spend your evening staring through the glass to check whether your cake is cooked, however, invest in an oven thermometer: many ovens run either hotter or colder than their temperature gauge suggests, so this will help you adjust the timing accordingly. Make sure too that you can actually see into the oven: opening the door unnecessarily will cool it down so the food takes longer to cook. If you have to peep in, do so quickly.

As even the most basic qualifications in science should have informed you, heat rises, so it makes sense that the higher you place food in the oven, the quicker it will cook. Most food cooks best in the middle, but if, for example, you're preparing a roast, it's better to put potatoes above the joint so they brown, while the meat cooks more gently beneath. Decide how to arrange the shelves before you switch the oven on: fiddling around with hot metal is the kind of fraught activity you don't need when you're trying to enjoy yourself in the kitchen.

Most ovens have a grill as well – I prefer a griddle pan, but if you do use it, remember that grilling has a tendency to dry food out. Baste it well with oil before cooking (and don't put it too close to the element: grill fires are scary).

Again, not appliances that really require an instruction manual, but still, ones that can benefit from a few pointers.

Don't overfill your fridge if possible: it interferes with the ventilation, so it won't work efficiently – and cool things to room temperature before chilling to avoid bringing the temperature up inside.

Conduct regular audits to remind yourself what needs using up and ensure nothing's mouldering at the back, and wipe the whole thing out with hot soapy water once every couple of months. (Ensuring that you cover everything well should help keep it clean in the interim, as well as preventing that Thai shrimp paste from tainting the gooseberry fool.)

The door will be slightly warmer than other parts, so if you're chilling wine fast, put it in the main body of the fridge. Ditto the salad drawers, which have a lower humidity, and so are also ideal for storing hard cheese if it's too warm to leave it out somewhere dry and cool, like a garage.

Always get meat out of the fridge a good half hour or so before you want to use it, to take the fridge chill off it so it cooks more evenly – the same goes for things like cheeses and many dairy products, whose flavour comes alive as they warm up.

If you've got anything more than a tiny freezer drawer, make the most of it: as well as storing stuff like frozen peas (double bagged, to prevent escapees), you can use it to thriftily squirrel away breadcrumbs from that old loaf that's too stale to eat, excess stock, leftover portions of lasagne, emergency rations like prawns, berries, mince and so on, ready for a rainy day when you can't face a trip to the shops. (NB: Never refreeze something that's already been frozen and defrosted.)

Wrap food well (if you can run to it, a vacuum-packing machine, available online, is an amazing boon for this) so it doesn't dry out, and label it clearly with a description of what's inside and the date, so you can eat up older things first. I find it useful to divide stuff like packs of bacon or loaves of bread up – that way you can just defrost what you need for breakfast.

Lastly, defrost raw food in the fridge, on a plate, overnight; pre-cooked food can be reheated from frozen if necessary, though I think you often get better results if you have time to defrost that first too.

FOODS YOU NEED

These are the ingredients you'll find it prudent to keep close to hand – not only because you'll probably find yourself reaching for them a lot, but because, with them in the house, you're never far away from a decent meal. Try to build up as well stocked a larder as possible, so you're good for a pretty long bout of flu, a flurry of unexpected guests or, indeed, an unexpected siege.

Storage-wise, remember to keep everything clearly labelled; buying spices in big bags from the 'foreign foods' section of the supermarket, or the appropriate grocers, has its benefits in terms of price, but it's easy to decant them into jars and then forget what they are, and ditto, tubs of different flours have the tendency to look pretty similar. (From bitter experience I'd advise storing anything that might be vulnerable to rodent attack in sturdy containers — you'd be surprised at the eclectic tastes of the common house mouse.)

On the subject of spices, deep drawers are ideal, so you can see at a glance what you've got, but in the absence of such luxuries, I keep mine in boxes, vaguely ordered by sweet, Oriental, etc.: so much easier to slide these off the shelf than it is to ferret around in a forest of jars in a dark cupboard. (If you're the kind of person who alphabetizes their record collection or library, then spices are another worthy candidate; I've tried, but I'm inherently too messy to sustain the order for more than a few weeks.)

Indeed, if your kitchen layout allows it, organize all your ingredients into broad categories: baking stuff in one cupboard, condiments in another, basics (oil, salt, pepper, garlic, etc.) within easy reach of the hob and so on. Eliminating time wasted searching for risotto rice or soy sauce will speed up the cooking process considerably.

Pantry

- *Plain flour, cornflour, baking powder, bicarbonate of soda, dried yeast, vanilla essence*

- *Caster sugar, soft brown sugar, golden syrup, honey*

- *Cocoa powder and plain chocolate*

- *English mustard powder, Dijon and wholegrain mustards, horseradish sauce*

- Red and white wine vinegar, cider vinegar, rice vinegar, balsamic vinegar
- Decent chicken, vegetable and beef stocks (liquid concentrates and organic stock cubes are more to my taste than those oversalted jelly pots)
- Soy sauce, Thai fish sauce, Tabasco, chilli oil
- Olive oil, extra virgin olive oil and a neutral oil such as vegetable or groundnut
- Anchovies, capers, olives, Marmite, Worcestershire sauce
- Tomato purée, good-quality tinned tomatoes, tomato ketchup
- Black pepper, sea salt (both fine and flaked), chilli flakes, bay leaves
- Basmati, risotto and pudding rice
- Long and shaped pasta
- Couscous, rice or egg noodles
- Dried or tinned chickpeas, lentils and split peas
- Dried fruit — raisins, currants, mixed peel, fancy jar of fruit in alcohol or syrup for emergencies
- Nuts — flaked almonds, pine nuts, peanut butter
- Breadcrumbs, preferably panko
- Pickle and chutney, to taste

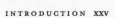

- Onions, garlic, potatoes
- Eggs

Freezer

- Peas and whole leaf spinach
- Berries
- Puff and shortcrust pastry
- Vanilla or plain ice cream

Fridge

- Parmesan cheese (or vegetarian alternative)
- Butter
- Milk

HELP!

SOS!

My melting chocolate has become a thick, grainy mass!
Chocolate 'seizes' when it comes into contact with water (steam from the bain-marie is usually the culprit). Strangely, however, adding liquid in larger amounts, such as hot cream or hot water, should rescue the situation, leaving you with a tasty chocolate sauce if nothing else.

My pastry won't roll out!
If your pastry is sticky and hard to roll, it may well be too warm, or too wet. Wrap it in clingfilm and chill for 20 minutes, then try again on a floured surface. If it seems dry and cracked when rolled out after chilling, then it may well be too cold. Gather it together into a ball and knead to warm it up slightly.

My cream won't whip!
Place the mixing bowl, cream and whisk in the fridge for 15 minutes to chill — it's easier to whip cold.

My egg whites won't form stiff peaks!
I hate to be the bearer of bad news, but either there's some yolk in there, or your bowl or whisk were dirty. In either case, unfortunately you'll have to start again with thoroughly scrubbed and dried equipment and meticulously separated eggs.

My mayonnaise has curdled!
Pour it into a food processor, or use a hand mixer to whiz it and see if it comes back together. If that doesn't work, start afresh with a new egg yolk mixed with 1 tablespoon of water, and very gradually whisk the broken mayonnaise into it.

My flour-thickened gravy/sauce is lumpy!
If it's already thick enough to use, simply strain it through a fine sieve. If not, mix 1 teaspoon of warm butter with 2 teaspoons of flour, then beat this into the hot sauce. Simmer for a couple of minutes until thickened, then strain before serving.

My gravy is bitter!
Sounds like those lovely browned bits on the bottom of the roasting

tin may in fact have been burnt. You can try to rescue the situation by stirring in something sweet, like port, or redcurrant jelly, or brown sugar, but you may still have to throw it away and reach for the Bisto.

My sauce is too salty!
People suggest adding potatoes or rice to soak up the salt, but in fact, the best thing to do is to dilute the sauce with water, wine, cream or any other non-salted liquid (stock is usually not a good idea) and then thicken it again with a roux or cornflour.

Dinner gone wrong?

Don't panic if things don't quite go to plan: a carefully stocked pantry has always got your back. To whip up a quick spaghetti aglio e olio, cook 100g of spaghetti per person in well-salted water until al dente, and meanwhile fry a finely chopped clove of garlic and a generous pinch of chilli flakes per person in 4 tablespoons of olive oil. Toss the drained pasta in the oil with a little of its cooking water, scatter with some chopped parsley if you happen to have it, and ta-da, dinner. Also nice with other pantry stalwarts like olives, anchovies, breadcrumbs, lemon zest, capers, sun-dried tomatoes, Parmesan and so on.

For pudding, keep good ice cream in the freezer, and a jar of fruit in booze on the shelf. They last for ages, and the two just need a scattering of chopped nuts to turn them into a sundae. And everyone loves sundaes.

Breakfast

*L*et's face it, most breakfasts in life will be nothing to write home about — a quick bowl of muesli, an apple on the train, a sad little yoghurt at our desk — if it really is the most important meal of the day, then frankly we're in trouble.

All the more reason, then, to make the most of the ones you can do justice to: the leisurely weekend brunches, the holiday feasts — the day you're snowed in and 'working from home'. Make a pot of tea, rather than the usual tannic mug, stick the radio on, and indulge yourself with a steaming bowl of creamy porridge, a stack of pancakes, or one too many blueberry muffins.

Indeed, such a breakfast is eminently achievable before work, and well worth getting up ten minutes earlier for; after all, even so-called instant oats actually take 3 minutes to cook, plus 5 wiping them off the inside of the microwave.

A canny cook always thinks ahead: if you devote a Sunday to making your own marmalade, then you'll always have the ingredients of a good day in the cupboard, ready for those mornings that need a little extra help. Happy is the man who gets up to find a stash of homemade granola in the cupboard.

Lastly, any breakfast is made better by freshly squeezed orange juice (of the kind you squeeze out of oranges yourself, rather than the stuff from Florida sold in bottles under that name), good tea or coffee, and a newspaper. Conversation, however, is entirely optional.

Perfect
Boiled Eggs

*B*oiled eggs aren't just for plonking under sweetly knitted cosies and serving with soldiers – though, paired with the brown bread on page 305, they're hard to beat. They're also the ultimate neatly packaged picnic food, and, soft-boiled and broken over a pile of steamed asparagus or sprouting broccoli spears, they elevate simplicity to an art form.

You'd think the clue to cooking them was in the name, but think again. Canadian foodie Susan Sampson claims, in her otherwise very useful book *12,167 Kitchen and Cooking Secrets*, that boiling is the worst thing you can do to an egg – instead, after bringing the water to the barest simmer, she likes to steep them off the heat. After peeling three hard-boiled eggs in succession that quickly reveal themselves to be all but raw, I crossly conclude that Susan must have kept one particular secret to herself.

She's right about not boiling them, though; Rose Prince, food writer and author of *The New English Kitchen*, starts her hard-boiled eggs off in cold water, on the basis that prolonged exposure to heat makes the whites rubbery, and after experimenting, I'm inclined to agree – soft-boiled seem to be fine dropped gently straight into a pan of boiling water (use a slotted spoon to avoid cracking them), but leave them in there too long and the whites become distinctly tough. Len Deighton, author of a wildly successful series of 'cookstrip' cartoons, as well as *The Ipcress File* and much other espionage literature, helpfully points out in *French Cooking for Men* that the Gallic word *frémir*, or shiver, perfectly describes the correct way to cook eggs.

Putting eggs into cold rather than hot water also makes them less likely to crack – and it's important not to overcrowd the pan for this reason, so they don't bump into each other during cooking. Once they're done, take the eggs straight out of the pan and run them under cold water for a couple of minutes; this will arrest the cooking process and allow you to peel them more quickly. To begin peeling the shell, rap the wide end sharply on a hard surface – rolling them on the counter may be satisfying, but you're more likely to end up picking splinters of shell out of the white.

Soft-boiled (just firm white, liquid yolk): Lower the eggs into boiling water, turn the heat down, and cook for 4 minutes

Medium-boiled (firm white, half-liquid yolk): Lower the egg into boiling water, then turn the heat down and simmer for 7 minutes

Hard-boiled (firm white, firm, sliceable yolk): Put the egg into cold water and bring to the boil, then turn the heat down and simmer for 7½ minutes

----

How to judge the freshness of an egg
Drop it gently into a bowl of cold water. If it sinks, it's very fresh, if it hovers on one end, then it's older but still edible, and if it floats, chuck it very gently in the bin – it's likely to be rotten. Interestingly, although fresher eggs make more stable meringues, and are easier to poach, as the protein networks that hold them together are stronger, very fresh eggs are a nightmare to peel, so don't use them for hard-boiling.

How to separate eggs
You don't need a special
gadget to separate eggs – in
fact, the best tool is right
in front of you. Break the egg
into your outstretched hand and
allow the white to run through your
fingers, while the yolk stays snugly on
top. If you need to whip up the whites, however, use
the eggshell instead, as your skin will give off grease
that may prevent them forming a proper foam –
toss the yolk from one half shell to the other, while
allowing the white to fall into a bowl below.

Perfect
Fried Eggs

*I*t's the star attraction of one of our most famous national dishes, yet fried eggs are still massacred by the great British caff on a daily basis — as a quick flick through Russell M. Davies' masterwork, *Egg Bacon Chips & Beans* (a survey of British caffs through the medium of his favourite order), indicates. A good fried egg is not as simple as it sounds. The whites must be firm and flavourful, yet still creamy, while the yolk should be just set, ready to spill at the merest caress of a knife. If there are people who savour the brittle lace of an overcooked white, this can only be through long and miserable habit.

Setting the white without spoiling the yolk is a precarious science, however. The notoriously perfectionist French chef Bernard Loiseau, who, haunted by the fear of losing his third Michelin star, took his own life in 2003, solved the problem by cooking them separately, in saucers of butter set in a pan of simmering water, and then sliding the cooked yolk back on to the white to serve. All well and good, monsieur, but it's pretty fiddly, and almost impossible to do in quantity. Also, it is *definitely* cheating.

A friend scornfully suggests I'm making too much of the issue: have I never heard of basting the white with hot fat during cooking? Not only is this process labour-intensive, causing me to burn the toast, but it doesn't really work: however hard I try, I'm still left with a ring of pale jelly around the carefully unsplashed yolk. The online food forum *chowhound.com* (hours of fun) suggests filling the pan with just enough fat to cover the white, but, of course, as well as effectively deep-frying most of the egg, this overcooks the bottom of the yolk.

The solution is much simpler – in this method, adopted from the great Lyonnais chef Fernand Point, the egg is fried, ever so gently, in warm butter. After playing around with timings for a bit, I hit upon the idea of covering it while it cooks, so it simultaneously steams and fries, which, if I say so myself, is pure genius, and absolutely foolproof. Point suggests drizzling the butter over the cooked egg before serving, but he was immensely fat and died before the age of sixty, so you might want to skip that part. The fresher the egg, by the way, the better the white will hold together in the pan.

Serves 1

    1 large free-range egg
    A generous knob of butter
    Salt and pepper

1.   Crack your egg into a saucer, and heat the butter in a heavy-based frying pan over a low heat. Have ready a saucepan lid – ideally one that is slightly too small for the pan, so you can wedge it inside, just above the egg.

2.   When the butter has melted fully, swirl the pan to coat, then slide in the egg; it should not sizzle as it hits the fat. Cover with a lid and leave for 2½ minutes, then check on it every 30 seconds – when it's done to your liking, lift it out with a slotted spoon, season gently, and serve.

Perfect
Poached Eggs

*P*oached eggs are the aristocrat of the breakfast table — a subtler pleasure than your workaday fried numbers, more luxurious than a safe soft-boiled egg, they're notoriously temperamental, making them a high-days and holidays treat for many. Crack their secret, however, and you can eat them every morning if you so desire.

Despite experimenting with the heat-and-leave methods favoured by Margaret Costa, the post-war cookery writer who deserves to be just as well known as her contemporary Elizabeth David, and Delia Smith, I reckon you can't make a proper poached egg without a vortex. After cracking numerous eggs into barely simmering water and allowing them to gently steep there until cooked, I remain convinced that a whirlpool is necessary if you're to end up with a well-shaped egg, rather than something that looks like it's come out of the pick and mix. It's the pressure of the water that pushes the egg in on itself; put it into still water and it will spread out as flat as a pancake.

Mark the words of Ramsay protégé Marcus Wareing, who learnt to poach eggs at the feet of the breakfast chef at the Savoy, and whisk your pan of boiling water vigorously, pause for a second, then gently slide the egg into the centre, turn down the heat and leave for 3 minutes. (Breaking it into a small jug or bowl makes this a lot easier — you don't want to be fiddling around with bits of shell at this crucial point in proceedings.) As chef and restaurateur Mark Hix points out, the deeper the vessel, the more teardrop-shaped the result, so use a saucepan rather than a frying pan. In an ideal world you'd only ever be called upon to poach spanking fresh eggs, but in reality, adding a drop of vinegar to the white helps to keep the egg together without imparting the overpoweringly acidic flavour that often results from tipping a capful into the water.

If I'm poaching a few eggs simultaneously, *Telegraph* food writer Rose Prince's clingfilm trick is unbelievably useful: crack the egg into a ramekin lined with lightly greased clingfilm, twist together the ends to seal, then lift the package out (it should resemble a goldfish at the fair) and dunk it into simmering water. The eggs don't have the perfect beauty of those cooked by the method below, but it does make life easier if they aren't absolutely fresh.

Poached eggs are a key ingredient in eggs Benedict (see page 273 for the hollandaise recipe), but they're also delicious on salads, with corned beef hash and smoked fish, and in soupy Japanese ramen dishes.

Serves 1

1 large fresh free-range egg
1 drop of malt or white wine vinegar

1. Half fill a medium saucepan with water and bring to the boil. Meanwhile, crack the egg into a small sieve, set over a bowl, and allow the runniest parts of the white to fall through before tipping into a small jug or bowl and adding a drop of vinegar.

2. Stir the boiling water vigorously with a balloon whisk until you have a whirlpool, then immediately slip the egg into the centre, lowering the jug a couple of centimetres into the water.
3. Turn the heat down low and cook for 3 minutes – use a timer to prevent overcooking.
4. Drain the egg on kitchen paper, and serve immediately. If you're poaching it in advance, drop it straight into a bowl of iced water instead, or it will carry on cooking; to reheat, simply warm the egg through in a pan of gently simmering water.

How to store eggs
Eggs should be stored at a constant temperature – it's not necessary to keep them refrigerated, except in midsummer, but they will keep longer in the cold. Bear in mind that eggshells are extremely porous, and will absorb the smell of anything you keep them near – this is useful if you happen to come into a truffle, but less so if you store them near some fish or strong cheese, so keep them in their box. Eggs should always be stored with the pointy end downwards; this keeps the air pocket at the top, which slows down the ageing process.

Perfect
Scrambled Eggs

*N*othing brings on a bad mood quicker than bad scrambled eggs. Equally, not much beats the lazy, luxurious pleasure of well-cooked ones, but unless you breakfast regularly in smart hotels, they're something best left to slow weekend mornings at home – scrambled eggs can't be hurried, although making them in a bain-marie, in the traditional French fashion, isn't worth the extra washing up, or the forty-five minutes you'll never get back.

Neither can they be bullied – don't whisk the eggs together as the godfather of modern French cookery, the great Escoffier, did before adding them to a hot pan, and don't add cream to the mixture in imitation of  Australian celebrity chef Bill Granger's famous scrambled eggs: overworking eggs makes them tough, and too much dairy masks their rich flavour. Instead, take a leaf out of Gordon Ramsay's book and crack the eggs straight into a cold pan, saving on washing up and making life easier for yourself in the process.

Gordon hasn't quite hit the egg jackpot, though; unless you like to start the day with an eggy purée, I'd avoid his way of furiously stirring them into submission – adopt Bill's more laid-back approach, and you'll end up with large, creamy curds which have a much more interesting texture – and look a damn sight more appetizing too. I don't think Ramsay's right that adding salt during cooking will ruin the texture either; it's essential for flavour. Sprinkle it on at the table, and you'll need a lot more to get the same effect.

The eggs will carry on cooking in their own heat after leaving the pan, so it's important to add some cold fat at the end to arrest this process, or you'll be sitting down to overdone eggs for all your pains. A knob of butter, as suggested by Delia, is good for everyday eggs, but if you're feeling luxurious, a dollop of Gordon's crème fraîche finishes them off perfectly, adding a deliciously subtle tanginess to proceedings — all you need is a slice of toasted sourdough and a few chives for the perfect Saturday morning breakfast.

Scrambled eggs aren't diet food — a poached version, as advocated by one *New York Times* writer, whisked together and decanted into simmering water, may be free from butter, crème fraîche and the like, but rubbery, watery and with a distinct whiff of space food about them, they certainly hide their virtues under a bushel. No, great scrambled eggs require a generous hand with the dairy and single-minded devotion to stirring and watching — leave them alone for a second, and they'll overcook. Get someone else to make the coffee.

Serves 1

2 large free-range eggs
A knob of butter
A pinch of salt
1 teaspoon crème fraîche

1. Break the eggs into a small, heavy-based frying pan or saucepan and add the butter and salt. Place over a medium-high heat, and stir the eggs together with a wooden spoon.
2. Once well combined, leave the eggs for 10 seconds, then stir again. If they're setting too quickly, take them off the heat to stir and then replace. Repeat until they begin to set, then stir continuously until they're nearly as cooked as you like them; always take them off the heat before they're done.
3. Whip the pan off the heat, stir in the crème fraîche, and serve immediately.

Good things to mix into scrambled eggs, from around the world, in no particular order

Britain: Wild garlic; chopped steamed asparagus; ham and spring onions; crumbled black pudding; flaked smoked mackerel or hot smoked salmon; crab and chives; steamed and squeezed spinach with Lancashire cheese

Spain: Cooked and sliced chorizo and green Padrón peppers, anchovies

Italy: Tomato, basil and Parmesan, nduja

Turkey: Onions, peppers, tomatoes and chillies with mint and crumbled feta (*menemen*)

Mexico: Onion, tomato, coriander and green chillies (*huevos a la Mexicana*)

India: Onion, garlic, chillies, fresh ginger, tomato and coriander (*akoori*)

China: Spring onions, soy sauce and prawns

Perfect
Omelettes

*T*here is something magical about a good omelette – the way a couple of eggs and a pinch of salt can, in less than a minute, achieve such greatness. Light yet rich in flavour, swift but satisfying, the omelette is the ultimate frugal supper. As with all very simple things, the omelette has attracted a certain mystique amongst those convinced that there must be more to it than meets the eye. In the titular essay from the collected short works of Elizabeth David, *An Omelette and a Glass of Wine*, the famously ferocious 'awful genius' of post-war food writing, who introduced a whole generation to the joys of continental cookery, tells of a certain Madame Poulard, celebrated throughout France for her omelettes.

The gourmands of France slavered over her light and fluffy creations, and indulged themselves with endless speculation as to her secret – water, foie gras, a special breed of hen, all were held responsible for these works of genius. Finally, David writes, someone saw fit to ask Madame herself for her recipe. 'I break some good eggs in a bowl, I beat them well, I put a good piece of butter in the pan. I throw the eggs into it and I shake it constantly. I am happy, monsieur, if this recipe pleases you.'

Before we start, let's clarify that the omelette of which I speak here is a classical French-style one, a rich cigar of fluffy deliciousness, rather than a dense yellow half-moon oozing cheese and ham. You can guess how to make those yourself, there's not much skill involved. This sort, however, aspires to delicacy, and height – and that's more difficult to achieve.

The classic French culinary encyclopedia *Larousse Gastronomique* adds milk to its recipe, and Darina Allen at Ballymaloe Cookery School suggests a couple of tablespoons of water, both ingredients which make the omelette fluffier, but which, in my opinion, dilute its rich eggy flavour. Really, you just need eggs (at room temperature or they'll take too long to set) and butter – not only does it impart flavour, but, unlike oil, butter helpfully foams when the pan is hot enough to add the eggs (that pan, by the way, should be heavy, and tailored to the size of your omelette – 23cm is ideal for one person. Le Creuset make a perfect cast-iron example which is well worth the investment if you eat them a lot). *Larousse* also helpfully suggests that, for a really spectacular omelette, you should whisk your yolks and whites separately, and fold them together before serving – but although the result is impressive, it lacks the deep flavour of a real omelette. Style over substance.

Purists such as Julia Child insist that stirring your omelette with a spatula will ruin the texture, but she must have had wrists of steel to flip her pan so dextrously – if Michel Roux Jr, Marcus Wareing and Ballymaloe Cookery School all allow it, then it's good enough for me.

For a great omelette, you need three things: good ingredients (and plenty of them, in the case of the butter), the right-sized pan, and fearlessly quick wits. Time is of the essence – it should be on a plate within a minute.

Serves 1

2 large free-range eggs
Salt and pepper
The filling of your choice (optional, but
  Parmesan, Gruyère, tomatoes, fresh herbs,
  shredded ham and smoked fish are all
  favourites of mine)
A generous knob of butter (about a tablespoon)

1. Whisk together the eggs until just mixed, then season. Lay out any fillings you are using by the hob.
2. Heat a 23cm pan over a medium-high flame, add the butter and swirl to coat. When the foam begins to die down, pour in the eggs. They should sizzle.
3. Shake the pan to distribute the eggs evenly, then leave for 20 seconds, until they begin to bubble. Add any filling.
4. Using a spatula or fork, draw in the sides of the eggs to the centre while shaking the pan to redistribute the liquid to the edges. The omelette is done when still slightly runny in the middle.
5. Take off the heat, and fold two edges into the middle. Shake the pan so they roll together, then tilt it and turn your omelette on to a warm plate (you can tidy it up before serving if you like). Season and eat immediately!

TIP

Egg guide

Although hens are the go-to egg producers in this country, they don't have a monopoly on the business. Here, from the smallest to the most mighty, are the different kinds you might come across:

Quail's eggs: Laid by the most diminutive of game birds, these prettily speckled eggs are about the size of a large stuffed olive, and have a higher proportion of yolk to white than a hen's egg. You can fry them and use them as a rather comical-looking garnish, but I like to soft boil them and serve with celery salt as a nibble. Simmer for 3 minutes, cool in iced water, then peel — or better still, get people to peel their own; they can be fiddly little things.

Gull's eggs: These have a very short season from mid-April to mid-May and, as they must be collected from wild birds, tend to be expensive — you're more likely to find them on a restaurant menu than at the supermarket. They have a rich, slightly minerally flavour, and can be treated in much the same way as a quail's egg.

Duck eggs: Slightly larger than hen's eggs, and higher in fat, they have a rich creamy flavour, and produce fluffier results when used in baking. Lovely soft-boiled too.

Goose eggs: Twice as large as a duck egg, these share their rich flavour and dense, translucent whites, which can turn rubbery at high heats. Better scrambled or soft-boiled than fried. Generally only available in spring and summer.

Ostrich eggs: If you come across one of these, bear in mind that it's the equivalent of 24 hen's eggs — and that you will need to boil it for an hour, and cut into the shell with a hacksaw, by which point the novelty will probably have worn off. You can, of course, also pierce a hole in the bottom, empty out the bottom to scramble, and decorate the shell instead.

Perfect
Pancakes

*I*t's such a shame we only make pancakes once a year in this country – they seem to have been a bit of a favourite in the seventeenth and eighteenth centuries, and no wonder; surviving recipes are laden with egg yolks, cream and sweet wine. These days we tend to favour more austere recipes to use up our eggs before the Lenten fast – although Australian food writer Jill Dupleix makes a brave stab at tradition with her rich, rum-soaked numbers. I prefer a plainer pancake, though – all the better to anoint with lemon juice and scatter with crunchy sugar.

While Jill and *Telegraph* writer Xanthe Clay beef up their batter with melted butter, *Good Food* magazine adds a dash of oil to the mix – the butter is nicer, but I think you can achieve the same effect by cooking them in a buttered pan instead. I do take a tip from the two ladies and use an extra yolk, however, which lends the pancakes a depth of flavour without that slight toughness that egg white imparts. Allowing the batter to stand for 30 minutes, as Hugh Fearnley-Whittingstall suggests, gives the starch a chance to soak up water, and helps get rid of any air bubbles, both of which improve their texture.

Although *Good Food* and Hugh Fearnley-Whittingstall counsel cooking the pancakes over a moderate heat, I prefer to follow

Professor Peter Barham, physicist and adviser to Heston Blumenthal, in getting the pan really hot, because I like mine thin and crisp – you can turn it down before cooking if you prefer a softer finish. Spread the batter as thin as possible for delicately lacy edges – and treat the first pancake as an experiment; it usually goes wrong, which is an excellent excuse to treat it as a cook's perk.

These are also good wrapped around a creamy seafood filling, stuffed with spinach and ricotta and gratinated – or slathered with chopped banana and chocolate sauce. Versatile, eh?

Makes about 8

125g plain flour
A pinch of salt
1 large free-range egg,
   plus 1 large egg yolk
225ml whole or semi-skimmed milk
30g butter, softened

1. Sift the flour into a large mixing bowl and add a pinch of salt. Make a well in the centre, and pour the egg and the yolk into it. Mix the milk with 2 tablespoons of cold water and pour a little in with the egg.
2. Use a balloon whisk to whisk the flour into the liquid ingredients, drawing it gradually into the middle until you have a smooth paste the consistency of double cream. Whisk the rest of the milk in until the batter has more of the consistency of single cream. Cover and refrigerate for at least 30 minutes.
3. Heat the butter in a crêpe pan or a 20cm non-stick frying pan

on a medium-high heat — you only need enough fat to just grease the bottom of the pan. It should be hot enough that the batter sizzles when it hits it.

4. Spread a small ladleful of batter across the bottom of the pan, quickly swirling to coat. Tip any excess away. As it begins to set, loosen the edges with a thin spatula or palette knife, and when it begins to colour on the bottom, flip it over with the same instrument and cook for another 30 seconds. (If you're feeling cocky, you can also toss the pancake after loosening it: grasp the handle firmly with both hands, then jerk the pan up and slightly towards you.)

5. Pancakes are best eaten as soon as possible, before they go rubbery, but if you're cooking for a crowd, keep them separate until you're ready to serve by layering them up between pieces of kitchen roll.

Perfect
American Pancakes

Americans may get a few things wrong in the breakfast department
— the sugar-glazed doughnut and bitter black coffee offered gratis at
every motel from San Antonio to Seattle for a start — but give me a
pillowy stack of maple-drenched pancakes, topped with a lattice of
brittle bacon, and I'll forgive them anything. Even Lucky Charms.

Despite eating my first stack at the age of twenty,
pancakes still remind me of my childhood: kids
in the Judy Blume books and Steve Martin films
I devoured over my Weetabix seemed to live on
the things.

Perhaps fortunately, given the quantities they tend to
be served in, American pancakes, unlike our own Shrove Tuesday
fare, chase an ideal of fluffy lightness. This is usually achieved with
baking powder, but I've taken a tip from the television show *America's
Test Kitchen* and added bicarbonate of soda as insurance. This reacts
with the acid in the buttermilk that gives them their tangy flavour,
creating bubbles of carbon dioxide for an extra feather-like result.

When creating this recipe I thought that I'd leave the pancakes
unsweetened, and let the toppings do the talking, but after much
tough testing, I decided to add a little sugar — maple syrup is pretty
pricey stuff over here, so plain pancakes are the surest way to
bankrupt yourself.

I've also allowed myself a bit of melted butter, like Nigella, to give the pancakes extra richness; after all, unlike the happy families of Hollywood, we're not eating these every day. Vanilla extract, as used by the Oklahoma blogger Ree Drummond, aka the Pioneer Woman, was a step too far for my taste though.

I am, however, completely sold on her suggestion to use a mixture of flour and cornmeal: it gives the pancakes a deep golden colour which makes them look hot-diggety wholesome, and, more importantly, a far more interesting flavour and texture – the toasted crust has crunch, while the insides are slightly gritty. (In a good way, I promise.)

One of the most important lessons I took from my research is not to overmix the batter – this will develop the gluten, leaving you with a breakfast of old shoe leather, rather than the melt-in-the-mouth feast you've got up early for. Be lazy about it, and you'll reap a rich reward.

Makes about 10

45g butter
115g plain flour
115g fine cornmeal
¼ teaspoon salt
2 tablespoons caster sugar
1 teaspoon baking powder
½ teaspoon bicarbonate of soda
1 egg
300ml buttermilk
100ml whole milk

1. Turn the oven on low to keep the pancakes warm, and prepare any bacon or other accompaniments. Melt the butter in a pan or microwave, and leave to cool slightly.
2. Put the flour, cornmeal, salt, sugar, baking powder and bicarbonate of soda into a mixing bowl and stir together with a whisk.
3. Put the egg, buttermilk and milk into a smaller bowl and whisk together, then stir in 2 tablespoons of the melted butter. Add this to the dry ingredients and mix briefly until just combined – then stop.
4. Put a heavy-based frying pan on a medium heat and brush the base generously with melted butter. Use a large spoon to dollop circles of batter into the pan (you'll probably need to do this in at least two batches) and cook them until they begin to look dry and bubbly on top; depending on the heat of your pan, this should take about 3 minutes.
5. Turn them over and cook for another couple of minutes, until golden. Put into the oven to keep warm while you cook the remaining pancakes (unless you have customers ready and waiting).
6. Serve, along with any toppings, and devour immediately, while they're still hot.

Some topping ideas
- Streaky bacon and maple syrup
- Banana and honey
- Fresh berries and Greek yoghurt
- Fruit compote and ice cream
- Ricotta, honey and lemon zest
- Melted chocolate and flaked almonds

- Sugar and cinnamon
- Lemon curd and blueberries (add the curd while the pancakes are still hot, so it melts a little)
- Chopped strawberries macerated with sugar and crème de cassis for half an hour, plus a dollop of clotted cream

Perfect
Granola

As a fully paid-up member of the Muesli Fan Club — the plainer and more puritanical the better — it took me a while to see the point of granola: if I'm going to indulge myself with something sugary at breakfast time, it's going to be much more interesting than mere cereal, thank you very much.

The way they're often marketed as health food is particularly irksome; Seb Emina (aka Malcolm Eggs) nails it in his book *The Breakfast Bible*: 'in the popular imagination, granola is to the world of mainstream breakfast cereals what folk music is to throwaway pop . . . it's unprocessed and authentic'. Two words guaranteed to get my goat, yet the concept is a good one. Granola involves the same base of cereals, seeds, nuts and fruit as muesli, but toasted for maximum flavour, and then bound together with something sticky and, yes, sweet.

If you make your own, however, you can add as much or as little sugar as you like — and leave out all those horrible banana chips or dried pineapple chunks that have been the ruin of so many good breakfasts. In the case of this recipe, once you've got the base, the other elements are largely a matter of personal preference, so please, muck about with it. Breakfast is too serious a matter to settle for second best.

Oats are a good start, preferably jumbo rolled oats for texture. I also like to cut them with another grain — rye, barley, spelt, or whatever looks interesting in the health food shop — but you certainly don't need to. Seeds, so beloved of commercial manufacturers for their alleged health-giving properties, also add a pleasant crunch: I like pumpkin, but again, go for whatever you fancy, and the same goes for the nuts – really the only important thing is that you coarsely chop them to give a more even distribution. Coconut shavings (not the desiccated dust) add a toasty sweetness, but they're certainly not mandatory – and if, unlike me, you do like chocolate at breakfast time, add the chips after baking, or you'll end up with a glossy mess.

I've left the amount of fruit to your discretion, as I'm aware I'm positively mean with the stuff: though I'd like to strongly suggest that sour cherries or cranberries work better than sugary raisins or sultanas, and a few chopped apricots or dates are even nicer. But the final word on the base should probably go to Seb Emina: 'Do not fret too much if you are lacking any one component. Haven't got hazelnuts? Use brazils! Short on pumpkin seeds? Top up with flax! Don't know what flax is? Don't worry, it's not that nice.'

What makes this jumble of ingredients more than muesli is the addition of sticky stuff and fat to bind them together into something almost addictively delicious. You could use almost any kind of syrup, from golden to maple, but I like the flavour of honey – plus a beaten egg white to add extra crunch. It may sound strange, but trust me, it works. My preferred fat is coconut oil, for its flavour, but butter, oil or even peanut butter will work too, though you may need to play around with the amount (let's be honest, testing granola is hardly a hardship). I also like to add a hefty pinch of salt, though you may not. You're missing out, but you'll probably live longer. (The decadent may like to add spice instead: cinnamon, vanilla, nutmeg, even cardamom are all possibilities.)

If you heed one piece of advice here though, don't overcook your granola. Let it cool completely before adding the fruit, and then dollop over fruit or yoghurt, drown in cold milk, or simply eat straight from a jar. It may not be muesli, but it's a pretty great substitute.

Makes 1 large jar

40g coconut oil
120ml honey
½–1½ teaspoons flaked salt
170g jumbo rolled oats
170g grain of your choice, e.g. spelt,
    barley or rye flakes (or twice the amount of oats)
200g mixed nuts, roughly chopped (I like almonds,
    pistachios, pecans and macadamias)
50g pumpkin seeds or seeds of your choice
50g coconut shavings (available at health food shops)
1 large egg white
80–100g mixed chopped dried apricots, dates and sour
    cherries (or dried fruit of your choice)

1. Heat the oven to 170°C/fan 150°C/gas 3 and line a baking tray with greaseproof paper. Stir the oil, honey and salt together in a small pan over a gentle heat until well combined, then allow to cool slightly.

2. Mix the dry ingredients, except the fruit, in a large bowl. Stir the honey mixture into the bowl. Beat the egg white in a separate bowl until frothy, then toss with the mixture.

3. Spread out on the baking sheet and bake for 30–35 minutes until golden, stirring occasionally so it cooks evenly, and more regularly if you'd prefer a looser texture.

4. Leave to cool and crisp up on the tray, then stir in the fruit. Store in an airtight container.

Perfect
Porridge

Simple to prepare, high in fibre and protein, and proven to lower cholesterol, porridge is the trendy modern face of the classic British breakfast — it's even (sound the bells!) low GI, which means the oats release their energy slowly, propelling you painlessly towards lunchtime. Or, at least, to the 11 a.m. tea break.

But, though it's simple to prepare, that doesn't mean it's easy — porridge making is an art. Apparently it is possible to produce a decent bowl from the microwave (although I've never managed it), but to even approach the foothills of perfection you need a pan, and a nice low heat. Anna Louise Batchelor, aka 'the porridge lady', and winner of the 2009 Golden Spurtle* award for her spotted dick variation (yes, she takes it seriously), uses a porringer, or bain-marie, to ensure the oats cook super slowly, but, heathen that I am, I haven't found this makes a significant difference to the end result.

What does, however, are the oats themselves. Aficionados sneer at the standard rolled or jumbo oat; indeed, Sybil Kapoor pronounces it 'tasteless and pappy'. For real flavour and texture, you need oatmeal — oats in their less processed, more nutritious form, superior in both flavour and texture. Like Sue Lawrence, the author of a number of books on Scottish food, I use a mixture of nutty, nubbly pinhead oats, and finer oatmeal for optimum texture: go

---

* A spurtle is a traditional Scottish porridge stirrer.

down the all-pinhead route, and you'll still be chewing it on the bus to work.

Dour traditionalists also insist that porridge should contain nothing more than oats, water and salt, but after reading in the *Oxford Companion to Food* that it's a descendant of that 'thoroughly English institution' the medieval pottage, I've decided milk is a permissible decadence. All-milk versions are delicious, but a bit rich first thing, so I've plumped for a combination of milk and water — plus the mandatory milk moat to finish, naturally.

Soaking the oats overnight does help to speed up the cooking time, but not significantly: it's no disaster if it slips your mind. More important is toasting them beforehand, which, as with the cream and raspberry dessert cranachan, gives the dish a glorious nuttiness.

I'll allow the Scots their salt, as it brings out the flavour of the oats, but there's no point adding it too early: though it doesn't seem to do much to toughen the oats as Nigel Slater believes, it is easier to judge the seasoning later in the cooking process.

What you top them with is, of course, up to you: I go for chopped dates and nuts on a weekday, and a good sprinkling of crunchy demerara sugar and some Jersey milk at weekends, but *Guardian* readers recommend golden syrup and a knob of butter, while Gordon Ramsay shows how far he's come from the Lowlands with Greek yoghurt and honey. I've included a few more suggestions under the recipe.

Per person

¼ cup pinhead oatmeal (about 25g)
¼ cup medium oatmeal (about 25g)
½ cup (about 100ml) whole milk
1 cup (about 200ml) cold water
A generous pinch of salt
Demerara sugar, golden syrup, chopped dates, etc.
A little more cold milk, to serve

1. Heat a frying pan over a medium-high heat and dry toast the oats until aromatic. Put into a bowl, cover with water and leave to soak overnight if time permits, draining them before cooking. Otherwise, use immediately as below.
2. Put the drained oats into a medium saucepan with the milk and water and bring gradually to the boil, stirring regularly with the handle of a wooden spoon.
3. Turn down the heat and simmer, stirring frequently, for about 10 minutes, until the porridge achieves the desired consistency. After about 5 minutes, add the salt.
4. Cover the pan and allow the porridge to sit for 5 minutes, then serve with the toppings of your choice and, of course, a moat of cold milk.

A few topping suggestions
The Moorish: chopped dates or dried figs or apricots with roughly chopped pistachios, cashews or flaked almonds and a sprinkle of cinnamon, ginger or nutmeg

The Diet Can Wait: butter or double cream, and golden syrup (as suggested by *Guardian* readers)

The Scot: raspberries and heather honey

The Compote: stewed plums, rhubarb, apple or any other seasonal fruit, with a grating of orange zest

The Berry Ripple: a handful of fresh berries (stir them in for the last 5 minutes of cooking so their vivid juices ripple through the porridge)

The Bircher: grated apple and natural yoghurt

The American: maple syrup and pecans

The Elvis: peanut butter, stirred into the hot porridge, topped with sliced banana (crumbled crispy bacon optional)

The West Country: clotted cream and raspberry or strawberry jam

The Congee: thinly sliced spring onions, soy sauce, soft-boiled egg

The Deep South: grated Cheddar and a knob of butter stirred into the cooking porridge, topped with plenty of black pepper or chopped chives

Perfect
Marmalade

I feel fiercely protective over marmalade, in the same way as I do about hedgehogs and water meadows, and other endangered, quintessentially British things.

There are as many recipes for 'perfect marmalade' as there are jars in your average WI sale. I've tried cooking the oranges whole, then chopping the squidgy poached peel as Jane Grigson suggests in *English Food*, but though the results were good, the whole operation was horribly fiddly. Adding the peel at the end of cooking, however, as in Johnny Acton and Nick Sandler's book *Preserved*, left it annoyingly chewy; the kind of thing you'd still be fishing out of your teeth come lunchtime.

Best, I decided, to follow the wise counsel of Delia Smith, and chop the peel from the raw oranges (so much easier), then boil the pith and pips in a muslin bag, which you can just fish out at the end.

She's right on the subject of pricey preserving sugar too: intended to give you a lovely clear set, it's a waste of money when peel's involved. Unlike Delia, however, I've used a mixture of brown and white sugars: Tamasin Day-Lewis says the refined stuff leaves a 'toxic froth' behind it, but I just think it has a less interesting flavour.

Once you've mastered the basics, it's easy to customize marmalade to your own taste, adding whisky, cardamom seeds, chilli — or even bacon. Personally, however, I prefer it in that other British classic, the bacon sandwich. Give it a try: I promise you won't regret it.

Makes 3 x 1½lb/700g jars

1kg Seville oranges
1 lemon
1 piece of muslin
1kg light muscovado sugar
1kg granulated white sugar

1. Place a sieve over a preserving pan or a very large, non-aluminium saucepan — you should have enough room in the pan to allow the marmalade to bubble vigorously without boiling over. Cut the fruit in half and squeeze the juice into the pan, using the sieve to catch any stray pips and pith.
2. Put the piece of muslin into a bowl and spoon the pips and pith into it. Slice the peel of the oranges to the desired thickness, tearing off any last large pieces of flesh and adding them to the muslin in the process. Put the shredded peel into the pan (any remaining flesh will dissolve during cooking), then tie the muslin up into a tight bag and add that to the pan too. Pour over 2.5 litres of water, bring to the boil, then allow to simmer gently for 2 hours, by which point the peel should be soft.
3. Take out the muslin bag and leave to cool in a bowl. It needs to be cool enough for you to give it a good squeeze, so unless you have heatproof gloves, you can leave the marmalade to sit overnight at this point if it's more convenient. Sterilize your jars

by washing in hot soapy water and cooling in a low oven before you embark on the next step.

4. Bring the marmalade back to a simmer, and vigorously squeeze the muslin bag into it – a satisfying quantity of gloopy juice should ooze out. Stir this in, add the sugars and stir well until dissolved. Put a few saucers into the freezer.

5. Turn the heat up and boil the marmalade rapidly until it reaches setting point – a sugar thermometer is ideal here (start checking when it reaches 104°C), but to confirm this, put 1 teaspoon of the marmalade on to one of your cold saucers and refreeze for a minute or so. If it wrinkles when you run a finger through it, and your finger leaves a clear line in its wake, it's ready. If not, check it at 5-minute intervals.

6. Once it reaches setting point, turn off the heat and allow it to sit for 15 minutes, then spoon into clean jars and seal immediately. Unopened, it should keep well for at least a year.

Perfect
Blueberry Muffins

I have a confession to make: I don't actually like muffins. Or, at least, I don't like 99 per cent of sweet American muffins. Give me a flat, bready English muffin any day, topped with hollandaise and a nice poached egg.

These, however, are different. And not just because I made them myself. They use a creaming method, as suggested by Thomas Keller in his *Bouchon Bakery* book, which gives a better rise than the classic combining method, in which the wet ingredients are simply stirred into the dry.

Keller's strict about beating the butter into submission first, until it's the consistency of mayonnaise, which gives the muffins an even fluffier result – be sure not to overmix the batter once the wet ingredients have been added, because this encourages gluten formation, which will yield a tough muffin. Even worse than a tough cookie.

I've also sided with the wonder-chef on raising agents: he uses both baking powder and bicarbonate of soda, which certainly helps on the lightness front, and his buttermilk adds a tanginess to balance the sugar, while being lighter than the magazine *Cook's Illustrated*'s sour cream, which I find rather cakey.

That sugar should, I think, be demerara: a compromise between the caramel flavour provided by the light brown sugar in *Joy of Cooking*'s recipe, and the crunch supplied by Keller's granulated stuff.

Buy the smallest blueberries you can find (wild bilberries would be even better, if you happen to live near a source and the season's right), and freeze half of them to prevent them bleeding too much juice as they cook.

Tossing the fruit in a little flour before adding them to the mix stops it sinking to the bottom during cooking, and I've also added a few mashed berries to the batter to supply an extra hit of blueberry flavour in every bite.

Unlike most muffin recipes, which urge you to bake them without delay, Bouchon rests his batter for up to 36 hours 'to allow the flour to hydrate'. I don't feel the results, though delicious, warrant such a pause, but at least you know there's no harm in making it the night before: then all you have to do is switch on the oven, dollop them into cases and go and have a shower while your house fills with the scent of blueberry muffins. A prospect even I can embrace.

Makes 9 muffins

75g **frozen blueberries**
75g **fresh blueberries**
240g **plain flour, plus a little extra**
110g **butter, softened**

200g demerara sugar
1 egg, beaten
1 teaspoon baking powder
1 teaspoon bicarbonate of soda
½ teaspoon salt
240ml buttermilk

1. Preheat the oven to 190°C/fan 170°C/gas 5 and line a muffin tin with 9 paper cases. Toss the frozen blueberries with a little flour and put back into the freezer until ready to use. Roughly crush the fresh blueberries with a fork.
2. Beat the butter with a hand or stand mixer until it is very soft – the consistency of mayonnaise. (NB: You may need to warm the bowl in a pan of hot water first if your butter is still quite hard.)
3. Beat the sugar into the soft butter, followed by the beaten egg, and mix until well combined. Stir in the mashed blueberries.
4. Sift together the flour, baking powder, bicarbonate of soda and ½ teaspoon of salt in a new bowl and mix together.
5. Fold half the dry ingredients into the mix, then half the buttermilk, then the remaining flour and buttermilk. Add half the frozen blueberries and mix in until just combined, but be careful not to overwork the batter. (At this point, the batter can be refrigerated for up to 36 hours.)
6. Spoon into the prepared tin and dot the remaining frozen blueberries on top. Bake the muffins for about 25–30 minutes, until well risen and golden.
7. Allow to cool slightly before serving, but these don't keep well, so don't wait too long.

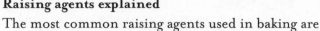

Raising agents explained

The most common raising agents used in baking are yeast, bicarbonate of soda and baking powder.

Yeast, as you probably know, is a living organism that eats sugar and emits carbon dioxide as it reproduces furiously in your dough – those bubbles of gas then expand to give the finished product an airy, fluffy lightness.

Bicarbonate of soda is an alkali that reacts with acids to produce bubbles of carbon dioxide which, again, will make your baking rise. Bicarb is always used in conjunction with something like lemon juice or buttermilk, both acidic liquids that will kickstart the reaction.

Baking powder simply puts the alkali and acid together in one tub; a mixture of bicarbonate of soda and cream of tartar, an acidic by-product of the winemaking process, all it needs to get going is moisture.

Salads, Soups and Snacks

You might be forgiven for dismissing this as the boring chapter — after all, what soup could hope to compete with pulled pork, and which salad or snack stacks up to a syrup sponge? As someone who habitually skims past the 'light bites' section of any menu, I sympathize: few things tempt me less than a badly made salad, all limp leaves and too much dressing, or a generic soup of the 'guess the vegetable' variety. So, naturally, I haven't included any here.

Instead, you'll find the real hard-hitters of the genre: the kind of dishes that you can happily tuck into without worrying you should have got a side of chips too. Which is not to say they're all rib-stickers: alongside the robust Scotch egg and the classic chicken penicillin for the soul there's fruity tomato soup, featherlight cheese soufflés, and the sunny Mediterranean flavours of a proper niçoise salad.

What they all have in common, however, is the simplicity of flavour — if you're making a tomato soup, I think it should taste of tomatoes. It may sound obvious, but there's no need for rich stocks or spoonfuls of spice if the raw ingredients are good enough — and that goes as much for the humble tomato as it does for the anchovies in your Caesar salad.

Rather than trying to confuse the issue, I've always tried to enhance the dish's natural assets — whether that's using chickpea cooking water to give hummus a silky smooth texture, or steering clear of boiled potatoes and tinned tuna to keep the niçoise as sunny and fresh as a Provençal morning, and I must say, I'm pretty pleased with the results. These are soups and salads to stake your appetite on. Delicate souls need not apply.

Perfect
Salade Niçoise

Until I went to Nice, I thought I didn't like salade niçoise – mulchy tinned tuna, floppy green beans and rubbery black olives are hardly the stuff of Mediterranean fantasy. Turns out that, in the Alpes-Maritimes, the ingredients are far more of a lottery, with my personal bête noire, tinned tuna, less popular than the far more handsome little anchovy. As Nigel Slater observes, 'whenever I say "hold the tuna" I am invariably told that I wasn't going to get any anyway'.

I do try Delia's niçoise recipe using the best quality tinned tuna I can find, in the interests of balance, but even the most committed tuna lovers admit that it doesn't have a hope against the stridently salty anchovies – it's just too mild. If you must use it, leave the anchovies out instead. Gary Rhodes uses fresh tuna, which seems very 1990s to me (Simon Hopkinson, less kind, describes it as 'a notion only to be entertained by the permanently bewildered' in *A Good Cook*): a fine, if extravagant choice, but chopping up and tossing it with the salad is a criminal waste.

Potatoes are another British classic pooh-poohed by the French – indeed, the former mayor of Nice, Jacques Médecin, pleads in his cookbook, 'never, never, I beg you, include boiled potato or any other boiled vegetable'. Now he may have been a convicted fraudster, but he has a point: the sunshiney flavour of the other ingredients is spoilt by the potatoes, and even crunchy French beans: juicy, sweet little broad beans are better in season, adding body to the salad without weighing it down. If you can't get them fresh, however, French beans are a better bet. Similarly, spring onions taste fresher than Delia's shallots or David Lebovitz's thinly sliced red onion.

The sweetness of red pepper is welcome with the saltiness of the anchovies, and cucumber adds a refreshing crunch, although deseeding is essential, so it doesn't make the salad too watery, and peeling the tomatoes isn't just a cheffy affectation on the part of Rowley Leigh — it helps them absorb the vinaigrette better.

And it should be a vinaigrette: however good the Provençal olive oil, it demands the balancing kick of vinegar, although not Delia's mustard: you really don't need it if you have salty anchovies (pounded into the dressing too, as Gary Rhodes cleverly suggests) and the inevitable French garlic.

Fresh basil adds the final, very Mediterranean touch to a dish that's worlds away from the petrol station favourite. Give it a try: even if, like me, you don't like salade niçoise, I promise you'll like this.

Serves 2

    2 eggs
    500g broad bean pods or 50g
       French beans
    4 ripe tomatoes
    ¼ of a cucumber
    2 spring onions, finely chopped

½ a red pepper, thinly sliced
50g small black olives, pitted
1 tablespoon capers
4 anchovies, cut into slivers
A few basil leaves, roughly torn

For the dressing
1 small clove of garlic
A pinch of coarse salt
2 anchovies, finely chopped
A small handful of basil leaves, torn
4 tablespoons extra virgin olive oil
½ tablespoon red wine vinegar
Black pepper

1. Put the eggs into a saucepan large enough to hold them in one layer, cover with cold water and bring slowly to the boil. Turn down the heat and simmer for 7½ minutes, then drain and cool in a bowl of iced water.
2. Meanwhile, pod and then peel the broad beans (if using French beans instead, top and tail them, then cook in salted boiling water until just tender and drop immediately into iced water to cool). Drop the tomatoes into a pan of boiling water, leave for 15 seconds, then scoop out, peel, slice and deseed. Peel the cucumber in stripes, then scrape out the seeds from the centre and cut it into half-moons.
3. To make the dressing, pound the garlic to a paste in a pestle and mortar along with a pinch of coarse salt. Add the chopped anchovies and then the basil, and pound it all to a paste, slowly dribbling in the olive oil and the vinegar along the way. Season generously with black pepper.

4. To assemble the salad, toss the beans, tomatoes, cucumber, chopped spring onion and sliced red pepper with two-thirds of the dressing and decant it on to a serving plate. Carefully peel the eggs, cut into quarters and arrange on top of the salad, along with the olives, capers, anchovy strips and remaining basil leaves. Drizzle the rest of the dressing over the salad and serve immediately.

Perfect
Caesar Salad

Not a Roman dish, or even an American one, but a salad created by a Mexican restaurateur struggling to cope with the number of thirsty visitors propelled across the border by Prohibition. The genius of Caesar Cardini's recipe was that it could be prepared at the table by waiters, taking the pressure off the kitchen — Julia Child recalls the sheer theatre of it: 'I remember the turning of the salad in the bowl was very dramatic. And egg in a salad was unheard of at that point.'

Well-documented provenance hasn't protected his creation, however — bacon, grilled chicken, even salmon are all common interlopers in modern Caesar salads, despite his original version containing nothing but leaves, dressing, croutons and cheese.

That's not to say there's no room for improvement: Tamasin Day-Lewis includes the original recipe in her book *All You Can Eat*, and I find it a bit underwhelming — pleasant enough, but hardly likely to cause a stir these days. For a start, though Caesar never thought of adding anchovies, I wouldn't dream of leaving them out: the salty, intensely savoury umami flavour makes the dish for me, although I do confine them to the dressing; having them draped across the lettuce like so many eyebrows is a step too far.

The dressing itself also contains, as Child noted, egg yolk; most recipes, apparently in obedience to the creator himself, lightly cook it, but I can't really see the point. It doesn't help thicken it, and it won't protect you against salmonella if that's what you're worried about – best to leave it out altogether if so.

Whisking the egg with the garlic-infused oil, lemon juice and Worcestershire sauce may lack the theatre of tossing each ingredient into the bowl individually, but it does help the dressing to emulsify so it coats the leaves better, which seems more important to me.

Those leaves don't need to be whole: Day-Lewis reports that the salad was originally finger food, but with this much garlic and anchovy involved, I think a fork is preferable, and Cardini himself apparently came to the same conclusion, if the *Dictionary of American Food and Drink* is to be believed – the recipe evolved to call for bite-sized pieces of lettuce. Tearing gives a more haphazard, rustic look to the dish, especially if you're attempting some 'tableside' drama.

Baked croutons are crunchier, and less greasy than the fried versions – but to be honest, they're not going to turn the dish into a health food. Salty, creamy and crisp, Caesar salad started life as a drinking companion, so please don't stint on the cheese or the oil. Refined it isn't, but by Caesar it's good.

Serves 4

> 2 cloves of garlic
> 150ml olive oil
> 4 thick slices of day-old white sourdough
>   or other robustly textured bread

2 anchovy fillets, rinsed
1 egg yolk
Juice of ½ a lemon
2 cos lettuces, torn into rough pieces
A large handful of finely grated Parmesan

1. Crush the garlic and whisk it into the oil. Leave them to infuse for at least an hour before starting on the rest of the salad.
2. Preheat the oven to 220°C/fan 200°C/gas 7 and cut or tear the bread into rough crouton-sized cubes. Toss these with a little of the garlic-infused oil to coat, then bake for about 15 minutes, until golden and crisp.
3. Mash the anchovies against the bottom of your salad bowl to make a paste, then beat in the egg yolk and, little by little, the rest of the garlic-infused oil until you have a thickish dressing. Add the lemon juice and taste – season if necessary.
4. Put the leaves into the bowl and toss until thoroughly coated with the dressing. Add the grated cheese and toss well again. Top with the croutons and serve.

Perfect
Coleslaw

*I*f you've never tried homemade coleslaw, you probably think it's
made with salad cream. I've given the matter some thought, and
that's the only explanation I can come up with for that oddly sweet,
vinegary flavour that most supermarket versions share – and as for
the aggressive raw onion that some of them sneak in, well, that can
ruin a romantic picnic before either of you have had a chance to
spill cider on the rug.

In fact, mayonnaise should be the base for coleslaw as we
know it – although, as Nigel Slater points out, it can
also be made with vinaigrette, which is particularly nice
in summer. Darina Allen's *Ballymaloe Cookery Course* adds
a dash of yoghurt, presumably for its tangy flavour,
but in practice, a little vinegar is more effective.
Simon Hopkinson and Lindsey Bareham macerate
the shredded vegetables for an hour in salt, sugar and vinegar before
mixing in the mayonnaise, which cuts through the richness of the
eggs perfectly.

Despite slicing it ever so thinly in obedience to Darina's
instructions, I can't get on with raw onion, but I find the chives get
lost in Simon and Lindsey's recipe, so I like to compromise with
spring onion. Horseradish, rather than Dijon mustard, gives a
touch of spice – the Germanic flavour seems more apt here,
somehow.

Serve as a side salad or sneak some into a ham sandwich — trust me, on brown bread, it beats pickle hands down.

Serves 4

2 medium carrots
½ a medium white cabbage
1 teaspoon salt
1 teaspoon caster sugar
1 tablespoon white wine vinegar
5 tablespoons mayonnaise (see page 276)
1 tablespoon creamed horseradish
2 spring onions (optional)

1. Peel the carrots and grate into a large bowl. Quarter the cabbage, cut the hard, woody core out of the centre, then shred finely with a sharp knife and add to the carrots.
2. Sprinkle over the salt, sugar and vinegar, mix well, then tip the vegetables into a colander or sieve and leave to macerate over the sink for about an hour. If you're making your mayonnaise, this is the time to do it.
3. Mix the mayonnaise and the horseradish in the bowl, and taste — add a little more if you prefer it hotter. Finely shred the spring onions, if using.
4. Press down on the vegetables to drain any excess liquid, then tip them back into the bowl and add the spring onions. Toss well until mixed, taste for seasoning and serve immediately: it will keep, but the dressing may begin to separate.

Perfect
Potato Salad

*B*ritish picnic foods tend to be hearty, in obedience to the prevailing climate – potato salad is perhaps the ultimate example, the word salad suggesting a seasonally light dish belied by the realities of starch and mayonnaise. Cold, but warming, it also happens to go very well with other classic picnic fare, like ham, or poached salmon.

The potatoes in this case must be waxy: floury versions crumble when I toss them with the dressing, leaving me with a potatoey mush. Plus, new potatoes are at their best in picnic season, so the more excuse to eat them the better.

Nigel Slater and I agree on the happy rusticity of unpeeled potatoes; it's not laziness, I promise, they add both texture and flavour to the dish. It also means you won't burn your fingers trying to peel them straight out of the pan – introducing the dressing while they're still warm prevents it running off and being lost to the bottom of the bowl.

That dressing should be vinaigrette: Jane Grigson's white wine just isn't acidic enough to cut through the buttery blandness of good new potatoes. Adding a little mustard, as suggested by Simon Hopkinson and Lindsey Bareham in *The Prawn Cocktail Years*, gives it a nice little kick. You could just stop there, as they do, but I'm with Grigson in preferring to finish things off with homemade mayonnaise, which, I think, makes the difference between a good potato salad and a truly great one. (You do also need the vinaigrette though, else the potatoes and mayonnaise remain two separate entities.)

As Constance Spry wisely advises, a decent potato salad 'should be garnished with some sharp ingredient such as capers, sliced gherkin or sliced pickled walnuts to relieve the somewhat cloying taste of potatoes'. Never one to stint, I've thrown in Signe Johansen's spring onions, capers and gherkins from *Scandilicious*, and Simon Hopkinson and Lindsey Bareham's chives, Sarah Raven's anchovies and fresh herbs for freshness, and a good dollop of wholegrain mustard for texture and warmth. And that last is something you might well be needing if it's a proper British picnic.

Serves 4

600g waxy potatoes
½ teaspoon Dijon mustard
1 tablespoon red wine vinegar
A pinch of salt
2 tablespoons vegetable oil
1 tablespoon extra virgin olive oil
115ml good mayonnaise (see page 276)
1 tablespoon wholegrain mustard
2 tablespoons finely chopped gherkins or cornichons
3 spring onions, thinly sliced
2 tablespoons capers, chopped
2 anchovies, finely chopped (optional)
A small bunch of chives, finely chopped
A handful of parsley, finely chopped
A handful of mint, finely chopped

1. Scrub the potatoes clean if necessary, then put them into a pan of well-salted water, bring to the boil and simmer for about 15 minutes, until tender.
2. While they're cooking, whisk together the Dijon mustard and vinegar with a pinch of salt, then slowly whisk in the oils to make a vinaigrette.
3. Drain the potatoes, and when just cool enough to handle, cut into halves, or quarters if large, and toss with the dressing, then leave to cool completely. (You can prepare the salad ahead up to this point.)
4. Stir the remaining ingredients into the mayonnaise, keeping back a little of each of the herbs for garnish. When the potatoes are at room temperature, drain off any remaining vinaigrette and toss them in the mayonnaise to coat. Garnish with herbs and serve.

Perfect
Hummus

*F*or a nation generally suspicious of pulses, Britain has really taken hummus to its bosom. Yet despite its popularity very few people actually make their own, which is a shame, because sour pasty supermarket hummus is a world away from the fresh stuff, which is simplicity itself to knock up.

Although, in extremis, passable hummus can be made from tinned chickpeas, purists frown upon these abominations: all wrong texturally, apparently. I try Claudia Roden's recipe with both tinned and dried, and find the latter indeed give a nuttier, slightly grainier texture which I prefer, although as Anissa Helou admits in *Modern Mezze*, 'you can now buy jars of excellent ready-cooked chickpeas, preserved in water and salt, without added artificial preservatives'. They're expensive, at almost four times the price of the tinned sort, but have a lovely buttery flavour: if you need to cheat, please, do it properly.

Nigella Lawson has bravely spoken out before about the global conspiracy to pretend chickpeas cook far quicker than they do, and it's true: despite lengthy pre-soaking, even the ones from my local 'Mediterranean supermarket', which I suspect has a fairly high turnover of the things, just aren't soft, even after 4 hours of diligent simmering.

You can use a pressure cooker if you have one, but if not, do as Helou and Yotam Ottolenghi recommend and add a little bicarbonate of soda to the soaking water. This stops the calcium in hard tapwater from glueing together the pectin molecules in the pea's cell walls — in fact, the newly alkaline water actually encourages them to separate. Too much can give the hummus an unpleasant soapy flavour, however, so err on the side of caution.

Homemade hummus can run the risk of clagginess; Nigella adds Greek yoghurt to match the 'tender whippedness that you get in restaurant versions' but it doesn't quite taste right to me, and I discover a similar texture can be achieved with chickpea cooking water, as suggested by Paula Wolfert.

Otherwise, I'm sticking to the classic recipe: chickpeas, tahini, lemon juice and garlic — with just a pinch of cumin. It may not be exactly standard in the Middle East, but it's by no means unknown, and it really livens up the end result, though purists may wish to leave it out.

Save any other embellishments for the topping: make it into a meal with minced lamb, caramelized onions and pine nuts, as the *Moro* cookbook does, or a salad with hard-boiled eggs and onion as Ottolenghi likes it, top with a little lemony za'atar — or just stick to a splash of olive oil and a few toasted flatbreads. Sometimes, simple is best.

Serves 4

200g dried chickpeas
1½ teaspoons bicarbonate of soda
6 tablespoons tahini
Juice of 1 lemon, or more to taste
3 cloves of garlic, crushed, or according to taste
A pinch of ground cumin
Salt, to taste
Olive oil, to top
Paprika or za'atar, to top (optional)

1. Put the chickpeas into a large bowl and cover them with twice the volume of cold water. Stir in 1 teaspoon of bicarbonate of soda and leave them to soak for 24 hours.

2. Drain the chickpeas, rinse them well and put into a large pan. Cover them with cold water and add the rest of the bicarb. Bring to the boil, then reduce the heat and simmer gently until they're really tender – they should be easy to mash, and almost falling apart, which will take between 1 and 4 hours depending on your chickpeas. Add more hot water if they seem to be boiling dry at any point.

3. Leave the chickpeas to cool in their cooking water, and then drain well, reserving the cooking liquid, and setting aside a spoonful of chickpeas as a garnish.

4. Beat the tahini with half the lemon juice and half the crushed garlic – it should tighten up – then stir in enough of the cooled cooking liquid to turn it into a loose paste. Put this paste into a food processor along with the chickpeas and whiz until smooth.

5. Add the cumin and a generous pinch of salt to the food

processor, then gradually, with the motor still running, tip in enough cooking water to make a soft paste — it should just hold its shape, but not be at all claggy. Taste, and add more lemon juice, garlic or salt if you think it needs it. Serve at room temperature, rather than fridge-cold, with a drizzle of olive oil and a little paprika or za'atar on top.

Perfect
Garlic Bread

'Anyone who says they don't like garlic bread must be fibbing' – never have I agreed with the authors of retro recipe bible *The Prawn Cocktail Years* more than this.

Garlic bread is the perfect food for the kind of party that's gone beyond the cheese straw and blini stage: where people congregate around the oven like vultures, and burn their tongues in their eagerness to eat the smell – Nigel Slater's ridiculously good Parmesan and garlic baguette was such a fixture at the annual Christmas parties I used to throw with my ex that people would request it on their RSVP. But times they have a-changed, and I'm prepared to move on – can Nigel's bread be bettered?

The answer is, happily, yes it can. Having tried a number of different recipes in my selfless quest for perfection, from Nigel's baguette to Jamie Oliver's pizza, Giorgio Locatelli's focaccia to Nigella's 'hearthbread' (a sort of puffy deep-pan pizza base), I slightly guiltily realize that it's Ina Garten's ciabatta that's stolen my heart. The American Barefoot Contessa's bread stands up to the copious amounts of garlic butter rather better than soft baguette, so the finished loaf is chewier and more satisfying to eat. Sorry, Nigel.

One thing he and I do agree on, however – well, actually, I reckon I'd agree with Nigel about most things in life, truth be told – is the importance of raw garlic. Nigella roasts a whole bulb and then purées it before adding it to the top of her hearthbread, while Locatelli confits it in milk and sugar until it's almost jammy. Even the Contessa drops it into hot olive oil to neutralize the flavour, which seems quite mad – garlic bread should taste of garlic! If you're worried about your breath, then believe me, they're almost certainly not worth it.

For maximum impact, that garlic needs to be incorporated into the butter (and only the richness of butter will do here, I'm afraid – recipes using oil are a greasy disappointment). Sprinkle it on top instead, as Jamie and Nigella do, and it will burn in the hot oven, giving the loaf an acrid flavour.

Nor is cutting the loaf laterally, as Garten suggests, a good idea: the garlic simply soaks downwards, leaving the top half dry and dull. Ciabattas might be flat (the name means 'slipper'), but it is possible to slice them vertically (especially if you take the pursuit of perfection really seriously, and bake your own – Richard Bertinet has an excellent recipe in his book *Crust*).

I can't now countenance garlic bread without Slater's generous helping of salty Parmesan – enough so 'that the cheese forms thin strings as you tear one piece of bread from the next' – but otherwise, I don't like many of the other additions: Garten's oregano in particular is too pungent. One modification I will be adopting, however, is Richard Bertinet's squeeze of lemon juice: a slight hint of citrus tanginess works brilliantly with the garlic and parsley.

Be warned: this bread is almost molten straight out of the oven, so be patient, and you will be rewarded.

1 ciabatta loaf
100g salted butter, at room temperature
4 cloves of garlic, crushed
A small bunch of parsley, finely chopped
40g Parmesan, grated, plus a little extra for topping
A squeeze of lemon juice

1. Preheat the oven to 220°C/fan 200°C/gas 7. Very carefully cut the ciabatta into slices roughly 4cm apart, making sure not to go right through so it holds together at the base, and place the loaf in the middle of a piece of foil large enough to enclose it.

2. Beat together all the other ingredients, apart from the extra Parmesan, until well combined and distributed, then gently force the butter between the slices of bread (this is messy work, but you won't regret it).

3. Sprinkle the top of the loaf with the remaining Parmesan, and seal the foil fairly loosely around it. It will sit quite happily for a few hours at this point.

4. Bake the bread for about 20 minutes, then open the foil and bake for another 5 minutes, until golden on top. Devour as soon as it's cool enough to tear into.

Perfect
Welsh Rarebit

*R*arebits (a corruption of the original rabbit) are generally made
with Cheddar, purely because that's what most of us tend to have
hanging around in the fridge on the kind of lazy Sunday evenings
the dish was made for. Mark Hix keeps things Welsh with Caerphilly
instead, but in fact, according to Simon Hopkinson and Lindsey
Bareham in *The Prawn Cocktail Years*, traditionally a rarebit would have
been made with hard English cheeses, 'Cheddar, double Gloucester,
Cheshire and Lancashire'.

I'm with Nigel Slater: Caerphilly doesn't have enough of a tang for
this particular dish – it just gets lost amongst the
other ingredients. Mature Cheddar is too strong
for my liking though – and I'm not sure what
Delia was thinking recommending intensely salty
Parmesan. Lancashire, however, as suggested by
Jane Grigson, has just enough bite to remain the star
ingredient, without steamrollering everything else in the
process.

Bread-wise, I like a seedy wholemeal for a really savoury flavour, but
I respect your right to use whatever you like, as long as it's robust
enough to stand up to the weight of the topping: toasting it on both
sides, as Hix does, helps with this. (The edges may char slightly
during the final grilling, but as they'll be covered in molten cheese,
you're unlikely to mind too much.)

Most rarebit recipes demand some sort of liquid to loosen the cheesy topping: ale or milk for Jane Grigson, cider for the Cheese Society, port for Mrs Beeton and stout for Hix, Hopkinson and Bareham. I find the cider too acidic, and port turns the cheese a slightly scary colour – the ale's not bad, but the moment I taste the stout versions, I'm sold. It gives the dish a rich maltiness which works fantastically with the salty, tangy cheese – and what's more, there are a number of good Welsh stouts on the market to soften the blow of that English Lancashire.

If the cheese isn't to turn rubbery the minute it's whipped from the grill, you either need a tabletop 'cheese toaster', as recommended by Mrs Beeton, or some other fat in the topping. Too much butter, as used by Nigel Slater and Jane Grigson, makes things greasy, and Mark Hix's double cream is too liquid. Egg yolks are by far the best option, adding richness while softening the cheese to a spreadable consistency.

English mustard (surely enjoyed in Wales too) adds a bit of kick, and Worcestershire sauce is a must for any cheese on toast – you could top it with a sprinkle of cayenne pepper too if you like, but frankly, that's quite enough flavour for me.

Serves 2

    1 teaspoon English mustard powder
    3 tablespoons stout
    30g butter
    Worcestershire sauce, to taste
    175g Lancashire cheese, grated
    2 egg yolks
    2 slices of bread

1. Mix the mustard powder and a dash of stout to a paste in the bottom of a small saucepan. Stir in the remaining stout and add the butter and about 1 teaspoon of Worcestershire sauce to the pan – you can always add more later if required. Heat gently until the butter has melted.

2. Tip in the grated cheese and as it begins to melt, stir to encourage it. Do not let the mixture boil. Once it's all melted, taste for seasoning and adjust if necessary, then take the pan off the heat and allow the cheese to cool until it's only just warm, checking regularly that it hasn't solidified.

3. Preheat the grill to medium-high, and toast the bread on both sides. Beat the egg yolks into the warm cheese mixture until smooth, then spoon this on to the toast and grill until bubbling and golden. Eat immediately.

Perfect
Quiche

*H*urrah for the prohibition on real men eating quiche – all the more for the rest of us. This classic French pastry has been done a major disservice by mass production: the flabby black sheep of the supermarket picnic basket bears little resemblance to the delicately wobbling, full-flavoured beauties you can turn out at home. (Elizabeth David is characteristically waspish on the subject in her essay 'Your Perfected Hostess'.) A quiche is essentially a rich baked custard, encased in crisp savoury pastry – and what's not to like about that?

Larousse Gastronomique informs me that, although quiche was made with bread dough in days of yore, both shortcrust and puff are now quite acceptable substitutes. Shortcrust is the classic in this country, but after experimenting with *Guardian* baker Dan Lepard's classic quiche, with its delectable flaky pastry, I realize the quiche's creamy filling is crying out for a bit of crunch. Rough puff it is – in their culinary survey of post-war Britain, *The Prawn Cocktail Years*, Simon Hopkinson and Lindsey Bareham suggest brushing the base with a little beaten egg to help seal it, which is helpful; a soggy bottom has been the ruination of many a picnic.

The filling should be emphatically egg-flavoured, rather than blandly creamy – I find *Good Food* magazine's ultimate quiche recipe, with its generous helpings of double cream and crème fraîche, rather insipid; the Elizabeth David version, which contains a greater proportion of egg, is much firmer and richer in flavour. The winner, however, is California's Thomas Keller, whose silky custard is so light it almost melts in the mouth, thanks to some vigorous whisking of the mixture before cooking. Keller is adamant that to be worthy of the name, a quiche must be made in a deep pan – you need something at least 3cm tall for a smooth, rich texture.

Adding the ingredients in stages helps to distribute them more evenly throughout the quiche, so you don't have to dig deep. One of the nice things about quiches is that you can add pretty much any ingredient you happen to have lying about – smoked bacon is the thing for the classic Quiche Lorraine, but I also like leek, goat's cheese and spinach, cheese and caramelized onion, spinach and salmon . . . the important thing is to ensure whatever it is won't leak any water into the filling. This means sautéing onions, leeks and bacon, and blanching and squeezing out leafy vegetables such as spinach before they get anywhere near your carefully baked shell.

Refrigeration will spoil the pastry, so eat this up as quickly as possible – but keep away from real men; they might forget themselves.

Serves 6

**1 quantity of rough puff pastry
(see page 363), rolled out on
a floured surface**

4 large free-range eggs and 2 egg
   yolks (keep 1 egg white for brushing
   the pastry)
200g dry cure smoked streaky
   bacon, chopped
300ml double cream
Salt

1. Preheat the oven to 200°C/fan 180°C/gas 6. Grease a deep (at
    least 3cm) 20-22cm fluted tart tin, and line it with the pastry,
    leaving an extra few centimetres of overhang to minimize
    shrinkage. Keep any extra in case you need it for remedial work
    later. Line with foil (shiny-side down) and weight down with
    baking beans or rice. Place on a baking tray and blind bake in
    the oven for 25 minutes, then remove the foil and beans and
    patch up any holes with the extra pastry if necessary. Bake for
    10 minutes, then brush the base with egg white and put back into
    the oven for 5 further minutes. Carefully trim the overhanging
    pastry to neaten. Turn the oven down to 180°C/fan 160°C/gas 4.
2. Heat a small pan and cook the bacon for 8–10 minutes, until
    cooked through, but not crisp. Drain and spread half over the
    hot base.
3. Put the cream and the eggs and yolks into a large bowl (or a food
    mixer if you have one) with ¼ teaspoon of salt, beat together
    slowly until combined, then give it a fast whisk for 30 seconds
    until frothy. Pour over the base to fill and then sprinkle over
    the rest of the bacon. Bake for 30 minutes and then keep an
    eye on it – it's done when it's puffed up, but still wobbly at the
    centre. Allow to cool slightly before serving – hot quiche tastes
    of disappointingly little.

Perfect
Cheese Soufflé

If you believe the hype, soufflés are temperamental little things,
liable to spectacular collapse if you so much as hiccough in their
presence – the stuff of masterchefs. In fact, there's not much more
to them than your average cake; they're simply a savoury or sweet
base enriched with egg yolks and then lightened with an egg-white
foam. The air bubbles in the foam expand dramatically in the heat
of the oven, causing the soufflé to rise – and then, of course, shrink
again in the cold of the room, which accounts for the dish's
celebrated tendency to collapse. There's really no more mystery to it
than that. As Harold McGee, the scientifically minded food writer
championed by Heston Blumenthal, points out, as long as you
manage to get some air into the mixture to begin with, your soufflés
will rise during cooking: it's a law of nature. (Sadly, of course, they
will eventually also fall.)

The question, then, is not how to get them to rise in the first
place, but how to achieve maximum height, and keep them
that way for as long as possible. I try adding extra egg
whites, as suggested in Darina Allen's *Ballymaloe Cookery
Course*, but although the rise is significantly more
impressive, the flavour isn't as good; egg whites and
air being, of course, largely tasteless. Folding the base
and egg whites together slowly and gently, as suggested by McGee in
contradiction to the general instruction to do so as quickly as possible,
does seem to result in less air loss, and his tip about cooking them in a

bain-marie to 'moderate' the bottom oven temperature is also a good one; the soufflé seems creamier somehow.

Most recipes suggest running a finger around the inside rim of the mixture before cooking, to create a neat 'top hat' effect in the oven, rather than the exploding cauliflower effect which plagues the amateur soufflé chef. This does work, if you do it straight before you put it into the oven, but I quite like the more eccentric look myself.

The higher the oven temperature, the higher the soufflé will rise, and the more spectacularly it will fall – but after some disappointing results between 160°C, as used by chef Tristan Welch, and 180°C, as in Raymond Blanc's recipe, I happen upon Xanthe Clay in the *Telegraph*, who blasts the soufflés in a very hot oven. They're boldly brown on top and still wonderfully quivery inside – and her heavy hand with the cheese (she carelessly pops in twice as much as Darina Allen) yields delicious results. More cheese is, as usual, a very good thing. However, I decide to turn the heat down slightly, so they aren't quite as dry on top.

Coating the inside of the ramekins with breadcrumbs, as suggested by *Leiths Cookery Bible*, apparently does nothing to help the soufflé to rise, as is popularly supposed, but it does provide a pleasing textural contrast to the egg. I also take a tip from Margaret Costa's *Four Seasons Cookery Book* and keep some of that lovely cheese back until the last minute, so it doesn't quite have time to melt into the sauce; as she observes, it's a real treat to encounter a string of Gruyère when you dig in with your spoon.

Good luck – and remember, you can slam doors, dance around, and even open the oven during cooking if you like; as long as the oven's hot, they'll still rise, I promise. Go on, be bold, give it a try.

Makes 6

40g butter, plus 20g melted butter for greasing the ramekins
40g plain flour
300ml whole milk
20g white breadcrumbs
4 large free-range eggs
½ teaspoon English mustard powder
100g Gruyère, finely grated
50g Parmesan, finely grated
Salt and pepper

1. Preheat the oven to 220°C/fan 200°C/gas 6. Melt 40g of butter in a small pan and stir in the flour. Cook, stirring, for a couple of minutes, then gradually whisk in the milk until smooth, and heat gently until the mixture comes to the boil. Simmer for 5 minutes, stirring until thickened but still pourable, then transfer to a large bowl and set aside to cool slightly.

2. Meanwhile, brush six ramekins or small ovenproof dishes or cups with the melted butter, using upward strokes, and coat with breadcrumbs. Separate the eggs, putting the whites into a large clean bowl (not a plastic one). Half fill a roasting tin with just-boiled water from the kettle, and put into the oven.

3. Stir the mustard powder, 75g of the Gruyère and all the Parmesan into the sauce until smooth, and then stir in the egg yolks one by one. Finally, add the rest of the cheese, season and give one brief stir to mix.

4. Whisk the egg whites with a pinch of salt until stiff, but still moist and glossy (beware of over-whipping them: they shouldn't look dry or grainy), and stir a couple of tablespoons into the cheese base. Then very slowly and gently fold in the rest with a spatula.

Divide the mixture between the ramekins and level the top with a palette knife.

5. Run your thumb inside the rim of each ramekin to create a groove in the mixture, then immediately put the ramekins into the roasting tin of water and cook for about 12 minutes, until they are golden and well risen. Serve immediately, before they shrink!

A soufflé for all seasons
Once you've mastered a basic cheese soufflé, you'll be empowered to experiment with other flavours: chopped ham and chives, sautéd spinach, leeks or mushrooms, crumbled goat's cheese and thyme – fold the extra ingredients through at the same point as the cheese in the recipe above. A classic addition is smoked haddock, cooked in milk and then broken into flakes – the milk is then used to make the soufflé base. Sweet soufflés work on the same principle, but usually start with a pastry cream, flavoured with chocolate, coffee or fruit purée.

For something so delicate, soufflés freeze surprisingly well. Freeze the ramekins as soon as you've filled them, and simply allow an extra 5 minutes in the oven.

Perfect
Scotch Eggs

*R*obustly portable, conveniently hand-sized, and absurdly delicious, Scotch eggs are the perfect snack.

The egg question is a simple one of preference: I like mine to be soft, but not runny, particularly if they're destined for a picnic, so I've plumped for a 5-minute boil, but you can cook yours for a couple of minutes more or less if you prefer. Rolling the peeled eggs in flour, as Angela Hartnett suggests, will help the meat to stick when you come to the assemblage.

The meat casing is more tricky. Many recipes just call for sausagemeat, which is an easy way to do things, but I find the all-sausagemeat eggs from Hartnett, Gary Rhodes and Heston Blumenthal a bit greasy for my liking. Tom Norrington-Davies' semi-lean pork mince, however, ends up a bit dry. You could mix the mince with pork fat, as the Ginger Pig suggests, but if you don't have an obliging local butcher, a mixture of sausagemeat and mince provides the perfect compromise.

As with a sausage itself, you can play around with the seasonings to suit the occasion: I find Hartnett's garlic and thyme too Mediterranean for a classic Scotch egg, while Heston's American mustard and smoked paprika is just confused. Instead, I'm plumping for traditional sausage seasonings like mace and mustard, with lots of fresh chopped herbs, as Norrington-Davies suggests, which gives the meat a bright, spuriously healthy appearance.

Less traditional, perhaps, are the panko breadcrumbs I'm using to coat it all – but if Yorkshire's Ginger Pig butchery has embraced these super-crisp Japanese crumbs then so can I. In fact, I like them so much that, like Gary Rhodes, I'm going to go for a double coating for extra crunch. Assembling them is a case of practice makes perfect: flouring the eggs, as Hartnett suggests, will help the mixture to cling to them, while rolling the sausagemeat out between clingfilm is a great tip from Gary Rhodes, helping, as it does, to ensure an even thickness.

Now for the bad news. Scotch eggs are so delicious because they're deep-fried, and sadly there's no way around it: baked versions are a tragedy waiting to happen. Instead, embrace the oil: as occasional treats go, these are corkers.

Makes 4

    6 eggs
    200g plain sausagemeat
    200g pork mince
    3 tablespoons chopped mixed herbs
       (I like chives, sage, parsley and thyme)
    A pinch of ground mace
    1 tablespoon English mustard
    A splash of milk
    50g flour, plus extra to dust
    100g panko breadcrumbs
    Vegetable oil, to cook

1. Put 4 of the eggs into a saucepan, cover with cold water and bring to the boil. Reduce the heat and simmer for 5 minutes, then drain the eggs and put them straight into a large bowl of iced water. Leave to cool for at least 10 minutes.

2. Put the meats, herbs, mace and mustard into a bowl, season and then mix together well with your hands. Divide into 4 balls while you've still got sausagey hands.

3. Carefully peel the eggs (see page 4 for tips). Beat the 2 remaining raw eggs together in a bowl with a splash of milk. Tip the flour into another bowl and season, then tip the breadcrumbs into a third bowl.

4. Put a square of clingfilm on the work surface, and flour it lightly. Place one of the meatballs in the centre, and also flour it lightly, then place another square of clingfilm of a similar size on top. Roll out the meat until it's large enough to encase an egg, and remove the top sheet of clingfilm (it can be reused for each subsequent egg).

5. To assemble the Scotch egg, roll 1 peeled egg in flour, then put it in the centre of the rolled-out meat. Bring up the meat to completely encase it, using the clingfilm underneath to help you, then smooth it into an egg shape with damp hands. Dip each egg in flour, then egg, then breadcrumbs, and then into just the egg and breadcrumbs again.

6. Use a deep-fat fryer or fill a large pan a third full of vegetable oil, and heat it to 170°C (or when a crumb of bread dropped in immediately sizzles and turns golden, but does not burn). Cook the Scotch eggs a couple at a time, for 7 minutes each, until crisp and golden, then drain well on kitchen paper and season

lightly before serving; I like mine with English mustard for dipping, but brown sauce, ketchup, mustard mayonnaise and tartare sauce (not just for fish!) all have their devotees. As a rule, if it goes with a sausage, it'll go with a Scotch egg.

Perfect
Tomato Soup

Although we may not be famous for our tomatoes, this is, I think, the finest possible dish for the British summertime. For a start, it makes use of seasonal produce: you have to wait until they're so ripe they're almost splitting. Secondly, it acknowledges that there are summer days – many, many summer days – which are in need of warming up.

There are good recipes using tinned tomatoes of course, and, having road-tested both Mark Bittman's wintertime tomato soup, as published in the *New York Times*, and one from the American department store chain Nordstrom, which apparently enjoys 'something of a cult following for those who love tomato soup', I can recommend both for a cold weather fix. But neither are a patch on the sweet and sour pleasures of the fresh version.

In really warm climates, no doubt fresh tomatoes are flavourful enough to need no special treatment, but I find recipes which simply simmer them in stock produce a sadly bland result. For a really tomatoey result, you need to roast the tomatoes, as Lindsey Bareham suggests – it concentrates the sweetness.

As it's a vegetable soup, you could use a matching stock here, but I always find them too assertively herby – better, if you don't mind meat, to substitute a good chicken stock, which will add savoury richness without contributing any distinct flavour of its own. My recipe uses less stock than many: although it shouldn't be thick exactly, a tomato soup should still have presence on the spoon.

That said, you don't need much in the way of added thickeners — cream of tomato soup is a classic, the natural wateriness of the fruit lending itself to a little added luxury, but too much double cream makes the Nordstrom recipe a bit sickly. Jamie mixes his double cream with egg yolks, which gives his soup a beautifully silky texture, but it's *Larousse*'s seasonally light fromage frais which seems to work best with the dish's summery flavours — and tangy crème fraîche is even better, amplifying the tangy flavour of the tomatoes. I'm not sure *Larousse*'s potatoes are entirely in keeping though — they make the soup far too cosy and fluffy.

Carrot and onion both accentuate the fruit's sweetness (helped along by a pinch of sugar), but I've eschewed their traditional companions celery and bouquet garni — they seem too wintery here, somehow. Garlic, however, is a natural match for tomatoes, as is fresh basil.

My final touch is a dash of balsamic vinegar — inspired by a River Café tomato sauce using both vinegar and sugar to boost the natural assets of the fruit, it makes up for any deficiencies in the tomatoes themselves, and adds a depth of flavour all of its own.

Note, though it's lovely hot in a summer rainstorm, this soup also goes down a treat chilled, should the weather forget itself for a few hours.

Serves 4

1kg ripe tomatoes
4 tablespoons olive oil
Salt and pepper
A pinch of sugar
1 onion, chopped
1 carrot, peeled and diced
2 cloves of garlic, finely chopped
A small bunch of basil, separated into leaves and stalks
600ml chicken or vegetable stock
1 tablespoon balsamic vinegar
2 tablespoons crème fraîche
Extra virgin olive oil, to serve

1. Preheat the oven to 190°C/fan 170°C/gas 5 and cut the tomatoes in half laterally. Place them, cut side up, in a baking dish, drizzle with 2 tablespoons of olive oil and season with salt, pepper and a pinch of sugar. Bake them for about an hour, until thoroughly softened and just beginning to blacken around the edges.

2. Once they're nearly ready, pour the remaining oil into a large, heavy-based pan over a medium heat and add the chopped onion, carrot and garlic. Fry, stirring regularly, for about 7 minutes, until thoroughly softened. Meanwhile, roughly chop the basil stalks. Add these to the pan and cook for another minute.

3. Tip in the baked tomatoes, plus any juices from the dish, and pour in the stock. Stir and bring to the boil, then turn the heat down, cover the pan and leave to simmer for 25 minutes, until all the vegetables are soft.

4. Use a blender to purée the soup, then stir in the vinegar and crème fraîche and season to taste. Reheat, then serve with a pinch of torn basil leaves and a drizzle of olive oil on top.

Perfect
Chicken Soup

*T*he answer to everything, according to the archetypal Jewish mamma – I hesitate to describe my recipe as penicillin for the soul, but it is very definitely Wholesome. For a start, it comes in big steaming bowls, a sight infinitely more restorative than anything you can get over the counter. Secondly, there's some evidence to suggest it may have anti-inflammatory properties, though no one quite knows why. And thirdly, making your own is thrift par excellence, which always lifts the spirits.

Claudia Roden makes the soup with a whole bird, but although she has kosher credentials, I'm not sure this is a good idea unless you're lucky enough to be able to lay your hands on a stringy old boiling fowl. Younger chickens don't boast enough flavour in the carcass, while the meat is too tender to benefit from prolonged simmering – it just goes rubbery.

A better and cheaper idea is to use wings, as Heston Blumenthal does – although there will be plenty of flavour in any bony bits, so feel free to swap – and only add a chicken carcass if you happen to have one left over from a Sunday roast or similar.

Purists may sneer, but to guarantee a good, chickeny flavour, I've also used chicken stock: if you make your own, or splash the cash on someone else's hard work, this isn't really cheating, and if Lindsey Bareham uses beef stock, then chicken must surely be acceptable.

Stock is as nothing to the heresy of adding fresh vegetables, however
– but I think the vitamins they bring with them are quite in the spirit
of the soup (after all, in the days when chicken fat was believed to be
a cure-all, chicken soup wasn't chicken soup without golden coins of
oil floating on the top: carrots are simply the modern equivalent).

To be truly comforting, a soup needs body: you could make matzo ball
dumplings (recipe below), or stick in some vermicelli, but wholegrain
barley seems more in keeping with the rest of the ingredients: chewy,
nutty, and pleasingly filling, it'll warm you from the inside out.

To finish, I won't be adding Heston's star anise (too Oriental), Skye
Gyngell's mint, coriander and lemon (too Middle Eastern), or
thyme, bay or decadent saffron: all this resolutely savoury soup
needs is the peppery pop of parsley to set it off to perfection.

Serves 6

Ikg chicken wings or drumsticks or a mixture,
   plus a leftover chicken carcass if you happen to have one
2 sticks of celery, chopped
2 onions, skin on and quartered
3 carrots (2 roughly chopped,
   I peeled and more finely chopped
   and kept separate)
3 leeks (2 roughly chopped, I more finely chopped and kept
   separate)
A small bunch of parsley, separated into stalks and leaves
750ml cold chicken stock
Pepper
200g wholegrain barley, cooked

1. Place the chicken in a large pan or stockpot and pour in just enough cold water to cover. Bring to the boil and skim off any scum that rises to the top — important because otherwise your soup will have a horrid, greasy flavour.
2. Add the celery, quartered onions (if they're clean, there's no need to peel these), the roughly chopped carrots and leeks, parsley stalks and stock to the pan. Season generously with pepper, then turn down the heat and leave to simmer gently for a couple of hours.
3. Strain the soup through a fine sieve; you can pick the meat off the bones and add it to the soup if you wish, although it may be rather chewy, but discard the vegetables.
4. Return the soup to the pan, add the finely chopped carrot and leek and cook for 10 minutes, until soft.
5. Tip in the cooked barley, season the soup to taste, and serve with the chopped parsley leaves on top.

Simple matzo ball dumplings

60ml sparkling water
2 large eggs
1 tablespoon neutral oil (or liquid chicken fat, should you happen to have some knocking about)
100g matzo meal
1 tablespoon finely chopped parsley or dill

1. While the soup is simmering, whisk together the water, eggs and oil, then stir in the matzo meal and herbs. Season generously and chill for half an hour.
2. Roll the dough into small balls about 1.5cm in diameter. Once you've strained the soup and returned it to the pan, add the

dumplings and simmer for 10 minutes before adding the carrot and leek.

3. Cook for another 10–15 minutes, until the dumplings are fluffy in the middle.

Perfect
Minestrone

Until recently, I thought I didn't like minestrone. This opinion was based solely on the strangely tangy powdered stuff, studded with suet-like strands of pasta, which was often the least-awful item on the school lunch menu. When the competition was stiffer than kidney stew, however, minestrone went out the window. Then I read Giorgio Locatelli on the subject – and discovered that, strictly speaking, minestrone isn't a *zuppa* at all, it's a kind of vegetable stew, with a few ladlefuls of broth on top, which makes it sound a lot more attractive. As Angela Hartnett observes, it should be a meal in itself.

In fact, as Locatelli and others point out, minestrone is more of a concept than a recipe, using whatever vegetables and thickeners happen to be available: courgettes, broad beans and peas in the spring, potatoes, chard and carrots in the winter. Common thickeners include broken bits of pasta, potato, beans, farro and rice – having tried all of them, I like to include cubes of potato, beans and risotto rice (at home, Locatelli admits he often makes a soup so thick with rice that his daughter can stand a spoon up in it – just as his grandmother did for him).

The really important thing to get right is the liquid which underpins the whole dish. Jamie comes down in favour of ham stock, while Locatelli uses vegetable stock for his light spring minestrone, and

Angela says chicken stock gives the best flavour, although she concedes one can also use vegetable at a pinch. Chicken is certainly the most versatile option; more subtle than ham, and more savoury than vegetable, it's the ideal base for most ingredients. I don't think you need the red wine or tinned tomatoes that Mr Oliver puts into his early autumn minestrone either – they make it too rich, overpowering the vegetables which should be the real stars of the show.

A good tip from Locatelli is to add the ingredients in the order they will cook, rather than sticking everything in together and hoping for the best. This way you should end up with soft, rather than mushy veg – and not a lump of soup powder in sight.

Serves 4

3 tablespoons olive oil, plus extra to serve
1 onion, chopped
1 clove of garlic, crushed
2 carrots, cut into 1cm dice
2 sticks of celery, cut into 1cm dice
Seasonal vegetables (e.g. autumn/winter – ¼ of a Savoy
    cabbage, roughly chopped, 1 bunch of spinach, roughly
    chopped, 1 leek, chopped; spring/summer – 1 courgette,
    diced, handful of fresh peas or broad beans, ½ a head of
    fennel, diced)
1.25 litres good-quality chicken stock (see page 169)
1 potato, peeled and cut into 2cm dice
100g drained tinned borlotti beans
200g risotto rice (optional)

Salt and pepper
A small bunch of basil, to serve
50g Parmesan, grated, to serve

1. Heat the olive oil in a heavy-based saucepan over a fairly gentle heat. Add the onion and garlic, cover and cook for 5 minutes, until softened but not coloured. Add the carrots and cook for a few minutes until softened, then do the same with the celery. Add the rest of the vegetables in order of cooking time — cabbage cooks very quickly, for example, while squash will take longer — but leaving very delicate vegetables like spinach, peas or baby broad beans aside at this stage. (Bear in mind they don't need to be cooked through at this point, just softened.)

2. Pour in the stock, and add the potato, beans and rice, if using. Bring to the boil, then turn down the heat and simmer until the potato and rice are cooked. Stir in any remaining vegetables, cook for a minute or so, then season to taste. Serve with torn basil leaves, a scattering of Parmesan and a drizzle of olive oil.

Meat and Fish

*T*hough I'd never want to give up the greasy joys of burgers, or the sensual pleasures of slow-cooked mutton curry, I don't, truth be told, eat that much meat or indeed fresh fish. (Or, at least, I don't when I'm not testing seven steak and ale pie recipes for the greater good, or pondering the thorny problem of how to get chip shop batter in a home kitchen.) By inclination, I'd probably only indulge about twice a week. But when I do, I like to make the most of it.

As you'll see, that doesn't mean treating yourself to the fancy bits – with the exception of the aforementioned battered fish, and beef wellington, almost all the recipes in this chapter make use of more economical cuts. They may demand a little more skill in the cooking department, but the rewards are infinite: I love the way a slow-simmered piece of beef shin melts into its gravy, or tearing into the juicy succulence of a slightly chewy chicken thigh. Anyone can sear a rump steak in a hot pan so it's halfway decent (though see page 109 for tips to upgrade to perfect), but making the most of stewing steak or fish scraps is rather more of an art, albeit an easy one to master with a few basic principles.

MEAT

For a start, much of that classic 'meaty' flavour is thanks to what's called the Maillard reaction — the scientific process responsible for the colour and flavour of toasted bread, chocolate, dark beer and, yes, roasted meat. Food scientist Harold McGee explains how the sugars in these foodstuffs react with amino acids when heated to produce 'a brown colouration and full, intense flavour' — the diagrams are in his book *McGee on Food and Cooking*, but for these purposes, all you need to remember is that browning meat is a very good idea, even if you're going to go on to cook it very slowly and gently.

The benefits of so doing are the other thing I think it's very important that you know before we get cooking. To keep the meat as tender and juicy as possible, the muscle should ideally be heated no higher than 60°C for very brief periods of time. But meat isn't all simple muscle — there's chewy collagen too, which won't dissolve into sticky, wobbly gelatine below 70°C, and indeed requires prolonged exposure to such a heat in order to break down at all.

All meat cooking, then, is to some extent a compromise, the method dependent on the makeup of the bit in question — but as it's melted gelatine that makes stews and casseroles and dishes like pulled pork quite so obscenely delicious, wherever possible I favour collagen-rich cuts, patiently simmered until they fall apart under the fork. No blandly tender fillet could ever hope to compete.

The other benefit of going for the less glamorous bits, the oxtails and lamb breasts of this world, is that they're relatively cheap, which means that, even if you're on a tight budget, you should be able to afford a better-quality piece than would be possible if you were buying the boring stuff.

Organic is usually a good indicator of careful, slow rearing, with ample space to breathe, but it's not the be-all and end-all: many small producers at farmers' markets, or who supply butchers, take just as much trouble over their animals without jumping through the hoops of certification. I know not everyone has such a market, or even a decent butcher, within easy reach, but good meat is easily available online, and, increasingly I must concede, in many supermarkets. If the provenance isn't clear on the packaging, then ask.

Lastly, always bring your meat to room temperature before cooking, except where specified, or it will bring the temperature of the pan or dish down, which sort of defeats the point. Oh, and remember, most things are enhanced by a good dollop of English mustard.

FISH

Most fish and seafood is best cooked very quickly and simply: squid, octopus and the like aside, the delicate flesh doesn't stand up well to the rigours of heat, and you're much more likely to over- than undercook it, so always err on the side of caution. After all, if your fish is fresh, eating a piece that's still slightly raw in the centre is unlikely to do you much harm.

To check whether a piece of fish is cooked, there's no need to faff about with a thermometer: once the flesh has turned opaque, a gentle prod with the finger to assess firmness will do the trick. And, as ever with cooking, practice makes perfect.

Gentle cooking methods, like poaching, or steaming in a foil parcel in the oven, tend to be safer bets than baking or frying when you've got yourself a nice fillet of gurnard, or a whole bream. That said, such dishes are so simple they don't really lend themselves to much perfecting, so the recipes in this chapter tend towards the more . . . if not complicated, then more interesting side of seafood. The creamy pies, smoky pâtés and spicy curries which, if I'm honest, I prefer to the poshest hunk of turbot or sole bonne femme.

As usual, if you have a fishmonger in the vicinity, I'd urge you to use them when you can. If a supermarket's all you have, then cruise the sell-by dates (the fresher the better, obviously), rather than just sticking the first piece you see into your trolley – and bear in mind that Oriental supermarkets tend to be an excellent and good value source of frozen seafood in particular, though some are more sustainably minded than others, as with all retailers.

Indeed, wherever you're shopping, the Marine Conservation Society website is a good place to check the status of whatever's on your list, and offers a handy list of good alternatives should it fall foul of their guidelines. I've developed a real fondness for gurnard and pollock, and would now choose them over their pricier rivals, but if there's something I haven't heard of on the slab, then I'll generally give it a try instead. After all, when it comes to variety, there are always plenty more fish in the sea.

Perfect
Roast Chicken

Jean Anthelme Brillat-Savarin, the nineteenth-century French gourmet – and inspiration for the unfeasibly rich triple-cream cheese of the same name – described the humble chicken as a culinary blank canvas, and he's got a point. Viewed with the appropriate respect, even the simplest of chicken dishes, the roast, is revealed as a veritable Tardis of gastronomic potential – it might sound like an easy option, but actually it's a surprisingly difficult thing to get right, which is why it's often used by chefs as a test for potential new recruits. The issue is not so much one of flavour – you get what you pay for in that department – but of texture: how do you achieve a crisp skin while keeping the meat nice and juicy?

Brining, stuffing, slow-roasting at 60°C, all have their advocates online, but lazily, I'm drawn to the Californian Thomas Keller's suitably laid-back recipe, which sounds perfect for a Sunday afternoon. No basting, no buttering – just a smoking hot oven and a little seasoning. It's easy, and the skin is tear-jerkingly crisp, but sadly, at the expense of the meat, which is rather dry.

Pierre Koffmann, whose Chelsea restaurant La Tante Claire was one of the first British kitchens to win three Michelin stars, has a more hands-on approach – but although turning the bird at regular intervals and basting it with goose fat makes the flesh undeniably succulent, there's no excusing its pallid, greasy skin. Slow-roasting it until the temperature reaches a bacteria-zonking 62°C, as the *Guardian* food writer Matthew Fort suggests, proves far too much hassle — I'm up until 1 a.m., and the thing still isn't cooked through.

Former Bibendum chef Simon Hopkinson's traditional approach, given in his much-fêted first cookbook, *Roast Chicken and Other Stories*, involves smearing the skin with butter and treating the bird to an initial blast in a hot oven, before turning the temperature down to a more reasonable 190°C. It's a successful enough result, but I'm finally won over by *Mail on Sunday* cookery writer Annie Bell's nifty poach and roast combo. The meat is deliciously tender, and, after turning the dial right up at the end, the skin is as crisp as a new banknote. Truly, the world holds no more beautiful sight.

**1 medium free-range chicken,
    about 1.6kg (removed from the
    fridge an hour before cooking)
1 head of garlic, cut in half laterally
4 sprigs of thyme, leaves only
1 tablespoon olive oil
Salt and pepper
1 lemon, cut in half**

1. Preheat the oven to 220°C/fan 200°C/gas 7. Bring a large pan of salted water to the boil, remove any trussing string from the chicken, and add it to the pan, breast side down. Turn down the heat and simmer for 10 minutes. Remove from the water and pat thoroughly dry: you can use a hairdryer to help if you have one handy.

2. Put the garlic into a roasting tin and scatter half the thyme over the top. Put the chicken on top of it and rub with the oil. Season generously, both inside and out, scatter with the rest of the thyme and put the lemon inside the cavity. Tip a couple of millimetres of just-boiled water from the kettle or hot stock into the bottom of the tin, and put into the oven for 1 hour and 15 minutes, or until the juices run clear: insert a skewer or the top of a knife into the thickest part of the thigh and then press down to check this.

3. Ten minutes before the end of cooking, tip out the juices to save for gravy if you're making one (see page 281), and turn up the oven temperature as high as it will go to help crisp the skin. Keep an eye on it to prevent it burning.

4. Allow the chicken to rest in a warm place for 15 minutes before carving and serving with the roasted garlic.

Perfect
Southern Fried Chicken

*F*ried chicken is taking over the world. Or, at least, taking over Britain. Deep-fried, wrapped in seasoned batter, and served in boxes and buckets – in London, at least, you can't move for branches of Kansas Fried Chicken and the singularly unappetizing-sounding Chicken Spot.

Done well, it can be pretty addictive stuff: juicy meat, served on the bone for flavour, in a crisp, spicy – and, let's be honest, ever-so-slightly greasy – crust is always going to be finger-licking good. But sadly, if the stuff being eaten on the top deck of the bus is anything to go by, it's not: flabby batter, stringy, fat-sodden chicken – give me a jumbo haddock and mushy peas any day of the week.

Much better to make it yourself. I'd recommend using only thighs and drumsticks: bland breasts take ages to cook through, by which time the batter is inevitably overcooked, and wings, in my experience, don't offer a good enough meat to batter ratio. And – controversially – I'd remove the skin: I know any good Southern housewife will stop reading at this point, but it doesn't crisp up under the batter, and chewy skin is not nice.

Marinating doesn't seem to be very traditional (and, when I try Laurie Colwin's recipe without it, it works perfectly well – so don't be put off if you need that fried chicken fast), but these days, you're no one if you don't have a signature soak. Though it does a good job in the juiciness department, however, I find that brining makes the chicken unpleasantly salty.

Better are dairy marinades, as recommended by Richard Ehrlich and Tim Hayward, author of *Food DIY*; I prefer the tanginess of buttermilk to the simple sweetness of plain milk. There doesn't seem to be much point in adding too many spices at this stage, though; it doesn't come through in the finished dish.

I'd say the coating is what makes the dish, however — and it's a tricky business to perfect. There's a fine line between that firm, satisfying crunch, and what Ehrlich memorably describes as a 'sarcophagus of stodge'.

The flour should be plain — in substance, but not flavour, because this is where you pack in that seasoning. I like Laurie Colwin's *Home Cooking* recipe, which sticks with salt, pepper and smoked paprika, because, like her, 'I adore [it], and feel it gives the chicken a smoky taste and a beautiful colour.'

If, like me, you don't adore the mess and drama of deep-frying, you'll be relieved to know that I preferred the shallow-fried versions — deep-frying is more difficult to control, and surprisingly, yields a less crisp coating, presumably because the crust hasn't had anything to form against. Covering the pan, as Colwin suggests, is a clever idea: though, as she says, the idea 'may make many people squeal', it means the chicken cooks through quickly, before the coating has time to burn, so it stays beautifully juicy.

OK, so fried chicken will never be a health food, or even a regular occurrence, both for the sake of your heart, and your soft furnishings. As Laurie Colwin observes, 'there are many disagreeable things about frying chicken'. Eating it hot from the pan, however, is not one of them.

Serves 2–3

300ml buttermilk
1½ teaspoons salt
6 pieces of chicken
  (I use a mixture of legs and thighs)
150g plain flour
½ teaspoon freshly ground black pepper
½ teaspoon smoked paprika
Vegetable oil, for frying

1. Put the buttermilk and 1 teaspoon of salt into a container large enough to hold all the chicken, and then add the meat and toss to coat. Cover and chill for about 8 hours if possible, allowing it to return to room temperature before cooking.
2. Put the flour, spices and ½ teaspoon of salt into a large, flat dish and whisk to combine. Pour 1.5cm of vegetable oil into a wide, straight-sided pan with a lid, and heat until very hot: a cube of bread dropped in should brown almost immediately (about 170°C).
3. Wipe as much buttermilk off the chicken pieces as you can, then roll them in the seasoned flour until thoroughly coated.
4. Put the chicken in one layer in the pan (you may need to do this in batches, depending on how big your pan is) and put the lid

on. Turn the heat right down and fry the chicken for 6 minutes, then turn the pieces over, cover again and cook for another 6 minutes. Prepare a rack, and lots of kitchen paper to drain the chicken.

5. Turn the heat up and fry the chicken until it's a deep golden colour on all sides. Lift on to the rack and dry with kitchen paper. Allow to cool slightly before serving.

Perfect
Chicken Tikka Masala

*L*ike so many classic dishes, the origins of CTM, as it's known to aficionados, are lost in the mists of time – though in this case, not that much time, since it only began appearing on British restaurant menus in the 1970s as an adaptation of Punjabi butter chicken. Whoever invented it deserves credit, however: rich, yet delicately spiced, it's deservedly famous, yet all too often passed over in favour of dishes with a longer, more 'authentic' provenance, which means it's even better made at home.

Though chicken breast is rarely the most interesting choice, when chargrilled, as Madhur Jaffrey recommends, to bring out its flavour, it makes a great mixture with juicier thigh meat. (If you happen to have a tandoor oven to hand, or indeed a barbecue, even better.) Both cuts will benefit from an initial marinade in lemon juice and salt to help tenderize them, before being immersed in a garlicky, gingery yoghurt bath overnight – you can leave them in there longer, as Dan Toombs (aka the Curry Guy) does, but it won't make much difference.

This is a dish that stands or falls on its sauce as far as I'm concerned; it should be savoury with tomato, but with a hint of sweetness too; buttery without being sickly; and moderately spiced, rather than fiery. At the base of almost every tikka masala sauce are onion, ginger and garlic; indeed, I miss the onions in Anjum Anand's

version from *I Love Curry*. Tomatoes lend both colour and sweet-sour flavour – unless it's midsummer, tinned versions are safer for northern European cooks at least, plus a dollop of purée, as Rick Stein suggests, to add extra oomph. Depending on your tastes you may like to add a pinch of sugar too, but keep some lemon juice on hand in case you need to squeeze in a little for balance. Whipping cream, as deployed by Jaffrey, proves the ideal choice of dairy to finish the sauce: satisfyingly thick without being overwhelmingly rich.

Every recipe has its own spice blend. Chilli powder is very popular, as is paprika for its vivid red colour – and I like the flash of green the fresh fruits bring. Sweet spices like cinnamon, cloves and cardamom are a must, but the elusive flavour of the classic restaurant dish proves to come from fenugreek leaves. Sprinkle with garam masala and fresh coriander and serve with pilau rice, naan bread and far too many side dishes for that authentic restaurant experience.

Serves 4

For the chicken tikka
4 boneless, skinless chicken thighs
2 boneless, skinless chicken breasts
Juice of 2 lemons
1 teaspoon salt
150ml plain yoghurt
1 tablespoon puréed ginger (use a fine grater or a pestle and mortar)
1 tablespoon crushed garlic (about 3 cloves)
1½ teaspoons ground cumin
1 tablespoon garam masala
1 tablespoon smoked sweet paprika

For the sauce

2 tablespoons ghee/clarified butter (or flavourless oil)
2 small onions, chopped
6 green cardamom pods
1 black cardamom pod (optional)
2cm cinnamon stick
4 cloves
2 tablespoons puréed ginger (use a pestle and mortar)
8 garlic cloves, crushed to a purée
400g chopped tomatoes
1 tablespoon tomato purée
2 small green chillies, split open
1 teaspoon sugar
50ml whipping cream
1 teaspoon paprika
½ teaspoon dried fenugreek leaves, ground
1 teaspoon garam masala
1 tablespoon lemon juice (optional)
A small handful of coriander leaves, to serve

1. Cut the meat into bite-sized chunks and marinate in the lemon and salt for 30 minutes. In the meantime, mix together the remaining marinade ingredients. Add to the bowl, stir well to coat, then chill for 8 hours. Bring to room temperature before cooking.

2. Heat the ghee in a frying pan over a medium-high heat and fry the onions until soft and golden, stirring regularly. While they're cooking, crush the cardamom pods and remove their seeds. Grind these to a powder with the cinnamon stick and cloves, using a spice grinder or a pestle and mortar.

3. Add the ginger and garlic to the onions and fry for a couple of minutes, stirring, then mix in the ground spices and cook for a minute or so. Stir in the tomatoes, tomato purée and 300ml water, bring to a simmer, then turn down the heat to medium and cook until you can see oil beginning to pool around the side.

4. Meanwhile, heat your grill to high and thread the chicken on to metal skewers, pushing the pieces close together. Put on a lined baking sheet and grill for 6–8 minutes on each side until lightly charred. (You can also do this on a hot griddle pan or a barbecue if you prefer.)

5. Use a stick blender to purée the sauce in the pan, then stir in any remaining marinade, along with the fresh chillies, sugar, cream and paprika – add more of the last if you'd like a deeper colour. Bring to a simmer, then stir in the chicken, fenugreek and garam masala and cook for about 5 minutes. Taste for seasoning. Add more salt or sugar or the lemon juice if you like, and serve with chopped coriander.

Perfect
Chicken Pie

*P*ies are God's gift to the cook – a medley of ingredients, prettily gift-wrapped in pastry, which will have your dinner guests falling over themselves in greed and gratitude. Just about any foodstuff is improved by a crisp, golden crust, but I think chicken works particularly well; the creamy white sauce keeps it moist, and is the perfect showcase for its delicate flavour. You can, of course, make this pie with leftover roast chicken, as Nigella does, but poaching a bird for it is well worth the effort; it gives a juicier result, and there's something for everyone inside. Buying a good-quality whole bird will also work out cheaper than buying enough chicken pieces for everyone.

Like Nigella, Angela Boggiano tops the chicken and tarragon pie in her recipe collection, *Pie*, with rich shortcrust, but I find I prefer a rough puff, as used by Jamie Oliver – crisp and flaky on top, pleasingly soggy beneath. Angela's chicken comes in a cream and white wine sauce which is a little bit thin for my taste, although I'm sold on the leeks and tarragon she uses to flavour it: both work brilliantly with chicken.

Skye Gyngell uses crème fraîche in her pie instead, but I don't like the slightly sour note this gives: sometimes the simplest ideas, like Nigella's white sauce, are the best. Here I've flavoured it with the poaching liquid (if you're using cooked chicken you can, like her, substitute chicken stock) and enriched it with a little cream so it wraps around the meat like a comfort blanket. Serve with steamed greens.

Serves 6

1 small chicken, about 1.4kg
1 large carrot, quartered
1 large onion, quartered
2 sticks of celery, quartered
A few parsley stalks
1 bay leaf
A few black peppercorns
40g butter, plus a knob for cooking
2 leeks, thinly sliced
4 rashers of streaky bacon, chopped
2 tablespoons plain flour
250ml milk
4 tablespoons single cream
A small bunch of tarragon, leaves chopped
Salt and pepper
1 quantity of rough puff pastry (see page 363)
1 free-range egg, beaten

1. Put the chicken into a pan large enough to hold it comfortably and add the carrot, onion, celery, parsley, bay leaf and peppercorns. Cover with cold water and bring to the boil, then lower the heat and poach for about an hour, until cooked through, skimming any scum from the top every now and then.
2. Remove the chicken to a plate, draining the juices from the cavity as you go. Strain the poaching liquid, put it back into

the pan on a strong heat and reduce the liquid by half, which should take about half an hour. Meanwhile, pull the meat off the chicken in large chunks.

3. Preheat the oven to 200°C/fan 180°C/gas 6. Put a knob of butter into a frying pan and gently sweat the leeks until softened; add the bacon and cook for 5 minutes, then turn off the heat. Melt the rest of the butter in a medium saucepan over a low heat, and stir in the flour. Cook, stirring, for a couple of minutes, without allowing it to brown (cooking the flour is vital; raw flour will spoil the taste of the sauce), then gradually whisk in about 150ml of the reduced poaching liquid, and then the milk and cream – if you add it too fast, your sauce will be lumpy. Beat until smooth, then simmer gently for about 10 minutes, until thickened. Stir through the tarragon and season to taste. (You can freeze the rest of the poaching liquid to use as a stock.)

4. Stir the chicken, leeks and bacon into the sauce, and spoon into a pie dish. Roll the rough puff out on a floured surface until about 5mm thick. Brush the edges of the pie dish with beaten egg, then lay the pastry over the pie and press down around the edges with a fork to seal it. Cut a small hole in the centre to let the steam out, and brush with beaten egg. Put into the oven and cook for about 45 minutes, until the pastry is well risen and golden.

Other great pies
Steak and ale; ham and leek; Cheshire cheese and onion; mince and potato; venison and red wine; lamb and thyme; spinach and feta; Stargazy (or Cornish pilchard pie)

Perfect
Chicken Liver Pâté

I mourn the loss of pâté from our culinary repertoire. Sometime in the noughties, probably while I was busy making melba toast, it quietly dropped off menus, to be replaced by deep-fried Brie, or tempura squid with sweet chilli sauce, or, horror of horrors, something involving a foam.

Well, they've all had their time, and now, I think, it's time to return to the hearty embrace of real food. The variations are near infinite – but for silky elegance, I don't think you can beat the simple chicken liver version. Winningly easy to make, and obligingly happy to sit in the fridge for a few days, it's possibly the perfect lunch party dish or dinner party starter. Or, indeed, the best thing to have in stock when you come home overtired from work, and perhaps a few more drinks than you intended, and require sustenance, fast.

There's no need to soak the livers first, as Raymond Blanc does – though common practice with stronger-tasting pig or ox livers, it robs the more delicate chicken version of its distinctive offally character. You should, however, brown them in a pan: using them raw, or poaching them in stock as several recipes suggest, denies the finished dish a layer of savoury flavour. They don't need to be cooked for 5 minutes, as Delia Smith suggests, though – leaving them blushing pink in the middle will give a better texture.

Those livers can be bound together with butter, as in Delia's recipe, butter and cream, like Julia Child's, or Raymond Blanc's butter and egg combination. Butter alone makes the pâté too oily, and eggs seem to give it a moussey texture — only cream and butter in combination hit the silky spot.

Flavour-wise, though I'm keen to let the livers themselves take centre stage, a little booze seems appropriate for such a rich dish. Having tried brandy and port, I've settled for the subtle sweetness of Madeira as a perfect match with the chicken, and the shallots I've taken from Raymond Blanc's recipe — others use garlic, spring onions, even yellow onions and anchovies, but I prefer their sweeter flavour with the livers. Sweet spices also seem appropriate: ginger and allspice supply a pleasingly festive feel.

Raymond Blanc and Constance Spry both bake their pâtés in a water bath, which gives them a firmer, lighter consistency, but, though they look impressive, I prefer the creamier texture of the quicker set version.

A seal of butter is only necessary if you're keeping the pâté a few days, but it does look pretty — and of course, it saves real gluttons the embarrassment of having to ask for the butter dish.

Serves 4

350g chicken livers, cleaned
175g butter, diced
1 shallot, finely chopped
1 teaspoon thyme leaves, finely chopped
75ml Madeira
75ml double cream
½ teaspoon salt
1 allspice berry, ground
¼ teaspoon ground ginger

1. Trim any stringy or green bits from the livers, and cut them into rough 1.5cm pieces. Heat a knob of the butter in a frying pan over a medium heat. Add the chopped shallot and thyme and soften in the butter, then turn up the heat to medium-high and add the livers. Sauté for a couple of minutes, until they're nicely browned on the outside but still pink within. Transfer the lot to a food processor.

2. Pour the Madeira into the same pan and bubble until it's reduced to a couple of tablespoons. Add this to the food processor, with the cream, salt and spices, and whiz it all together until smooth.

3. Add all but 75g of the butter, and whiz again until thoroughly combined. Taste and adjust the seasoning if necessary.

4. Pass the pâté through a sieve into a serving dish, or individual ramekins, and chill for half an hour. Melt the remaining butter and pour on top. (You can clarify it if you have the time – melt it in a pan over a gentle heat, then allow to simmer until you spot the first dark flecks on the bottom. Watch it carefully, or it will burn. Strain it through some butter muslin, or two sheets of kitchen roll.) Then refrigerate until set.

Perfect
Coronation Chicken

A word of warning. This isn't the kind of Coronation chicken you can knock up for an impromptu picnic in the time it takes your partner to find the rug.

The original recipe, created by the founder of the Cordon Bleu cookery school, Rosemary Hume (rather than her better-known partner in the venture, florist Constance Spry, as is often claimed), calls for a whole poached chicken, rather than the usual leftovers from Sunday's roast. Although I did try roasting one, on the assumption that this would give the bird a better flavour, in fact the poached version, once I've added some spices to the pot, is much nicer: juicy and subtly exotic-tasting.

Instead of using just mayonnaise, which can be rather too rich and claggy, I've gone for a half-and-half mixture of mayo and Greek yoghurt to make the dish creamier and lighter, after finding crème fraîche too buttery, and double cream too runny.

Generic curry powder feels like a very 1950s ingredient, but it adds just the right touch here – make sure you toast it first though, or the raw flavour will spoil the dressing.

The original Coronation chicken was a more delicate affair than we're used to today, and to be honest, rather underwhelming to a modern palate, so I've given the sweet, mildly spicy sauce a bit more oomph. Mango chutney goes in, courtesy of Hugh Fearnley-Whittingstall's recipe, to add an Indian fruitiness, and Worcestershire sauce, itself an Anglo-Indian creation, contributes a pleasing tangy, savoury flavour. Chopped apricots and toasted almond flakes finish the whole thing off nicely, giving it a more interesting texture than your average yellow gloop, while coriander adds freshness and colour.

I suspect the results would have been regarded as rather bold back in 1953, but this is a dish crying out to be dragged into the twenty-first century and given the respect it deserves. As Simon Hopkinson tartly observes, 'those cowboys who continue to think that bottled curry paste mixed with Hellmann's is in any way a reasonable substitute here need a good slap with a cold chapatti'. Try it, and you'll see why.

Serves 6

    1 chicken, about 1.5kg
    1 cinnamon stick
    5 black peppercorns
    A pinch of saffron
    1 teaspoon salt
    1 bay leaf
    A 4cm piece of fresh ginger
    5 tablespoons good-quality mango chutney (I swear by Geeta's)
    50g ready-to-eat dried apricots, finely chopped
    2 tablespoons good curry powder
    2 teaspoons Worcestershire sauce

200ml homemade mayonnaise (see page 276)
200ml Greek yoghurt
A small bunch of fresh coriander, chopped
50g flaked almonds, toasted
Green salad and basmati rice, to serve

1. Put the chicken, breast side up, into a large pan with the cinnamon, peppercorns, saffron, salt, bay leaf and half the ginger. Fill with cold water until only the top of the breast is sticking out. Cover with a lid and bring to a simmer, then turn down the heat, so only the odd bubble can be seen. Cook gently for about 1½ hours, until the juices run clear. Take the chicken out of the pan and set aside to cool, then, when lukewarm, remove the meat in bite-sized pieces.

2. Peel and finely chop the remaining ginger. Put the chutney and chopped apricots into a large bowl. Toast the curry powder in a dry pan until aromatic, then stir into the bowl with the chopped ginger, followed by the Worcestershire sauce, mayonnaise and yoghurt. Season to taste.

3. Fold the cooled chicken through the dressing and refrigerate for at least a couple of hours before bringing to room temperature, folding in the coriander (reserving a couple of sprigs for garnish) and serving topped with the almonds and coriander sprigs, preferably with a green salad and basmati rice.

Perfect
Steak

Some myths can be as irritatingly persistent as a dog at a barbecue. Most of us, I think, can accept that margarine isn't a health food, and that the world didn't hatch from an eagle's egg — yet still we cling to the idea that searing meat magically 'locks in' the juices, and no wonder, with the likes of Delia and Gordon waffling on about sealing things.

In fact, every time you hear a chef on TV mention the word 'seal', you should fire off a meatily worded letter of complaint, because this idea, which has been hanging around since Aristotle was a lad, has been acknowledged as bunkum for about eighty years. The clue is in the lovely sizzling noise that meat makes when it hits a hot surface like a pan — that's the sound of water evaporating. You will notice that it doesn't stop when, after a minute or so, you decide that side of the joint is sealed. That's because it isn't; moisture is still leaking out through that gorgeously charred surface, and will continue to do so for some minutes after you finish the 'sealing' process.

However, after experimenting with a variety of cooking heats and times, from slower cooking as favoured by Alain Ducasse (who collects Michelin stars like most chefs collect blue plasters), which works well for very thick pieces of meat, less so for more

normal-sized steaks, to finishing them off in the oven à la John
Torode, I realized that Hugh Fearnley-Whittingstall was, as usual,
right: although briefly searing steak on a high temperature doesn't
make it perceptibly juicier — if anything, it was slightly drier — it does
improve the flavour, thanks to the workings of the Maillard reaction
in that wonderfully savoury, carbonized crust. (The Maillard
reaction is another name for the browning of sugars and amino
acids which is responsible for much of the flavour of roasted and
grilled foods.) Even advocates of very slow cooking, like Heston and
his eighteen-hour fore rib, finish steaks off with a quick blast in a
hot pan.

Buy the best-quality steak you can afford — depending on the cut,
it should have a good marbling of creamy fat, and be slightly
dark, rather than bright red, indicating that it's been aged to
tenderize the meat and improve the flavour. For cooking at home,
I like rump — it has bags of flavour and is easy to get right. Look
for one that's about 4cm thick — any thinner and you'll risk
overcooking it.

> **Steak of your choice — allow about**
>   **300g per person, depending**
>   **on appetite**
> **A knob of butter**
> **Salt and pepper**

1. Bring the steaks to room temperature before cooking, and put
    plates in a low oven to heat. Put a heavy-based frying pan on
    a high heat, and grease it with a little butter — a good piece of
    rump or sirloin will give off its own fat, and too much liquid
    will interfere with your flavourful crust. Cut off a small piece of

meat to use as a test – it should sizzle when it hits the pan, but the pan shouldn't be smoking.

2. Add the steaks to the pan – don't overcrowd them, and cook in batches if necessary. Leave them for a minute, then turn them over. If the pan's at the right temperature, they should be nicely browned, but not black. Season, and cook for another minute before repeating the process: although exact cooking times will depend on the size of your steak, Hugh Fearnley-Whittingstall's suggestion of 3–4 minutes for rare, 5–6 for medium rare, 6–8 for medium, and 10 for well done always works for me. The old rule of thumb (page 112) is a good one.

3. Remove the steaks from the pan and put on to warm plates for 5 minutes to rest before serving. When you've finished, you can deglaze the pan with a little red wine and pour the juices over the steaks.

Marinade

Marinating a good steak is a crying shame, but it's a useful tool to have in reserve for tougher cuts, such as onglet (also known as thick skirt in this country), and also works well with lamb leg or shoulder steaks, or chicken thighs – particularly on the barbecue. This recipe, based on the flavours of an Argentinian *chimichurri*, but harnessing the tenderizing properties of yoghurt instead of vinegar, which I found made the meat tough, is a great one to keep in mind for barbecue season.

Makes enough for 6 steaks or chicken breasts

200g Greek yoghurt
A large bunch (about 40g) of
    fresh herbs of your choice, finely
    chopped (parsley, mint and
    coriander work particularly well)
2 teaspoons salt
4 cloves of garlic, crushed
6 spring onions, finely chopped
1 small green chilli, finely chopped

Mix all the ingredients together, then use to coat each piece of meat well. Put the meat into a freezer bag or a shallow bowl and refrigerate for at least 3 hours, or overnight. Bring to room temperature before cooking.

Rule of thumb

Although it's not an exact science, this is a useful way to judge how your steaks are cooked without cutting into them, as well as being a slightly gruesome reminder that we're all made of meat. Prod the thickest part of the steak with a clean finger, and then compare it to your own hand.

Rare: will feel like the pad of flesh at the bottom of your thumb when your hand is completely relaxed – soft but springy.
Medium rare: will feel like that same pad of flesh

when you touch the tip of your index finger to the tip of the thumb on the same hand.

Medium: will feel like that flesh when you touch the tip of your middle finger to the tip of the thumb (are you getting the idea?).

Medium well done: will feel like that flesh when you touch the tip of your ring finger to the tip of the same thumb.

Well done: will feel like that flesh when you touch the tip of your little finger to the tip of the same thumb.

Perfect
Burgers

*T*he hamburger may well have European origins – it's thought to have crossed the Atlantic with the German immigrants of the early nineteenth century – but it took the Americans to recognize what North Carolina-born author Tom Robbins called this 'companionable and faintly erotic' chunk of seasoned beef as comfort food extraordinaire. Even if you tuck into seven colours of caviar every weekend, I bet the scent of grilling burgers still gets you all Pavlov's dog around the chops. It's that primal, charred, slightly crunchy exterior, the soft juiciness within – and of course, that perfect combination of toppings, chosen in childhood and sacred thereafter.

There's no place for lean, or finely ground beef in a burger – both produce a dry, crumbly patty unworthy of the name. Heston Blumenthal recommends a 2:1:1 combination of chuck, short rib and brisket, but in my experience, plain old chuck will do nicely. Ideally, of course, you would mince your beef yourself, but if you have neither the time, nor the appropriate food processor attachment, ask your butcher to do it for you – a coarse mince gives the best texture.

Homemade burgers can be disappointingly dense; throwing in a few breadcrumbs is a surefire way of lightening the texture. They will also soak up whatever liquid you use to bind the burger together, keeping it nice and juicy: egg, as recommended by *Larousse Gastronomique*, gives an oddly crunchy result once cooked, and the dollop of cream used by Charles Campion in his excellent barbecue book, *Food from Fire*, makes them unnecessarily rich – you couldn't top these babies with cheese.

Campion's Guinness burgers are inspired, however – the stout makes the burgers tender, juicy and super beefy, while caramelized onion adds a touch of sweetness. Poking a dimple in the middle before cooking is a handy tip from *Leiths Meat Bible* to stop them turning into cannonballs on the grill. Chilling the burgers before cooking will help keep them together when you cook them; whatever you do, don't press them down in the manner of a Hollywood diner cook, however – you'll lose all those delicious juices.

I must add that, in the interests of food safety, the Department of Health advises we should cook all minced meat products right through, until the juices run clear and there is no pink meat left. This is obviously particularly important for young children, pregnant women and the elderly, or anyone else with what is known as a 'compromised immune system'. The rest of you should weigh up risk versus reward, and make your own decision on the matter – but if you come down in favour of reducing quality beef to a dry puck of overcooked protein, you're not coming to my barbecue.

Serves 6

1 tablespoon olive oil or soft butter,
   plus extra to brush
1 large onion, finely chopped
1kg coarse-ground beef mince
100ml stout
2 tablespoons brown breadcrumbs
2 teaspoons finely chopped herbs
   (parsley or thyme work well)
1 teaspoon salt
Black pepper
Garnishes as desired (6 small sesame rolls, 6 x 20g slices of
   mature Cheddar, sliced pickles, sliced tomato, iceberg
   lettuce leaves, mustard, ketchup, tomato relish – the choice
   is yours)

1. Heat the oil or butter in a frying pan over a low heat, and cook
    the onion for 20 minutes, until soft and slightly browned. Leave
    to cool.
2. Spread the beef out on a tray and sprinkle over the onion. Add
    the stout, breadcrumbs, herbs and seasoning and mix together
    with a fork, being careful not to overwork it.
3. Divide the meat into twelve flattish burgers, putting a dimple in the
    centre of each to help keep them flat during cooking. Cover and
    refrigerate for an hour. Lightly brush with melted butter or oil.
4. Cook the burgers on a medium to hot barbecue or griddle pan:
    leave them undisturbed for the first 3 minutes so they build
    up a good crust on the bottom, then carefully turn them over,
    adding a slice of cheese on top if using. Cook for a further

4 minutes for rare, and 7 for well done, and allow to rest for a few minutes before serving. (You can toast buns, cut-side down, on the barbecue at this point.) Put the garnishes and sauces on the table, so people can build their own perfect burgers.

Barbecue tips

Take the barbecue seriously. If you've put the effort into buying the food, there's no point in wandering off to watch the football while it burns. Barbecues are notoriously unreliable, so keep an eye on it, even if you're reading the paper or following a match with the other one.

Oil the grill itself, but only once the barbecue is hot enough to actually cook on – it will just be burnt off if you put it on too early.

Don't add any food until the flames die down to reveal grey embers.

Although barbecues and ovens are very different beasts, it's helpful to think of the heat it's giving off in the same terms. In *12,167 Kitchen and Cooking Secrets*, Susan Sampson reveals a no-pain-no-gain approach to judging the temperature of a grill. If you can hold your hand just above the grill for less than a second before it's too hot for comfort, then it's very hot (260°C or more); 1–2 seconds and it's hot (between 200 and 260°C); 3–4 seconds and it's medium (180–200°C); 5 seconds and it's medium-low (160–180°C) and 6 or more seconds means the temperature is low (150°C or less).

Perfect
Beef Wellington

I'd always assumed this was a dish created in honour of the great
duke's famous victory at Waterloo — but in fact, it seems that the
name at least is almost certainly a twentieth-century invention,
awarded to mark the dish's resemblance to a brown, shiny wellington
boot. Rather less glamorous, isn't it?

The concept of cooking a piece of meat in a pastry case to keep it
moist is much older, however — and whatever the
history, this is one dinner party classic in sore
need of a revival. Not only does it look and
taste impressive (who doesn't love putting a
great big boot on the table?) but it's surprisingly
simple to prepare, and can be done ahead of time,
making it perfect for the host who'd actually like
to spend some time with their guests. Not always a given, I'll
admit.

That said, it doesn't come cheap: fillet of beef is sadly
non-negotiable — you need its buttery softness for the dish to work.
Fortunately, however, you don't need pâté de foie gras (far too
overpowering for the poor beef), or Parma ham, or any of the other
expensive ingredients some chefs stick in.

Truffles are similarly de trop; though mushrooms are an integral
part of the dish, a porcini duxelles, with a little Madeira for

sweetness (the duke was, apparently, a fan) and double cream as a nod to the special occasion, is quite sufficient. (You can use fresh chestnut or field mushrooms if you prefer, but I think the meaty flavour of dried porcini works best with the beef.)

Chopped shallot, meanwhile, adds a subtle sweetness – Delia uses onion instead, which gives a puzzlingly pasty-like quality to her wellington, making it about as posh as an old pair of galoshes.

The pastry should be puff – I tried a flaky alternative as suggested by *The Prawn Cocktail Years*, but found it too heavy for this rather refined dish. Unless you're weighed down with time and a yen to spend a morning chilling, folding and rolling, one of the excellent all-butter ready-made varieties will do you proud. (You can salve your conscience by decorating it with poppy seeds instead, just to make it look even less like its namesake.)

Traditionally, the pastry would be lined with crêpes, to soak up the meat juices and stop it going soggy, but as Simon Hopkinson and Lindsey Bareham observe, 'if the pastry is good and thin, buttery and rich, nothing is nicer than a meat-soaked crust', and James Martin's pancakes just add an unnecessary layer of stodge.

Add some spinach to the filling if you like, as Madalene Bonvini-Hamel of the British Larder does, but though it looks pretty, I prefer to serve greens on the side in more generous portions. The beauty of the wellington is in its simplicity.

Serves 4

10g dried porcini mushrooms
50g butter
2 shallots, finely chopped
300g mixed mushrooms
    (e.g. chestnut, oyster, shiitake, field),
    roughly chopped or torn
1 sprig of thyme, leaves picked
200ml Madeira
Salt and pepper
2 tablespoons double cream
1 tablespoon vegetable oil
500g beef fillet
250g all-butter puff pastry
1 egg, beaten, to glaze
1 tablespoon poppy seeds

1. Soak the dried porcini in 150ml of boiling water for 20
    minutes, then, reserving the soaking water, squeeze them out
    and finely chop.
2. Meanwhile, melt the butter in a frying pan over a medium heat
    and cook the shallots until pale golden. Add the mixed
    mushrooms, porcini and thyme to the pan and cook until the
    mushrooms have softened. Pour in 150ml of Madeira, season,
    turn up the heat and cook until the wine has all but evaporated.
    Scoop three-quarters of the mixture into a bowl. Mix in the
    double cream, taste for seasoning, and set aside.
3. Preheat the oven, and a flat baking sheet, to 220°C/fan 200°C/
    gas 7. Heat the oil in a frying pan over a high heat and, when
    smoking, add the fillet and sear briefly on all sides until well

browned and crusted. Season generously and allow to cool. Don't wash the pan yet — you'll need it for making the sauce.

4. Roll out the pastry to a rectangle measuring a few centimetres wider than your fillet, and long enough to wrap it in, and 3mm thick. Brush this all over with beaten egg, then spread with the duxelles mixture. Put the beef at one end and carefully roll it up, making sure the join is on the bottom, then trim the edges and tuck them in to seal the parcel, using the tines of a fork to press the edges together. Brush with beaten egg and sprinkle with poppy seeds.

5. Put the wellington on the hot baking sheet and bake for 30 minutes, until golden, then set aside to rest for 15 minutes.

6. Meanwhile, make the sauce. Heat the pan in which you seared the beef, pour in the remaining Madeira, and scrape the bottom to dislodge any crusty bits of meat. Add the rest of the mushrooms, plus the porcini soaking liquid, and allow the mixture to reduce slightly. Taste, season, and serve with the beef wellington.

Perfect
Ragù Bolognese

*T*o write on spag bol is to wade into a mire of controversy thicker and darker than any ragù that ever came out of nonna's kitchen. People feel very strongly indeed about what is, basically, a meat sauce of no more particular merit than, say, a shepherd's pie, or a chilli – and almost every cookery book has its own 'authentic' version.

I'm all for keeping things simple, but the minimalist beef, vegetable and tomato purée version in the classic Italian recipe bible *The Silver Spoon* fails to deliver on flavour, and although a dollop of cream can generally be relied upon to improve any dish, Italian cookery teacher Ursula Ferrigno's bolognese is rich but bland. I like the dark and intensely savoury ragù in Locatelli's *Made in Italy*, but the mixture of red wine and tomato passata doesn't seem to be typical of the traditional sauces of the area, unlike Marcella Hazan's combination of milk and white wine. The Italian-American food writer claims the dairy counteracts the acidic 'bite' of the alcohol – and it certainly adds a hint of sweetness to the end result. Bologna, in the north-east of Italy, is cow country, so this addition makes sense.

Although mixing meats is quite usual in the dish's homeland, I find adding pork overpowers the beef: chicken livers and pancetta, however, as used by Elizabeth David, add a subtle smokiness to the sauce. (She takes her recipe from one Zia Nerina, 'a splendid woman, titanic of proportion but angelic of face and manner', who ran a renowned restaurant in Bologna in the 1950s, when David was researching *Italian Food*.) Lastly, cooking the dish very slowly and gently in the oven, in obedience to Heston Blumenthal, makes the meat tender, and wonderfully rich. It may seem a lot of faff for such a common or garden dish, so remember, this is *ragù alla bolognese*, not spag bol – and you certainly won't regret it.

The fact is that there is no definitive recipe for a bolognese meat sauce, but to be worthy of the name, it should respect the traditions of the area: white wine, meat and milk, rather than tomatoes or Chianti, should be the key flavours. Cook long and slow, freeze any extra for week-night suppers, and serve with anything but spaghetti; in Bologna, rich meat ragùs such as this are eaten with fresh tagliatelle, or spinach-tinted lasagne verdi. (Tag bol doesn't have quite the same ring to it though, does it?)

Serves 4

A generous knob of butter
100g smoked pancetta or dry-cured
    streaky bacon, finely diced
1 onion, finely diced
1 carrot, finely diced
2 sticks of celery, finely diced
250g coarsely minced beef, at
    room temperature
Salt and pepper
40g chicken livers, finely chopped
150ml whole milk

Nutmeg, to grate
150ml dry white wine
1 x 400g tin of plum tomatoes
500g homemade pasta (see page 243)
   or dried pasta of your choice
100g Parmesan or pecorino, to serve

1. Melt the butter in a large flameproof casserole set over a gentle heat, then add the pancetta. Cook for 5 minutes, until the bacon has started to melt, then add the onion and cook gently for a further 5 minutes, until softened. Tip in the carrot and cook for 5 minutes before adding the celery and cooking for a further 2 minutes.

2. Turn the heat up, crumble the beef into the pan, season generously and brown for 5 minutes, stirring occasionally to break up any lumps. Stir in the liver, and let it cook for another 5 minutes.

3. Preheat the oven to 140°C/fan 120°C/gas 1. Pour in the milk, and grate a little nutmeg over the top. Turn the heat down and simmer gently for 30 minutes, until almost all the milk has evaporated.

4. Pour in the wine and the tomatoes, breaking them up with the back of a wooden spoon, and stir well. Bring to a simmer. Put the casserole into the oven, with the lid slightly askew, and cook for at least 3 hours (4 is even better), until the meat is very tender. Check on it occasionally, and top up with a little water if it seems too dry, although this probably won't be necessary.

5. Cook the pasta in a large pan of generously salted water and drain. Add the sauce to the pasta and toss together well to coat before serving with freshly grated Parmesan or pecorino.

Pasta, meet sauce

Although you're free to eat vermicelli with wild boar ragù, or strozzapreti with pesto if you so wish – hell, you can top it with custard and call it Sheila if that's what floats your boat – certain shapes just go better with particular sauces. The general rule is, the more delicate the pasta, the more delicate the sauce – angel hair (capellini) goes well with a simple oil and garlic dressing, for example, while chunky rigatoni can stand up to baking with minced beef. Here's a brief guide to matching some of the more widely available shapes with recipes – you'll notice the most versatile shapes are the thicker noodles, like fettuccine, and smaller shapes, like farfalle (bows), which go with just about everything.

Baked: bucatini, fusilli, lasagne, macaroni, orzo, penne, radiatori, rigatoni, rotini

Butter or oil-based sauces: capellini, farfalle, fettuccine, fusilli, linguine, macaroni, penne, spaghetti, tagliatelle

Cream or cheese-based sauces: capellini, farfalle, fettuccine, fusilli, lasagne, linguine, macaroni, penne, rigatoni, rotini, spaghetti, tagliatelle

Meat: conchiglie, farfalle, fettuccine, fusilli, lasagne, linguine, macaroni, orecchiette, pappardelle, rigatoni, spaghetti alla chitarra, tagliatelle

Pesto: capellini, farfalle, fusilli, linguine, trofie

Seafood: capellini, farfalle, fettuccine, linguine, spaghetti, spaghetti alla chitarra, tagliatelle

Tomato: bucatini, capellini, conchiglie, farfalle, fettuccine, fusilli, lasagne, linguine, macaroni, orecchiette, penne, radiatori, rigatoni, rotini, spaghetti, spaghetti alla chitarra, tagliatelle

Perfect
Chilli con Carne

We may love chilli, but, as a nation, we haven't been particularly kind to it. Lumps of mince made fiery red with cayenne pepper, topped with kidney beans and served bursting forth from a microwaved jacket potato – hardly the proud culinary heritage so celebrated in its American homeland.

The International Chili Society, an organization devoted to the 'promotion, development and improving of the preparation and appreciation of true chili', credits the dish to south-western cattle drivers, who had to survive on what they took with them, and the raw ingredients they found along the trail. Which might, I suppose, include Nigella's tomato ketchup, but is unlikely to have taken in her cardamom pods, or Hugh Fearnley-Whittingstall's chorizo.

In this recipe, I've stripped the dish right back to its roots: meat and peppers. No tomatoes – the only recipes I find using them are British – and no cayenne, although I have kept the dubiously authentic minced meat, because, although I enjoyed Jamie's brisket, and Hugh's pork shoulder, without it, it isn't chilli to me. You won't find any lumps here though: after two and a half hours in the pot, it should almost melt in the mouth.

My spice mixture, which might seem a bit daunting if you were hoping to pick up the ingredients from the corner shop, is based on that apparently used by the long-gone Chilli Queens of San Antonio: Mexican women who once sold their highly spiced stews from street carts 'to a cadre of customers who rode in from all over the prairies to singe their tonsils'.

The coffee, meanwhile, is stolen from Jamie Oliver's American road trip — cowboys travelled on caffeine apparently, and I love the smoky, almost campfire bitterness it gives to the dish. Add sweet, charred onions and copious amounts of garlic, plus the mealy beans strictly forbidden by the Institute of Texan Cultures, and you have a meal fit for a chilli queen herself. Serve with rice, Nigella's wonderfully fluffy cornbread — or, of course, a good old jacket potato. Just call it Anglo-Texican fusion.

Serves 6–8

Beef dripping or vegetable oil, to fry
1kg minced meat
2 onions, thinly sliced
5 cloves of garlic, minced
350ml freshly brewed coffee
2 chipotle chillies
2 ancho chillies
A pinch of rock salt
1 teaspoon cumin seeds, toasted
1 tablespoon Mexican oregano
2 teaspoons chilli powder, or to taste
2 tablespoons dark muscovado sugar
2 fresh long green chillies
400g cooked kidney beans

1. Heat the dripping or oil in a large, heavy-bottomed pan on a high heat, then brown the mince well (to a deep brown, rather than beige) in batches, stirring regularly. Don't be tempted to do it all at once, or it won't brown properly. Remove from the pan once cooked and set aside.
2. Add the onions to the pan and stir-fry briefly, until slightly browned at the edges.
3. Turn the heat right down and add the garlic. Stir and cook until the onion has completely softened, then add the browned meat, brewed coffee, 300ml of water and a generous pinch of salt. Bring to the boil, reduce the heat again, then cover and simmer for 2 hours.
4. Meanwhile, remove the stalks and seeds from the dried chillies and discard. Grind the chillies together in a pestle and mortar, or grinder, along with a pinch of rock salt and the toasted cumin seeds. Mix in the oregano and chilli powder.
5. Add the spices to the pan along with the sugar and the whole fresh chillies, stir well and simmer, partially covered, for another 30 minutes, adding a little more water if it seems dry, or you prefer a saucier chilli.
6. Ten minutes before the end, add the drained beans, taste, and adjust the seasoning and spicing if necessary. If possible, leave overnight and reheat to serve.

Perfect
Steak and Ale Pie

What a noble thing is the pie. Everyone, with the puzzling exception of my own mother, loves plunging through that pastry portal to discover the riches that lie beneath – and whether that's cheese and potato, apple and blackberry, or, as here, a classic meat and gravy number, the pie rarely disappoints.

The most important thing to bear in mind about steak and ale pie is that you shouldn't use steak. Or at least, not the kind generally recommended for pies – stewing, braising and chuck steak all came out tough in my experiments.

Much better were the shin beef recommended by Hugh Fearnley-Whittingstall and the ox cheek and oxtail deployed by the London steak restaurant Hawksmoor in their cookbook: flavoursome, rich, and yes, melt in the mouth. Generously-sized chunks of bacon add another layer of smoky flavour (lest there be any remaining doubt, this is not a dinner for dieters).

I'm not keen on the slimy mushrooms which seem bafflingly common in pie recipes, or indeed on the classic, but inevitably mushy carrots, but baby onions make the cut, adding a little sweetness to what is otherwise a defiantly savoury dish.

For the gravy, ale is obviously non-negotiable, although be sure to go for a full-bodied, slightly sweeter variety — as beer writer Melissa Cole explains, using just any old stout can make your gravy bitter. You could top it up with water, but I think the Hairy Bikers' beef stock gives a more satisfyingly meaty result.

And then, despite what I've said about the ale, I've added some cocoa powder, like chef Tom Norrington-Davies — unless you're a super-taster you'll be hard pressed to identify it in the finished gravy, but somehow it rounds things off perfectly.

Finally, to top the dish, I've eschewed the usual feather-light puff in favour of a crumbly suet version: crisp on top, soft, almost doughy beneath, and the perfect thing for soaking up all that lovely gravy. I don't, unlike Hugh, believe it's necessary to line the entire dish with the stuff, because I'm not keen on the gumminess that lurks at the bottom, but if you feel strongly that a pie ought to be encased in pastry to be worthy of the name, by all means make double the quantity and do so. Serve with steamed greens, as a nod to a balanced diet.

Serves 4

A large chunk of dripping
700g boneless beef shin or ox cheek,
   cut into large chunks
20g plain flour, seasoned
200g smoked bacon lardons
225g whole baby onions
400ml sweetish dark ale

400ml beef stock
4 sprigs of thyme, leaves roughly chopped
1 bay leaf
1 tablespoon dark muscovado sugar
1 teaspoon red wine vinegar
1 teaspoon cocoa

For the pastry
400g plain flour, plus extra to dust
1 teaspoon baking powder
2 teaspoons mustard powder (optional)
½ teaspoon salt
175g suet (or chilled, grated bone
    marrow if you have it)
Iced water
A little milk, to glaze

1. Preheat the oven to 170°C/fan 150°C/gas 3. Melt a generous
   knob of dripping in a large frying pan over a high heat, and toss
   the chunks of beef in seasoned flour to coat. Sear it in batches,
   taking care not to overcrowd the pan, until well browned.
   Transfer to an ovenproof casserole once done.
2. Reduce the heat a little, and add the lardons and the onions to
   the pan. Cook until the bacon fat begins to melt, and the onions
   are deep golden, then tip them into the casserole along with any
   fat and juices.
3. Pour a glug of ale into the frying pan and bring it to a simmer,
   scraping the bottom to dislodge any bits, then pour the whole lot
   into the casserole along with the meat. Add the remaining ale,
   the stock, herbs, sugar, vinegar and cocoa and bring it all to a
   simmer.

4. Cover the dish and bake for 2¼ hours, then uncover and cook, stirring occasionally, for another 1½ hours, until the meat is tender and almost falling apart (it will cook further in the pie). Allow to cool to room temperature.

5. Meanwhile, make the pastry. Mix the flour, baking powder and mustard powder in a bowl with ½ teaspoon of salt. Stir in the fat, then add just enough iced water to make a dough. Shape into a disc, wrap in clingfilm and chill for at least an hour.

6. Preheat the oven to 190°C/fan 170°C/gas 5. Spoon the filling into a dish, and roll out the pastry on a lightly floured surface to about 1cm thick. Wet the rim of the pie dish, then place the pastry over the filling, pushing down around the edge to seal. Cut a hole in the middle to let the steam out. Brush with a little milk and bake for about 50 minutes, until golden.

Perfect
Steak and Kidney Pudding

*T*he British can be justly proud of the pudding. Done well, as it so rarely is these days, it's a marvellous combination of rich and delicate — a meaty, savoury interior, steamed to perfection in its light, spongy pastry jacket, complete with the kind of gravy that can make even grown men a little damp around the eye.

But traditional puddings are thin on the ground these days, even on pub menus — sad, yes, but also an excellent reason to make your own. People seem to think that steaming anything more complicated than a head of broccoli is hard work, but in fact, as long as you remember to keep topping up the water during ad breaks, making your own pudding is gratifyingly easy.

Steak and kidney is the classic combination, although those who are still trying to suppress a smile of relief at every bite that turns out to be the former rather than the latter should bear in mind the myriad alternative options (including a rather lovely vegetarian leek pudding from the north-east). That said, if you use veal or lamb's kidney, rather than Constance Spry or Jane Grigson's ox variety, it does tend to fade obligingly into the background, providing only a hint of offaly excitement — take your pick according to preference.

The beef, meanwhile, should be neck or chuck: something with a good amount of sinew to break down during cooking. Mrs Beeton extravagantly calls for rump steak, but it turned out to be a mistaken extravagance, dry and disappointing.

The pastry must, of course, be suet – the creamy fat encasing the kidneys (a pleasing synergy) has a relatively high melting point, which means the pastry shell has already set by the time it melts away, leaving only a rash of tiny bubbles in its place. This is why something that sounds so heavy (suet pastry, a great lump of an idea) is actually so remarkably light.

If you can get fresh suet, which butchers will be able to order in for you, then it gives a better flavour than the dried pellets in jaunty coloured boxes. I also add mustard powder and chopped thyme to make it even more delicious.

Braising the meat before adding it to the pastry not only gives your gravy a better flavour, but also prevents the singularly unattractive grey, claggy look that bedevils Constance Spry's filling. She's also rather sparse in her flavourings – rationing's over now, and I feel confident that we're allowed to use stock and stout rather than plain old water to make a gravy, although Jane Grigson's red wine, and Gary Rhodes' garlic, may both be a step too far in the name of progress; this remains a very British dish. Which doesn't mean you have to serve it with over-boiled vegetables – unless you really want to.

Serves 4

1½ tablespoons beef dripping or oil, to cook
I onion, thinly sliced
I carrot, peeled and diced
I bay leaf
A small bunch of thyme, leaves picked
Salt and pepper
I tablespoon plain flour
400g chuck or stewing steak, cut into chunks
150g rose veal kidney, halved, trimmed and cut into chunks
150ml stout
150ml beef stock

For the pastry
250g plain flour
2 teaspoons baking powder
¼ teaspoon salt
½ teaspoon English mustard powder
125g chopped suet
3 sprigs of fresh thyme, leaves finely chopped
Oil, to grease

1. Melt the dripping in a large, heavy-based pan over a medium heat and cook the onions and carrots along with the herbs until they are beginning to caramelize. Remove them from the pan and set aside.

2. Season the flour well, and toss the steak and kidney in it to coat. Add more fat to the pan if necessary, then brown the meat in batches: if you do it all at once, it will steam in its own juices.

3. Pour in the stout and scrape any beefy floury bits from the bottom of the pan, then add the stock, the vegetables and all the meat. Bring the liquid to a simmer, partially cover and simmer gently for 1¾ hours, until the steak is very tender. Season to taste and allow to cool.

4. Two hours before you want to eat, sift the flour and baking powder into a mixing bowl and add the salt and mustard powder. Rub in the suet briefly to mix, then add the thyme and enough cold water to make it into a firm dough. Set a quarter of the dough aside, then roll out the rest on a lightly floured surface to about 0.5cm thick. Generously grease a 1 litre pudding basin and line with the pastry, being careful not to stretch it too much.

5. Fill the pastry-lined bowl with meat and gravy, stopping about 2cm from the top, then roll out the rest of the pastry to make a lid and seal it on with a little cold water. Cover the basin with foil, leaving enough slack for the pastry to rise, and fashion a handle out of string to lift the basin out of the water when required.

6. Put the pudding into a large pan half filled with boiling water, cover and simmer for 1½ hours, checking the water level regularly and topping up as necessary. Turn out and serve immediately.

Perfect Cottage Pie

*T*his is neither the time nor the place to get into an argument about the semantics of shepherd's versus cottage pie. I think we can all agree that it makes sense, logically speaking, for the first to refer to a dish made with lamb, and that by long custom, the second has come to suggest beef, whatever the original relationship between the two.

The truth is, although you may choose to vary the herbs, the two meats are largely interchangeable in this context, as most recipes acknowledge. Once lubricated by a rich, savoury gravy and entombed beneath a blanket of crisp-topped mash, few hungry souls would notice the difference in any case.

What is important is to have juicy, robustly textured meat – although Hugh Fearnley-Whittingstall's leftover roast beef and Nigel Slater's mince both work fine here, it's Jane Grigson's finely chopped shin which proves the perfect partner for the fluffy potato topping. It has a more robust feel to it, rather than simply melting into the sauce. (I think you do need to peel the spuds, here, by the way, to enjoy the contrast in textures.)

Forget her garlic and white wine though – this homely dish needs no such Mediterranean makeover, nor does it require Simon

Hopkinson and Lindsey Bareham's tomato ketchup, which I can taste even after forty minutes in the oven. Nigel's simple sauce of stock, Worcestershire sauce and thyme is perfect, the condiment giving the meat depth and a hint of spice without overpowering it – I've just added a touch of cornflour to make a more satisfying gravy. Any further additions are at your own risk.

Serves 4

600g shin of beef* (trimmed weight),
   chopped into small pieces
25g beef dripping or butter
2 onions, finely diced
2 carrots, finely diced
2 sticks of celery, finely diced
1 teaspoon dried thyme
350ml good-quality beef stock
1 teaspoon cornflour
1 teaspoon Worcestershire sauce
1kg floury potatoes, such as
   Maris Piper, peeled
Salt and pepper
125g butter

1. Cut the trimmed beef into evenly-sized dice, then gather these together on a chopping board. Grasp the handles of two knives together in one hand, and using your other hand to keep the two tips in place, move the knives back and forth across the meat to chop it into 1cm pieces.

---

* NB substitute 600g minced lamb for shepherd's pie.

2. Meanwhile, heat the dripping, if you have any left over from your last roast, or 25g butter in a pan over a moderate heat, then add the vegetables and cover. Cook for 20 minutes, until soft but not brown.

3. Add the thyme, then turn up the heat and add the beef. Cook for 5 minutes, stirring to brown all over, then add half the stock. Whisk the other half with the cornflour, and stir into the meat mixture. Add a generous dash of Worcestershire sauce, turn down the heat, and allow to simmer uncovered for 1 hour and 15 minutes, until the meat is tender.

4. Meanwhile, cut your potatoes into evenly-sized chunks and put into a large pan of cold, salted water. Bring to the boil and simmer until tender. Drain and mash with 100g of the butter. Season to taste.

5. Taste and season the meat, adding more Worcestershire sauce if necessary. If it looks dry, pour in a little water.

6. Preheat the oven to 200°C/fan 180°C/gas 6. Put the meat into a large baking dish (30 x 28cm would be ideal) and allow to cool slightly if you've got time — it will make adding the potato easier. For a nice crispy top, I like to spoon it on in lumps: you can run a fork over the top if you prefer. Dot with the remaining 25g of butter.

7. Put into the oven and bake for 40–50 minutes, until the potato is crisp and slightly brown, then serve.

How to keep cut herbs fresh
Treat them like a bunch of flowers: cut a few millimetres off the bottom of the stem, then put them into a couple of centimetres of water in

the fridge, making sure no leaves are submerged. Change the water every day.

Alternatively, you can wrap the bottom of the herbs in a damp piece of kitchen roll and put them in an open plastic bag in the salad tray of the fridge.

Perfect
Beef Stew and Dumplings

*S*tew and dumplings reeks of institutional catering, when in fact, done well, it's one of the most comforting dishes around.

Stewing steak, despite the name, is not the best cut to use here – Delia Smith hits the nail on the head when she confesses that for years she was put off shin by its unattractive appearance, until she realized all the stuff that looked so off-putting would melt during cooking, adding flavour and richness to the gravy. 'Now,' she says in her *Complete Cookery Course*, 'for an old-fashioned brown stew, I wouldn't use anything else.' And on the matter of 'brown stew', Delia knows best – it may take longer to cook, but shin falls apart under the fork, and gifts a gorgeous richness to the surrounding sauce.

You could make that sauce with water, as recommended by Francatelli's *Plain Cookery Book for the Working Classes* (1852), but frankly, the working classes deserve better in the form of stock and stout – they both go brilliantly with beef (see also steak and kidney pudding, and steak and ale pie), to produce what is, in my opinion, an unbeatable gravy. If you can find what used to be known as 'milk stout', made in Britain, the slight sweetness gives a more well-rounded result than the ubiquitous Irish variety. Thicken the gravy with a little flour to give it a respectably robust consistency.

Add potatoes to the pot if you like, but I think that, together with the dumplings, they're carb overload. Instead I've used sliced onions, carrots and baby turnips for sweetness, the latter two added towards the end of cooking, so they keep their texture. Mushy vegetables are almost as unwelcome in a stew as gristle.

Lastly, keep an eye on the temperature. You need to cook the meat slowly, so it isn't tough, but bear in mind it still needs to bubble — as Harold McGee (him again) explains in his book *The Curious Cook*, strands of beef collagen don't even begin to unravel until the temperature gets above 60°C, and it needs to be 20° higher for them to dissolve into gelatine 'in any appreciable quantities'. In other words, to turn chewy meat into something really delicious, keep your stew hot, but not too hot: a gentle simmer is what you're after.

Apart from that, it can be happily left to its own devices for a couple of hours — bear in mind that like many slow-cooked dishes, this stew is even better reheated, which makes it the ideal thing to prepare ahead for guests. And who says you can't serve stew and dumplings at a dinner party anyway?

Serves 4—6

800g shin of beef
2 tablespoons flour, seasoned with salt and pepper
Beef dripping, butter or oil, to cook
2 onions, sliced
300ml beef stock
300ml stout, preferably milk stout
Salt and pepper
1 bay leaf

3 sprigs of thyme
2 carrots, peeled and cut into chunky slices
2 small turnips, peeled and cut into chunks

For the dumplings
100g plain flour
1 teaspoon baking powder
50g suet
A small bunch of chives and parsley,
   finely chopped

1. Trim any outer sinew off the beef and cut it into large chunks.
   Coat these with the seasoned flour.
2. Heat a heavy-bottomed casserole or large pan on a medium heat
   and add a knob of dripping or butter, or a couple of tablespoons
   of oil if you prefer. Brown the meat well in batches – be careful
   not to overcrowd the pan, or it will boil in its own juices –
   adding more fat if necessary, then transfer the pieces to a bowl.
   Scrape the bottom of the pan regularly to prevent any crusty bits
   from burning.
3. Add some more fat to the pan and fry the onions until soft and
   beginning to brown. Put these into the same bowl as the beef,
   and then pour a little stock into the pan and scrape the bottom
   to deglaze it. Put back the beef and onions, pour in the rest of
   the stock and the stout, season, and top with the herbs. Bring to
   the boil, then partially cover, turn down the heat to a gentle
   simmer, and cook for 2 hours.
4. Add the carrots and turnips to the pan, and leave to simmer for
   about another hour, checking occasionally, until the meat is
   tender enough to cut with a spoon. Leave to cool, overnight if
   possible (this will improve the flavour), then remove any
   solidified fat from the top and bring the stew to a simmer.

5. Meanwhile, make the dumplings by sifting the flour into a bowl. Add the rest of the ingredients and just enough cold water to make a dough. Roll this into 6 round dumplings and add these to the top of the stew. Partially cover again and simmer for 25 minutes, until the dumplings are cooked through, then check the seasoning of the gravy, and serve.

Good cuts of meat for slow cooking
Cheaper cuts of meat generally come from older animals, or hard-working bits of younger animals – they will have a high proportion of tough connective tissue, which must be broken down by long, slow simmering. This also breaks down the muscle fibres, and results in meat so tender it can be cut with a spoon. Getting the best out of these cuts takes time – although not necessarily much of yours; they're quite happy to simmer away quietly for hours on a low heat while you read the paper, or watch a film – but I think the results are infinitely more delicious than the most tender fillet steak.

Beef: blade, brisket, chuck, flank, leg, middle/short ribs, neck, oxtail, shin, silverside, skirt
Lamb: breast, chump, leg, neck and middle neck, scrag end, shank, shoulder
Pork: belly, chump end, hand, leg, loin, spare rib
Chicken: thighs and legs

Perfect
Boeuf Bourguignon

*T*his Gallic classic must surely rank among the world's great dishes: for a meat eater, there are few greater pleasures than slow-cooked beef in a deliciously savoury red wine sauce studded with tender baby veg.

Simon Hopkinson and Lindsey Bareham call for 'well-hung sinewy beef – chuck, shoulder or shin' in their book *The Prawn Cocktail Years*, Anthony Bourdain's *Les Halles Cookbook* for *paleron* (featherblade), Richard Olney's much-lauded *French Menu Cookbook* for heel and Michel Roux Jr's *The French Kitchen* for 'braising beef (chuck is good but cheek is best)'. Harry Eastwood is also a fan of cheeks, writing in *Carneval* that they 'are the perfect vehicles for a Bourguignon since they absorb all the flavours in the pan and the meat surrenders completely' – and I'm with her; though shin and heel are other good options, they don't have quite the same ratio of meat to fat.

A few chunks of oxtail add a beefier richness than Hopkinson and Bareham's pig's trotter, though boeuf à la bourguignonne almost always contains cured pork too, preferably unsmoked (that said, as Eastwood and Roux's recipes confirm, Olney is wrong: smoked bacon is better than no bacon). Last Minute Larries will be relieved to learn there's no need to marinate the meat in wine before cooking: as Roux warns, it makes for 'a gamey flavour that's not entirely true to the original'.

The traditional Burgundian garnish of mushrooms and onions is non-negotiable, preferably sautéd until golden in bacon fat. The *Prawn Cocktail Years* recipe adds the vegetables to the stew for the entire cooking time, while Roux and Olney cook them separately, which is a bit of a faff — I prefer Eastwood's method, which adds the sautéd veg to the beef for the final half hour of cooking.

Bourdain uses caramelized onions instead, which makes his dish taste more like *soupe à l'oignon*.

If you can't find pearl onions, small shallots will do, though they're more of a faff to peel. The baby carrots favoured by Eastwood and Roux are the most pleasing garnish aesthetically, but ordinary ones, cut into large chunks, work just as well in the flavour department and the same goes for the mushrooms.

The principal flavour here ought to be dry, fruity red wine, though it needn't be a Burgundian Pinot Noir unless you're made of money. Puzzlingly, Bourdain uses only a cup: a whole bottle is required for maximum impact, preferably reduced with a few aromatics to concentrate its flavour. A splash of brandy adds complexity, and beef stock, rather than Bourdain's water, gives the wine a savoury boost.

Lastly, you can cook it on the hob if you prefer, but I find it's much easier to keep the heat constant in a moderate oven. Ideal served with a mountain of mash, and a lake of red wine.

Serves 6

1 bottle of fruity, relatively light dry red wine
1 onion, peeled and cut into 6 wedges
1 large carrot, scrubbed and cut into 2cm chunks
2 garlic cloves, peeled and squashed with the back
   of a knife
1 bay leaf
A small bunch of parsley, plus a handful for
   garnish
2 sprigs of thyme
2 tablespoons olive oil
35g butter
200g unsmoked bacon lardons, or a thick piece of unsmoked
   bacon, cut into 2cm cubes
18 baby carrots
200g button mushrooms
24 pearl onions, or 12 small shallots, peeled and trimmed
2 tablespoons flour
Salt and pepper
1kg beef cheeks, cut into 3cm chunks
400g oxtail
60ml brandy
250ml good beef stock

1. Pour the wine into a saucepan and add the onion, carrot, garlic and
    herbs. Bring to the boil, then simmer for 30 minutes until reduced
    by about half. Heat the oven to 170°C/fan 150°C/gas 3.
2. While it's reducing, put the oil and butter into a large casserole
    dish over a medium-high heat, and once the butter has stopped
    foaming, add the bacon and fry until golden. Scoop out with a
    slotted spoon and set aside.

3. Repeat with the carrots and mushrooms, putting them into a fresh bowl once coloured. Add the onions to the pan, turn down the heat a little and fry until just beginning to brown.

4. Meanwhile, tip the flour on to a plate, season with salt and pepper, then roll the meat in it. Add the onions to the carrots and mushrooms, and turn up the heat under the now empty pan. Fry the meat in batches until deeply browned, being careful not to overcrowd the pan (add a little more oil if it feels like it's burning rather than browning). Scoop out and set aside in a bowl.

5. Pour the brandy into the pan and scrape the base to dislodge any caramelized bits. Strain in the reduced wine (discarding the vegetables and herbs), and add the stock. Return the meat to the pan and bring to a simmer.

6. Cover, put in the oven and bake for 2½ hours, at which point add the onions, mushrooms and carrots and bake for a further half an hour.

7. Scoop out the oxtail and strip off the meat. Stir this back into the pan with the lardons and season to taste. Add the remaining parsley before serving.

Cooking with wine
The old adage, never cook with wine you wouldn't be prepared to drink, is true – to an extent. Do you really want the dominant flavour of your dish to be thin and acidic, overpoweringly oaky, or just plain off? Steer clear of anything marked cooking wine for a start; it'll be overpriced rubbish. Saying that, neither should you splash out on a Châteauneuf du Pape, which Elizabeth David records one Nîmois cook bringing out for a beef and olive stew in *French Provincial Cooking* (in fact, simmering that kind of wine

for two hours might well be a prosecutable offence across the Channel). Do try, however, to match the strength and character of the wine to the dish. The most versatile whites are clean and fresh-tasting — avoid anything strongly oaky, or too aromatic: dry white vermouth is a useful standby. Reds should be full-bodied and fruity, but not overpoweringly so: you don't want the sauce to be sweet, or tannic and bitter; depending on the dish, Beaujolais or Merlot are reliable choices.

Perfect
Meatballs

With apologies to Lady and the Tramp, I'd be hard pushed to describe meatballs as romantic, but there aren't many other occasions where they don't fit the bill. From our very own faggots to the Chinese lionhead variety, via Turkish koftes and Iranian sparrowheads, they're a dish with universal appeal. It's tough to pick a favourite, but, possibly thanks to those damn dogs, I'm pretty soft on the Italian variety, served with a big plate of spaghetti and what's known in America as 'red sauce'.

Beef-only meatballs are sadly dull, tasting of dripping and little else, and veal, despite claims it makes the best meatballs of all, has too delicate a flavour to stand up to such treatment. Better to do as they do in Italy, and mix in some pork for good measure.

Binding is key – there's nothing sadder than a meatball that crumbles in the pan. Egg, as used by Hugh Fearnley-Whittingstall and the *Ginger Pig Meat Book*, works wonders, but makes the finished meatballs rather dry and dense. Even just using the yolk is disappointing; far preferable to do as Angela Hartnett suggests in *Cucina* and go for breadcrumbs soaked in milk: 'the secret of making light meatballs' apparently.

Onions are a classic flavouring – I don't think you need garlic as well, although I wouldn't rule it out of the sauce – but I found classic Italian cookery bible *The Silver Spoon*'s anchovies overwhelming, and though Hugh and Angela both use Parmesan, I prefer to save it for the top. I have allowed myself one impromptu addition though: fennel seeds, which work wonderfully with the pork, and add a pleasing crunch to the cooked meatballs.

The cooking, annoying as it sounds, should be done separately; otherwise, the meatballs seem to lose their flavour to the sauce (which is fine, if you're happy to make that sacrifice; personally, I'd like both parts to taste equally fantastic). Cooked alone, they remain juicy, while also developing a tasty caramelized crust.

This is a three-pan job: one for the meatballs, one for the sauce (I'd obviously recommend the perfect tomato sauce recipe on page 296), and one for the pasta. It's well worth it though, I promise.

Serves 4

> **6 tablespoons milk**
> **1 thick slice of white bread, crusts removed**
> **300g minced beef**
> **200g minced pork**
> **1 onion, finely chopped**
> **2 tablespoons finely chopped flat-leaf parsley**
> **3 teaspoons fennel seeds, toasted (optional)**
> **Salt and pepper**
> **Olive oil, to fry**

1. Put the milk and bread into a shallow bowl and leave to soak for about 10 minutes. Meanwhile, put the other ingredients, except for the oil, into a large bowl, season generously, and mix well with your hands.

2. Use a fork to mash the bread into a milky paste and then add this to the meat and mix in well. Heat a little olive oil in a large pan over a medium-high heat and fry a pinch of the mixture until cooked through. Allow to cool slightly, then taste and adjust the seasoning of the mixture if necessary.

3. Shape the mixture into balls with damp hands — I like to make them about the size of a chocolate truffle — then add another 2 tablespoons of olive oil to the pan and fry them in batches until nicely caramelized all over. Turn down the heat and fry more gently until cooked through.

4. Serve with a tomato sauce and spaghetti.

Perfect
Roast Pork with Crackling

I'm happy to confess to being an out-and-proud fat-fancier. The tender, melting wobble of it, that satisfying oily crunch — how can mere meat hope to compete? Good as it tastes, fat is largely a textural pleasure, and crackling is surely the supreme example of this: a blistered top, as dry and crunchy as an autumn leaf, hiding a layer of rich, creamy deliciousness beneath.

The basic principles of great crackling are simple enough. You must score the rind in vertical lines about a finger's width apart, to allow the heat to penetrate the fat, but without cutting into the meat itself — go down too far, and all the lovely juices will come rushing out, which is definitely not desirable. Further than that, authorities beg to differ. I try everything from sticking it in the oven with no more than a coat of salt, as suggested by Delia, to the Chinese-duck-style treatment espoused by Simon Hopkinson, who has me scalding, air-drying and salting like Ken Hom himself, but the clear winner is, obviously, the slightly nutty recipe suggested by food blogger Gastronomy Domine. In an effort to dry the meat out as much as possible, she treats it to a rub down, gives it the once-over with a hairdryer, and leaves it in the fridge overnight, covered only with a tea towel, until the skin is as desiccated as an old camel bone in the Kalahari — then, and only then, is it ready for the oven. (The fridge is a very dry environment, which is why it's best not to store bread in there.)

As well as a bone-dry rind, perfection requires generous levels of salt, and a quick blast in a blisteringly hot oven, in accordance with the teachings of Hugh Fearnley-Whittingstall. Adding extra fat, as *Good Housekeeping* does, is an unnecessary decadence.

To rescue disappointing crackling, carefully detach it from the meat and either put it back into a very hot oven for a few minutes, or stick it in the microwave for a couple of minutes, to give it a texture reminiscent of a porky Aero – not ideal, but better than admitting defeat, and far superior to popping it under a hot grill, which, in defiance of all logic, does disappointingly little for the texture.

I joint of pork with a generous
coating of fat
Salt

1. The day before you want to eat the pork, score the skin with a sharp knife if your butcher hasn't already done so – cut a regular diamond pattern into the fat, but don't go as far down as the meat. Pat the joint dry with kitchen paper, and rub vigorously with salt. Now, take a hairdryer, and gently blow-dry the joint until the skin is absolutely dry – you'll feel ridiculous, but it's worth it, I promise. If you don't own a hairdryer, you'll need to be extra diligent with the paper towels. Cover the joint with a tea towel and put into the fridge overnight.

2. On the day itself, preheat the oven to 240°C/fan 220°C/gas 9, take the joint out of the fridge while it's heating, and rub some more salt into the skin. Put it into a roasting tin (you can add sliced onions, herbs, garlic – whatever flavourings you fancy – into the tin as well) and roast for half an hour, then turn down the heat to 190°C/fan 170°C/gas 5 and roast for 35 minutes per 450g until the juices run clear.

3. Check the crackling — if it isn't quite crisp enough for your liking, you can very carefully cut it from the joint and put it back into the oven for another few minutes — turn it up as high as it will go, and keep an eye on it.
4. Take the meat out of the oven and allow to rest in a warm place for at least 20 minutes before carving.

Perfect
Baked Ham

*T*his recipe was originally created for Christmas, but having made it in midsummer, if you can bear to have the oven on, it's a winning cold centrepiece for lunch or dinner. It also makes superlative sandwiches. In short, there's no need to wait until that last Advent chocolate has been eaten: this truly is a ham for all seasons.

Those who are of an obsessively DIY bent might want to cure the pork themselves – all it takes is a big bowl of brine and a few days' notice – but if you leave everything until the last minute, like me, then a piece of ready-cured meat, known as a gammon (unless you're cooking the whole leg, in which case, confusingly, it's a ham from the get-go), is what you're after. I find unsmoked versions are best, so the flavour of the meat itself comes through: modern gammon tends to be less salty than its ancestors so you rarely need to soak it, but do check the packaging or ask your butcher, just in case.

Because gammon is cured, but not cooked, it's generally poached or baked before the final glaze is added. After trying both methods, including a recipe which involves baking it in a rack above a pan of stock, I decided that the former is a more effective way of infusing flavour into the meat.

You can use just about any liquid you fancy for this purpose, from cider to mulled wine to Coca-Cola (courtesy of Nigella Lawson), but I've gone for a treacly, spicy mixture inspired by Jane Grigson's Bradenham ham recipe, which makes me think of festive gingerbread and other similarly happy memories. It also has the benefit of giving the ham a rather striking black rim, which should draw admiring glances its way.

Once poached, the ham is crowned with its ceremonial glaze – a stiffish paste is required if it's to develop a crunchy crust, which means it needs to have a dry base. Toffeeish brown sugar and hot English mustard powder do the trick, with a little orange zest as a nod to the traditional marmalade ham (marmalade itself threatens the structural integrity of the crust) and a drop of spicy ginger wine, just to make it loose enough to spread.

A final sprinkling of extra sugar, as suggested by Delia Smith, gives a nice even caramelization – and of course, you can't have a ham without cloves. They just look so wonderfully Dickensian. With a big baked ham on the table, what could be wrong with the world?

Serves 8

I boneless gammon joint, about 2kg
3 tablespoons molasses or black treacle
4 teaspoons cloves
A pinch of mace
I bay leaf
I teaspoon allspice
I tablespoon black peppercorns
Peel of ½ an orange, cut into thin strips

For the glaze
5 tablespoons dark brown sugar,
   plus extra to sprinkle
1½ tablespoons mustard powder
Finely grated zest of ½ an orange
20ml ginger wine

1. Place the ham in a stockpot or large saucepan, and cover with cold water. Bring slowly to a simmer, skimming off any scum, then add the molasses, 1 teaspoon of cloves, the mace, bay leaf, allspice, peppercorns and orange peel and simmer very gently for about an hour and a half, until the internal temperature of the ham reaches 68°C.

2. Preheat the oven to 220°C/fan 200°C/gas 7. Lift the ham out of the liquid (which can be used to make really brilliant baked beans), allow it to cool slightly, then use a sharp knife to carefully cut off the skin, leaving as much fat beneath as possible. Score the fat in a diamond pattern, and stud the intersections with cloves. Place the ham in a foil-lined roasting tray.

3. Mix together the glaze ingredients to make a thick paste, and brush this all over the scored fat. Bake the ham in the hot oven for about 25 minutes, basting twice during this time, and adding a sprinkle more sugar each time, until the top is nicely caramelized and bubbling. Allow to cool completely before serving.

Perfect
Pulled Pork

*I*n the US, barbecue suggests long, slow cooking, patiently allowing the smoke to do its work while you sink a few beers and set the world to rights. In this country, it means burning meat in the rain.

You could never cook pulled pork on a British grill – it takes hours of loving devotion to get meat this tender. Ideally, of course, you'd dig a barbecue pit for your piece of hog, but in the absence of available spots in my garden, I've chosen to stick with my trusty oven. If real, living, breathing Americans reckon decent pulled pork can be made without ever lighting a match, then who am I to quibble?

The traditional cut for pulled pork everywhere but eastern North Carolina, where they barbecue the whole hog, is Boston butt, or the top of the shoulder. Neil Rankin, the chef behind several of London's best-loved barbecue joints, tells me to ask for 'bone-in neck end, with a good layer of fat on top'. This is one you'll have to go to a butcher for.

Myths swirl around barbecue like wreaths of smoke – brining does not make your meat any juicier, as far as I can tell, and curing it in salt and sugar before cooking just leaves it stringy. In fact, in terms of flavour, you can make pretty decent pulled pork with just pork, as Rankin suggests, adding spices and sauces to taste once it's done, but I like the smokiness of burnt sugar, so I add half the rub before putting the meat in the oven, and half when it comes out.

If you're to pull the meat apart with your fingers, you need to cook it low and slow – but doing this robs it of the burnt, savoury flavours which make roasted meat so delicious. As a compromise between taste and texture, I decide to give it an initial blast of heat to caramelize the outside, then turn the oven right down, before whacking it back up again for a final crisping. Resting the meat in a tent of foil so it gently steams as it cools, as *Guardian* reader and barbecue enthusiast Jonathan Dale suggests, gives it a final prod in the tenderness department.

You can add any old sauce you want once it's done, but I'm a purist – the same salt and sugar I use for the rub, with a little smoked paprika for spice and smoke, and, the secret ingredient, liquid smoke. Imported from the States and easily obtainable on the internet, it's optional if you're worried about carcinogens (in which case, also stay away from barbecues), but it does give a satisfyingly charred tanginess at a lot less cost to the garden than digging your own pit. And I firmly believe this is the best recipe you're going to get without doing so. Serve stuffed into soft white rolls. Disposable bibs entirely at your discretion.

Serves 6

1.6kg shoulder of pork from the neck end, bone in
2 tablespoons salt
2 tablespoons dark muscovado sugar
1 tablespoon smoked paprika
2 teaspoons liquid smoke (optional)

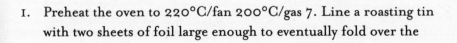

1. Preheat the oven to 220°C/fan 200°C/gas 7. Line a roasting tin with two sheets of foil large enough to eventually fold over the

top of the pork, then pat the meat dry with kitchen paper and put it in the tin. Mix the salt, sugar and paprika and rub about half of this mixture into the meat.

2. Cook the pork, uncovered, in the hot oven for about 40 minutes, until well browned, then take out and turn down the heat to 140°C/fan 120°C/gas 1. Pour the liquid smoke over the meat if using, then fold the foil securely over the top to make a sealed parcel. Return to the oven and cook for about 6–7 hours, until the internal temperature measures 89°C and, more importantly, it's soft enough to spoon. Pour off the juices and reserve for later.

3. Turn the heat back up to 220°C/fan 200°C/gas 7 and cook the pork, uncovered, for 10 minutes, until crisp. Remove, cover with a tent of foil, and leave to rest for 30 minutes.

4. Use two forks or your fingers to pull the meat into shreds, cutting up any crackling too, and then add a sprinkle of the remaining seasoning, plus any meat juices from the tin, and stir in.

5. If possible, leave to soak for 24 hours before reheating in a warm oven to serve. Or just eat immediately.

Perfect
Moussaka

I'd made many assumptions about moussaka, including that it was Greek, that it always contains lamb, and that it should be served hot, all systematically shot down by about five minutes of research. Although the name is actually Arabic, and it pops up in various forms from Egypt to Romania, I've stuck with the Greek version, simply because that's the one most familiar to Britons from a thousand Ionian holidays.

Talking to Greek cookery teacher Elisavet Sotiriadou, who modestly concedes she makes a moussaka nearly as good as her mother's, I discovered 'the mince used is veal, or pork and veal', although in the UK she goes for beef. Elizabeth David also suggests beef in *A Book of Mediterranean Food*, and Tessa Kiros a beef and pork mix in *Falling Cloudberries*, but, heathen that I am, I use just lamb: the sweet, robust flavour seems to work so much better with the spices than blander beef. (Hugh Fearnley-Whittingstall uses leftover roast lamb, finely chopped, which is a great idea if you happen to have drastically over-catered.)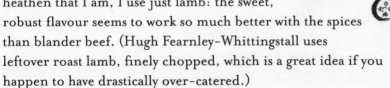

Tomato sauce is a must (indeed, the name moussaka apparently comes from the Arabic for to moisten, such is the importance of this ingredient) – in Greece, thin perasti (like the Italian passata) is traditional, but I can't help falling for the richer, more intensely flavoured tomato purée and red wine versions used in *The Prawn*

Cocktail Years, and by Hugh Fearnley-Whittingstall. Along with the traditional cinnamon, I'm adding oregano, for a touch of sun-baked herbaceousness, parsley and a generous amount of garlic.

It's aubergines that I think really set moussaka apart from the likes of lasagne or shepherd's pie, however: a layer of silky soft, wonderfully juicy and ever so slightly bitter purple slices, too often let down by too much grease. Salting them helps, as, according to Nigel Slater, it allows them to 'relax, allowing them to soak up less oil', but it's baking the slices rather than frying them which really makes the difference — and that way there's no need to pre-salt either, which speeds things up a bit. Thanks, Hugh.

My mum, who makes excellent moussaka, finishes things off with a simple béchamel, but actually a thicker sauce, made with beaten eggs and seasoned with salty sheep's cheese, is a richer, more satisfying crown for this truly regal dish. Eat with plenty of rustic red wine, and holiday memories.

Serves 4, generously

4 tablespoons olive oil
I large onion, finely chopped
4 cloves of garlic, finely chopped
I½ teaspoons ground cinnamon
I teaspoon dried oregano
500g minced lamb
2 tablespoons tomato purée, mixed with 150ml water
150ml red wine
A small bunch of flat-leaf parsley, chopped
3 medium or 2 large aubergines, sliced

For the béchamel
500ml milk
60g butter
60g plain flour
50g kefalotyri or pecorino cheese, grated
2 eggs, beaten
Nutmeg, to grate

1. Put 2 tablespoons of olive oil into a large frying pan over a medium-high heat and cook the chopped onion until golden and soft. Add the garlic, cinnamon and oregano to the pan and cook for a further couple of minutes, then stir in the lamb.
2. Turn up the heat slightly, and brown the lamb well (by which I mean a deep brown), cooking until the mixture is quite dry. Stir in the tomato purée and wine, bring to a simmer, then turn the heat down low and cook for 30–40 minutes, until most of the liquid has evaporated. Season and stir in the chopped parsley.
3. Meanwhile, preheat the oven to 200°C/fan 180°C/gas 6. Cut the aubergines laterally into 0.5cm slices, and arrange in one layer on oiled baking sheets. Brush with a little olive oil and season with salt and pepper, then bake for about 25 minutes, until they're soft, golden and floppy (keep an eye on them towards the end, as smaller slices may char faster).
4. While they're cooking, make the sauce. Bring the milk to just below the boil, and melt the butter in another, larger saucepan. Whisk the flour into the butter and cook for a couple of minutes until you lose that raw flour smell, then very gradually whisk in the hot milk until smooth. Simmer gently to make a thick sauce, then add the cheese, stirring it in until melted.
5. Remove the sauce from the heat and allow it to cool slightly, then beat in the eggs, season to taste and add slightly more

nutmeg than you might think wise (it's a strong flavour, but this dish can take it — use ½ teaspoon at least).

6. Line the base of an ovenproof dish with a third of the aubergines, and top with half the meat. Repeat these layers, finishing off with a layer of aubergine, then top with the sauce.

7. Bake at 200°C/fan 180°C/gas 6 for about 45 minutes, until well browned on top, and leave to cool for half an hour before serving.

Perfect
Lancashire Hotpot

One of the great stews of the world, Lancashire hotpot is a dish that makes a virtue of simplicity – even the name is likely to refer to the hodgepodge of ingredients that might go into it.

It's well worth tracking down the mutton or hogget this dish would traditionally have been made from: it's easily available online if you don't have a local butcher that stocks it, and the flavour is well worth the minimal hassle. Contrary to the dish's frugal billing, however, it's long been made with tiny delicate cutlets, though I prefer them from the meatier middle neck if you can get hold of them. Local Michelin-starred chef Nigel Haworth also sticks in thriftier neck and shin, which will break down to silky succulence during cooking. The gelatine in these latter cuts also helps give the gravy body, as will flouring the meat before cooking – and using stock rather than the traditional water (Gary Rhodes' wine would surely have them manning the barricades in Blackburn).

Using floury, rather than waxy potatoes for the topping will give a rich, meaty mash next to the meat, while those above turn crisp and golden in the heat of the oven – and two layers of spuds, as in Margaret Costa's recipe, will double the pleasure.

Onions are the final part of the hotpot trinity; there's no need to pre-cook them, as Paul Heathcote suggests. Lamb is a meat that tends towards fattiness, so adding any more takes the dish perilously close to greasy – though the fresh flavour of thyme helps counteract that. You can add carrots, celery, even garlic if you like, but all this dish really needs is a big dollop of pickled red cabbage on the side.

Serves 4

Flour, sugar, salt and pepper, to dust
4–6 best-end or middle-neck lamb, hogget or mutton cutlets
400g diced lamb, hogget or mutton neck fillet or shoulder
3 largeish floury potatoes, such as Maris Piper
2 sprigs of thyme, leaves picked
1 bay leaf
2 onions, sliced
500ml good lamb stock
20g butter, melted, plus extra to grease

1. Heat the oven to 190°C/fan 170°C/gas 5. Cover a plate with flour and sprinkle with a pinch of sugar, salt and pepper. Toss the meat to coat. Peel the potatoes and thinly slice.
2. Grease a high-sided casserole dish with butter and put about a third of the potatoes in the base. Season and sprinkle with a little thyme. Top with the meat and bay leaf, followed by the onions, all seasoned in the same way.
3. Arrange the remaining potato slices on top like overlapping fish scales, and season. Pour enough stock over the potatoes to just come up to the base of the topping (take a piece off to see this better), then brush the top with melted butter.
4. Cover and bake for 2 hours (2½ hours for mutton), then uncover and bake for another 30 minutes, until the potatoes are golden and crisp.

Perfect
Stock

*L*ife might seem too short to make your own stock, until you realize that it saves you a fair amount of washing up after the Sunday roast – temporarily at least. Chuck in the bones, the vegetable trimmings and a few elderly herbs, cover with cold water, do a bit of skimming, then sit back in front of a film while time works its traditional magic. Even if you don't have a roast handy, most butchers will give you bones for free, which means you can make one of the cornerstones of culinary greatness for practically nothing. (Although they tend to be over-salted, stock cubes are fine for many things, but when stock plays a pivotal role in a dish, such as a soup or a risotto, you need to step things up a notch.)

There are a few rules to bear in mind when it comes to stock:

- Raw bones will give a clearer stock than cooked ones, but home cooks are unlikely to be unduly troubled by a cloudy stock. Ask your butcher to chop them up to make them easier to fit into your stockpot.

- Stocks made from poultry or vegetables are known as white stocks, and are simply made by simmering bones and aromatics together to extract the flavour. For richer beef, lamb or veal stocks, known as brown stocks, the bones and vegetables are roasted before simmering.

- Adding veal bones or a pig's trotter to any stock will add collagen to the stock, which will help it set to a jelly. This will keep longer than a liquid stock.

- You need more than just bones – I find it helpful to do as Hugh Fearnley-Whittingstall does and think of it as a broth in its own right, rather than just a raw ingredient: that way, it's easier to work out how to make it taste good.

- A good way to do this is using vegetables: carrot, onion, celery and herbs will all add pleasing flavours and aromas to the finished stock; although they can be tops or bottoms, or slightly past their best, never put anything rotten in a stock, because if it didn't taste good to begin with, you can bet your boots it will be even worse when boiled down to a concentrate. There's no need to peel vegetables, as long as they're clean, and extra peelings and tops are also good – herb stalks are ideal. Vegetables to avoid in any quantity are anything starchy (potatoes, yams, etc.), which will make your stock murky, beetroot, which will make it gruesomely pink, and the cabbage family, including broccoli and cauliflower, which will leave it tasting of overcooked sprouts.

- You must start a stock with cold water: hot, according to *Leiths Meat Bible*, will melt the fat in the bones into the stock, making it greasy and unpleasant tasting. With cold, the fat will rise to the surface, where you can skim it off; do this frequently.

- Don't add salt to your stock – it's easier to add salt to the finished dish than it is to correct an over-salted one, and remember, all that reducing will concentrate the flavours.

- Don't boil the stock; keep it at a gentle simmer, so the surface just trembles, or it will be cloudy.

- Don't make the mistake of thinking that the longer you cook your stock, the better it will be — as I've found to my cost, after a while, the flavours turn murky.

- All the recipes below can be scaled up, so you may wish to freeze your ingredients until you have enough to make a really big batch — stock keeps in the fridge for a few days, and freezes well.

The below are basic stocks — for more information, see *Leiths Meat Bible*, which covers the subject very thoroughly.

Vegetable stock

50g butter
2 onions, roughly chopped
2 large carrots, roughly chopped
2 sticks of celery, roughly chopped
Vegetable trimmings of your
    choice, apart from those listed
    above (e.g. leeks, mushrooms,
    fennel, turnips, lettuce,
    beans, etc.)
1 bay leaf
A few parsley stalks
A few black peppercorns

1. Melt the butter in a large pan, and stir in the vegetables. Cover the pan and cook over a low heat for about 10 minutes, then add the herbs and peppercorns, cover with about 2 litres of cold water and bring to the boil.
2. Reduce to a simmer and cook for 20 minutes. Pass through a sieve and it's ready to use.

Meat stock

1kg beef or lamb bones
2 onions, quartered
2 carrots, quartered
2 sticks of celery, quartered
100g button mushrooms
1 tablespoon tomato purée
A handful of parsley and/or thyme stalks
1 bay leaf
A few peppercorns

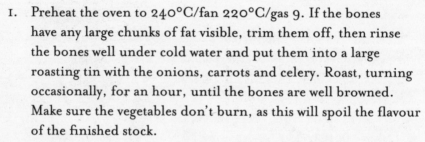

1. Preheat the oven to 240°C/fan 220°C/gas 9. If the bones have any large chunks of fat visible, trim them off, then rinse the bones well under cold water and put them into a large roasting tin with the onions, carrots and celery. Roast, turning occasionally, for an hour, until the bones are well browned. Make sure the vegetables don't burn, as this will spoil the flavour of the finished stock.

2. Using tongs, carefully transfer the hot bones and vegetables into a stockpot, but drain off any fat. Add the rest of the ingredients, including any other vegetables you're using.

3. Pour about 300ml of water into the roasting tin and put it on a medium heat. Bring to the boil and deglaze by scraping up all the caramelized bits from the bottom, then tip this into the stockpot. Cover the bones with cold water, and bring to the boil.

4. Skim off any scum from the surface – you can add a little cold water to help solidify it – then simmer gently (so the surface just trembles, rather than bubbles), uncovered, for 5 hours, skimming from time to time.

5. Strain the stock through a sieve and discard the vegetables – don't press them, as this will make your stock murky.

6. Bring the stock to your required strength by boiling rapidly until reduced; you'll be able to tell how strong it is by tasting it. A useful way to store stock is to boil it until thick and syrupy (a *glace de viande*) – it will keep in the fridge for several weeks like this, and you just need to add water to bring it back to a stock consistency.

Chicken stock

1 chicken carcass (raw or cooked),
  plus any giblets but not the liver,
  which will make the stock bitter
1 small onion, roughly chopped
1 carrot, roughly chopped
1 stick of celery, roughly chopped
A few parsley and/or thyme stalks
½ bay leaf
A few peppercorns

1. Put all the ingredients into a large pan and cover with cold water. Bring to the boil and skim off any scum from the top – you can add some cold water to solidify the fat and make this easier.
2. Turn down the heat and simmer for around 4 hours, skimming occasionally, then pass through a sieve, and allow to cool.
3. If you aren't using the stock immediately, you can leave the fat, which will solidify on top as a handy natural seal – otherwise, lift it off before adding to your chosen dish. You can also reduce the stock to give a more intense flavour if required. As above, if you're not using it immediately, reduce the stock by boiling it until thick and syrupy (a *glace de viande*) – it will keep in the fridge for several weeks like this, and you just need to add water to bring it back to a stock consistency.

Fish stock

1kg fish bones, fish heads or prawn,
   crab or mussel shells
3 leeks, roughly chopped
1 fennel bulb, roughly chopped
2 sticks of celery, roughly chopped
3 carrots, roughly chopped
A handful of parsley stalks
A few peppercorns

1. Wash the bones thoroughly under cold water to remove any trace of blood. Put them into a large pan with the rest of the ingredients, cover with cold water and bring to the boil. Skim off any scum that rises to the top.
2. Turn down the heat and simmer very gently for 30 minutes, skimming occasionally, then strain and it's ready to use.

How to clarify a stock

If you want a clear stock, for making a consommé, or simply for showing off, once you've strained it, put it back into the pan and simmer for about 5 minutes. Meanwhile, beat an egg white per litre of stock, and drizzle it over the top of the stock. Throw in the eggshells for good measure, simmer for a further 5 minutes without allowing it to boil, then take the stock off the heat and allow to stand for about an hour. A thick foam should have risen to the top – push this aside and ladle out the stock (if you try to pour it, it will go murky again) into a sieve lined with cotton or muslin for a final strain. Ta da – it should now be completely clear!

Bright ideas for a batch of stock
Gravy, risotto, soup, Irish stew and Lancashire hot pot, daube of beef, braised celery, fennel or lettuce, boulangère potatoes, steak and ale or chicken pie, paella, fish stew . . . convinced yet?

Perfect
Fish Pie

Who says beige is boring? Fish pie, with its kaleidoscope of off-white hues, is delicious proof that food doesn't have to be all the colours of the Mediterranean rainbow to beguile. Just thinking about it on a cold day can make me feel all warm and fuzzy inside — so it's worth making two and keeping one in the freezer for comfort food emergencies.

A word about that seductive golden top — Angela Boggiano uses a pastry crust for her smoked fish and cider pie, and Nigel Slater suggests a most unorthodox crumble, but for sheer comfort you can't beat a cloud of fluffy mash. In homage to J. Sheekey, purveyors of the finest fish pies in London, I've topped mine with a few breadcrumbs to give it a bit of crunch. Adding cheese to a properly seasoned mash is de trop as far as I'm concerned, but you can follow their example and sprinkle over a little Parmesan if you're feeling decadent.

A firmly traditional white sauce is the backbone of Nigel's crumble-crust fish pie; it's comfortingly thick, but I prefer the flavour of Marco Pierre White's gorgeously savoury fish stock reduction with double cream. As a compromise, I retain the texture of the white sauce, but add a bit more flavour by using wine and stock to poach the fish instead, in homage to Tom Aikens' recipe.

Jamie Oliver includes a characteristically unusual recipe using a double cream, mustard and cheese sauce in *The Return of the Naked Chef*, which, while admittedly delicious, utterly overpowers the delicate flavour of the fish. (He also puts the fish in raw, which makes the pie a bit watery, as it gives off liquid as it cooks.) I've gone for more subtle flavourings: parsley adds a fresh note, and anchovy salty richness, but I do like his use of spinach – I often put in a few handfuls, or some sautéd leeks, to bulk out the filling.

Serve with plenty of steamed greens to mop up the creamy sauce – anything else is overkill.

Serves 4

1kg floury potatoes (e.g. Maris
    Piper or King Edward)
Salt and pepper
50g butter
100ml milk
350g white fish and/or salmon fillets
350g smoked white fish
500ml homemade fish stock
    (see page 174) or ready-made
    stock (but not cubes)
100ml dry white wine
A small bunch of flat-leaf parsley,
    separated into leaves (finely
    chopped) and stalks
50g butter
50g plain flour

100ml double cream
2 anchovy fillets in oil, drained
   and finely chopped
200g small peeled prawns
25g white breadcrumbs

1. Peel the potatoes and cut into evenly sized chunks. Put into a
    large pan, cover with cold water, add a generous pinch of salt,
    and bring to the boil. Simmer for about 20 minutes, until
    tender. Drain, allow to sit in the colander for a few minutes,
    then mash until smooth, beating in the butter and a splash of
    milk. Season well and set aside.

2. Preheat the oven to 200°C/fan 180°C/gas 6. Remove any skin
    from the fish and check for bones. Pour the stock into a large
    pan with the wine and parsley stalks and bring to a simmer. Add
    the fish, simmer for a couple of minutes, then lift out with a
    slotted spoon and cut into large chunks. Discard the parsley
    stalks.

3. Melt the butter in a medium pan over a lowish heat, and stir in
    the flour. Cook, stirring, for a couple of minutes, being careful
    not to let it brown. Gradually stir in the stock. Bring to the
    boil, then simmer very gently for about 20 minutes, stirring
    frequently.

4. Take the sauce off the heat, stir in the double cream, chopped
    parsley leaves and anchovies and season. Add the fish and prawns
    and toss to coat.

5. Put the seafood and sauce into a large baking dish (30 x 28cm
    would be ideal) and top with the mashed potato. Bake for 20
    minutes, then sprinkle over the breadcrumbs and bake for a
    further 20 minutes, until the top is golden brown.

5 fish to eat and 5 fish to avoid

Nearly half the fish eaten in the UK is from just three species: cod, salmon and tuna – what an unadventurous lot we are. Not only is this downright dull, but it's putting undue pressure on stocks, so next time you're making a fish pie, stick something new in there. You never know, you might even enjoy it. Visit www.fishonline.org for the full list.

Eat
Grey or red gurnard
Cornish sardines
Dab
Sprats
Pollock

Avoid
Bluefin tuna
Wild turbot
Dogfish/rock salmon
Eel
Skate

Perfect
Fishcakes

*P*roof, if any were needed after the pie, that seafood and potato go together like Sharky and George. I've long been a secret fan of those day-glo curling stones served in chippies, but I really fell in love with fishcakes on my eighteenth birthday, when a boyfriend of the time whisked me to lunch at Le Caprice. Ah, the heady taste of house white, fishcakes and sorrel sauce, with Dame Judi Dench at the next table.

Fishcakes don't have to be grand, though — as Simon Hopkinson and Lindsey Bareham point out in their recipe in *The Prawn Cocktail Years*, they're often the resort of leftover fish, and none the worse for that. As you're only heating the cakes through, the ingredients all need to be pre-cooked, making them the perfect vehicle for that cold bit of salmon or morsel of smoked mackerel. They use crushed potato rather than the more traditional mash, which gives the fishcakes a more interesting texture, but you don't need the double cream in their recipe, unless you're after a particularly rich result. The same goes for the melted butter in gastropub stalwart Trish Hilferty's *Lobster & Chips* recipe: a humble egg should be binding enough. Chill before use to firm them up, or you'll end up with a fish hash instead. Still delicious, but less likely to impress your guests.

Flavourings are up to you – I tried out spring onion, hard-boiled egg, parsley and chopped gherkins before deciding on capers and anchovies, which add the salt and vinegar that's all the seasoning you need with fish and potatoes. Although Le Caprice simply coat their fishcakes in flour before frying, I like the crunch of breadcrumbs; perhaps it reminds me of the chippie. Serve with sautéed spinach.

Serves 2

400g floury potatoes
(e.g. Maris Piper)
Salt and pepper
250g fish: salmon, firm white
fish or smoked haddock work
particularly well
1 tablespoon chopped chives
1 tablespoon capers
2 anchovy fillets in oil, drained
and finely chopped
1 egg, beaten
40g flour, for coating
50g fresh white breadcrumbs
A generous knob of butter
1 tablespoon vegetable oil

1. Peel the potatoes and cut into evenly-sized chunks. Put into a large pan and cover with cold water. Add a generous pinch of salt and bring to the boil, then turn down the heat slightly and simmer until tender, but not mushy. Drain and put back into the hot pan for a minute to dry off, then roughly crush

them with a fork, so they're a mixture of mash and larger lumps.

2. Meanwhile, put the fish into a large pan and just cover with water. Bring to a simmer, then gently cook for 3–5 minutes, depending on the size of the fillets, until the skin, if any, pulls off easily, and it's just beginning to flake. Drain and set aside to cool, then skin if necessary, break into large flakes and add to the potatoes.

3. Stir in the chives, capers and anchovies. Season lightly, and mix together gently, adding a little of the beaten egg to bring the mixture together into patties – it shouldn't be too sloppy. Use your hands to form into four large cakes or six smaller ones.

4. Put the remaining egg in a shallow bowl, and tip the flour and breadcrumbs on to separate saucers. Dip each fishcake in turn into the flour, the egg, and finally the breadcrumbs until thoroughly coated. Put into the fridge for at least half an hour to firm up.

5. Heat a frying pan with the butter and oil until the butter begins to foam. Add the fishcakes, in batches if necessary, cook for 5 minutes on a medium-high heat until golden and well crusted, then turn them carefully over and repeat on the other side.

- -

How to tell if your fish is fresh
First off, unless you're buying farmed fish like salmon or trout, avoid buying fish on a Monday – fishing boats don't go out on a Sunday. The rest of the week, don't be afraid to get up close and personal with your prospective dinner when giving it the once-over – fresh fish should smell of the

sea, so any unpleasant 'fishy' odours are bad news. Look for clear rather than cloudy eyes on whole fish, and shiny, slick skin or a full complement of bright scales. Fillets should look wet — if they feel dry, or are already flaking apart, they're probably not fit for anyone but the cat.

Perfect
Battered Fish

As long as the fish isn't dry or, of course, off, then I'll forgive many things for a light, yet crunchy savoury coating, preferably standing proud on its own solid little batter legs. Utter heaven with well-salted, really potatoey chips (page 199), and a decent helping of mushy peas.

The choice of fish, therefore, is up to you – pollock, gurnard (go beyond the usual boring cod and haddock and you'll not only get points for sustainability, but you might just find a new favourite), skin-on, skin-off depending on your degree of northernness – what really matters is getting air into the batter.

This is usually done in two ways: by adding a raising agent like yeast or baking powder to the batter, or by including something carbonated, like beer or sparkling water. Using one or the other seems to give disappointing results: Rick Stein's baking powder and still water gives a crisp, but quite solid coating, while the River Cottage plain flour and beer mixture is crunchy, dry and dense, though the beer supplies a good flavour.

Trish Hilferty, gastropub legend, uses fresh yeast, which gives her batter a quite incredible volume, but it seems to soak up more oil than the others. Simon Hopkinson's secret weapon is potato flour, which, he claims, 'retains its crispness like no other' – but actually I find it just gives the batter a weirdly grainy texture. In fact, there's no need to add anything more than plain flour, beer and baking powder — eggs and milk are both so rich that the fish can't compete on flavour.

Gary Rhodes explains that it's important that the batter is thick, 'almost too thick', to ensure that as the fish cooks, the batter billows obligingly around it. His self-raising flour and lager combination gives the lightest of results of all the recipes I try — and I'm pleased to note there's no need to rest it before use, as many of the other recipes suggest. Indeed, it seems counter-intuitive: allowing a Yorkshire pudding to stand before baking helps the flour absorb the liquid, but here we want to keep the mixture as effervescent as possible to help it rise, and as any fool knows, a fizzy drink left to stand will quickly become a flat one.

The best tip I get, however, comes from Matthew Silk, co-owner of 149 in Bridlington, winner of the Fish & Chip Shop of the Year 2011, who reckons the batter must be 'seriously cold, say 6°C, so that when it hits the fat at 185°C the reaction happens'. He's right: chilling the ingredients beforehand gives the batter an almost ethereally light texture.

I'd strongly urge you to fry the fish in dripping if you're prepared to leave the windows open for the rest of the day: the rich flavour is absolutely peerless. Otherwise, vegetable oil gives a pretty decent result at less risk to your soft furnishings — but, personally, I'd happily sacrifice a set of curtains for really good fish and chips.

Serves 4

Dripping or oil, for frying
3 teaspoons baking powder
400g plain flour, put in the freezer
for 15 minutes before using
½ teaspoon salt
550ml very cold beer
4 pieces of sustainable white fish (I used pollock)

1. Heat the fat in a deep-fat fryer or a chip pan to 185°C.
2. Whisk the baking powder into the chilled flour with the salt, then, working quickly, whisk in the cold beer to make a thick paste. This all needs to be done just before you cook the fish.
3. Place the bowl of batter next to the fryer or pan. Prepare a plate lined with kitchen paper.
4. Dip each piece of fish into the batter to coat, then carefully lower it into the hot fat and agitate the frying basket to prevent the fish sticking to it. (This will also give the batter a more craggily interesting texture.) Cook one or two pieces at a time: don't overcrowd the fryer or the fish will steam.
5. Cook the fish for about 4–6 minutes, depending on size, keeping an eye on it; it should be crisp and golden when ready. Lift out of the fat and drain on kitchen paper, then serve as quickly as possible.

Perfect
Goan Fish Curry

I'd never been adventurous enough to try a fish curry before I went to India at the age of eighteen – to be completely honest, I'd never graduated beyond the chicken tikka masala. The hot, sour, boldly peppery fish dishes of Goa were a revelation well worth all those months of work saving up for the ticket. As we travelled further south, I realized that Goa doesn't have a monopoly on great fish curries, but they remain some of my favourites.

Though you're unlikely to find the same varieties of fish used in India over here, heed the wise words of Madhur Jaffrey: 'better to get very fresh fish, whatever it be, than to hunt all day for a specific fish preferred in a recipe'. Anything robust enough not to fall apart in the pan will work: I like pollock and prawns, but ask your fishmonger for advice.

Concentrate instead on the spice paste which forms the base of the sauce. There are some ingredients common to all the recipes I try – garlic, turmeric, red chillies, coriander seeds – and a few more unusual additions. Vivek Singh includes star anise for example, a spice more typical of points further east but which, according to Madhur Jaffrey, is a legacy of Goa's trading past, and I love the slightly mentholated character it gives his sauce. He also uses cloves, which add a deep sweetness to the dish. Ginger provides extra warmth, and brick red Kashmiri chilli-powder colour, though paprika will also work if that's what you have.

The Goan taste for sour flavours, as in their most famous dish, the vindaloo, is said to come from their former Portuguese masters — and, like vindaloo, this fish curry benefits from a glug of vinegar, and a pinch of palm sugar and some coconut milk to balance it. The sweet and sour flavour of onions and tomatoes proves the perfect complement.

Finish the dish with a tadka of sizzling spices as recommended by Goan cook Maria Teresa Menezes, and serve with fluffy rice, preferably on a beach.

Serves 4

3 tablespoons vegetable oil
1 onion, finely chopped
1 large tomato, grated
1 x 400ml tin of coconut milk
2 fresh green chillies, slit lengthwise
400g firm white fish (e.g. pollock), cut into 2cm chunks
200g prawns (or 200g more fish)
½ teaspoon mustard seeds
10 curry leaves
Coriander, to garnish

For the masala

1 teaspoon cloves
1 tablespoon coriander seeds
1 teaspoon cumin seeds

8 dried red Kashmiri chillies
2 star anise
½ teaspoon turmeric
1 tablespoon palm sugar
1 teaspoon salt
5 garlic cloves, peeled and crushed
3cm root ginger, peeled and grated
1½ tablespoons white vinegar

1. Start with the masala. Toast the spices in a dry pan until fragrant, then grind to a powder in a food processor or a pestle and mortar. Stir in the remaining ingredients to make a smooth paste.

2. Heat 2 tablespoons of oil in a large pan over a medium high heat, then fry the onion until soft and lightly golden. Stir in the masala mix and cook, stirring, for a minute or so until you can smell the spices, then add the tomato and cook until most of the liquid has evaporated.

3. Pour in the coconut milk and 100ml of water, add the fresh chillies and bring to a simmer. Turn down the heat and bubble for about 10 minutes until slightly thickened. Taste for seasoning, then add the seafood and leave undisturbed for about 5 minutes until cooked through.

4. Meanwhile, heat the remaining tablespoon of oil in a frying pan on a high heat, and add the mustard seeds and curry leaves. Cook for 30 seconds, until they begin to pop, then stir into the curry. Serve with rice and coriander to garnish.

Perfect
Prawn Cocktail

After years languishing in the doldrums of naffness, this classic 60s starter has enjoyed a small renaissance of late, largely thanks to our national passion for nostalgia — and Marie Rose sauce. This, of course, is the element on which the dish's flimsy integrity stands or falls, which is why I'd urge making homemade mayonnaise the backbone. Nigella reckons salad cream works like a dream, but I found it made the sauce rather vinegary, and adding mascarpone, as suggested by a recipe on the Waitrose website, seemed to serve no discernible purpose except for selling more cheese. Keep it firmly trad.

You don't want to muck around too much with the flavourings either — as Nigel Slater points out. Tomato ketchup (Simon Hopkinson and Lindsey Bareham say it has to be Heinz, and as they named a book after the dish, they must know a thing or two about it) is a must; tomato chutney, as used by *Good Food*, just doesn't give the same wonderful sweet and sour flavour. Tabasco, that stalwart of the veneer cocktail cabinet, provides a subtle kick, and a dash of brandy suggests true 1960s sophistication. That, and a dash of lemon juice, is really all you need: Delia's Worcestershire sauce takes over the party (in fact, in combination with prawn cocktail, it reminds me powerfully of swapping crisps in the playground), and her lime adds a jarring freshness to the cosily retro flavours. Again, don't try to be too clever; this is not a dish which needs fixing.

Little gem lettuces are a favourite here, but this is perhaps the only occasion for which I reckon iceberg is a must (other possibilities include hamburgers, and tacos – in fact, come to think of it, they deserve a revival too). The very blandness that renders iceberg so pointless in a salad is a boon here – stronger flavours, like watercress or, God forbid, rocket, would compete with the cocktail sauce – and it adds a pleasingly crunchy counterpoint to the softness of the prawns. I've stolen the idea of green pepper from a relative, who turns up every Christmas with the best prawn cocktail I have ever tasted: that herbaceous slight bitterness works wonderfully with the sweetness of the ketchup. Avocado is also a nice touch if you're feeling decadent – it takes the dish into the 1970s, which is about as far as you want to go before you hit the sun-dried tomatoes.

Serves 4

**5 tablespoons mayonnaise
(see page 276)
¼ of a green pepper, finely chopped
1 tablespoon tomato ketchup
1 teaspoon brandy
Tabasco sauce
½ a lemon
Salt and pepper
400g peeled prawns
½ iceberg lettuce, finely shredded
½ a cucumber, diced
A small handful of chives,
finely chopped
Cayenne pepper, to serve**

1. Mix the mayonnaise with the green pepper, ketchup and brandy and add a couple of drops of Tabasco and a squeeze of lemon. Season, taste and adjust if necessary. Toss with the prawns.
2. Divide the lettuce and cucumber between 4 serving dishes, then spoon the prawns on top and drizzle any extra sauce over them. Sprinkle with chives and dust with a little cayenne pepper.

Perfect
Smoked Mackerel Pâté

We're always being told how healthy oily fish are for us, but for some reason, they have a bad rep – too fishy, apparently, which is an odd accusation to level at a fish. Anyway, this recipe, one of my mum's favourites, is entry-level mackerel, the risky gateway to increased consumption of omega-3 oils and their super healthy ilk.

You need hot-smoked fish: the cold-smoked sort is too delicate, and making it into a pâté would be a crime. Add this to cream cheese – Delia gets too exotic with her grainy ricotta, and David Cameron (yes, *that* David Cameron)'s homely cottage cheese recipe, which he's submitted to a number of charity collections, is weirdly lumpy.

Cheeseless recipes, like those from the *River Cottage Fish Book* and Matt Tebbutt, are too emphatically mackerelly to eat in any quantity. Cream cheese, favoured by no less a person than the afore-mentioned parent, provides the silkiest of textures.

To stop the pâté becoming claggy, something more liquid and preferably also tangy is needed to cut through the richness, like Delia Smith's sour cream, or the River Cottage boys' crème fraîche; *Country Life* magazine's double cream is far too bland for the task.

I must salute mackerel: it's a rare fish that stands up so well to spice. Cameron goes for Tabasco, and Delia for cayenne, but I've decided to add both heat and flavour with fresh horseradish: cleaner than the creamed sort, and a brilliant pairing with the smoke.

Dill is another obvious match: the sweet, aniseedy flavour works wonderfully with both the oily fish and the heat of the horseradish — it's not an essential, but it does look pretty (and let's face it, a dish that, unadorned, has a tendency to look a bit like a bowl of Polyfilla can use all the help it can get in that direction).

I've also left a few flakes of fish whole for texture — and to remind everyone that there is mackerel in there, and actually it's really rather nice. Delicious served on rye bread, or crisp toast, preferably with a nice watercress salad and some pickled capers or beetroot for that authentic Scandi feel.

Serves 4

3 hot-smoked mackerel fillets
150g cream cheese
100g crème fraîche
3 teaspoons freshly grated horseradish
Black pepper
Lemon, to squeeze
A small handful of dill, finely chopped

1. Peel the skin from the mackerel fillets and do a quick check for any rogue bones. Flake three-quarters of the fish into a food

processor along with the cheese, crème fraîche and grated horseradish and whiz until smooth.

2. Add a generous grinding of black pepper, and lemon juice to taste, check the seasoning, then fold through the dill and the remaining flakes of fish. Serve with rye bread or crisp toast.

Vegetables, Pasta and Rice

*I*t may say something about my tastes that so many of the recipes in
this chapter involve potatoes – but I prefer to keep my greens
blessedly simple. At least, that's my excuse though to be honest, I'm
a complete carbohydrate junkie. Forget chocolate – I'm rarely
happier than when contemplating a big bowl of silky pasta, some
soupy noodles or enough fluffy rice to bury my head in.

On the subject of potatoes, for a country that eats so many of the
things (by tonnage, the British are the biggest consumers in
Europe), we're remarkably careless about them: how often have you
struggled to find out what variety is inside that supermarket bag of
'white potatoes', or even where they come from?

The fact is that all potatoes were not made equal: most are better for
some things than others – the firmer, waxy sort, with dense, often
yellow flesh, hold their shape well during cooking, making them the
superior choice for salads and dauphinoise. Floury potatoes, by

contrast, yield to heat, making them the only option for fluffy mash and baked potatoes.

The most common waxy varieties in this country are probably Maris Peer, Desiree and the smaller Charlottes, while Maris Piper and King Edwards are ever-reliable floury sorts, but it's well worth giving more unusual names a try if you come across them.

You'll notice I always leave potato skins on where possible, both out of laziness and because that's where most of the flavour (and much of the fibre) seems to reside – even if you don't want the skins in the finished dish, it's worth cooking the potatoes in them where possible, and peeling them off afterwards.

(Potato lecture over, I'd happily eat every single one of these recipes on its own with no further accompaniment.)

While they tend to be good value, it's still worth paying a little extra for the main attraction. Value pastas are actually pretty rubbish value in that, though the ingredients are the same (though the quality of the flour may vary), the manufacturing process isn't.

Better-quality pastas are made in bronze dies, giving any sauce a rough, textured surface to cling on to – and also making them more interesting in the mouth. Cheaper brands use easy-clean dies, which produce a smooth, boring result. It may sound silly, but trust me, it makes a difference.

And don't make the mistake of thinking that fresh pasta is always the best option when you can afford it – all the recipes in this chapter are better with the dried variety (fresh tends to suit richer cheese or meat sauces, or filled pastas like ravioli).

The same goes for rice; it's easy to taste the difference between aromatic basmati, or jasmine rice, and bog-standard long-grain, and no use at all using any of the above for paella, or indeed risotto, because they behave in completely different ways when cooked.

If you eat a lot of any of these carbs, they keep so well that it's worth buying in bulk — rice and noodles can be purchased in large quantities at Asian supermarkets, and multipacks of pasta are available online. Even with postage, you'll save money on the supermarket price, which will, of course, leave you more cash to spend on the toppings.

So please don't just regard this chapter as 'sides' — yes, a dal is nice with rice and curried vegetables, and aubergine parmigiana is lovely with roast lamb, but both are also great dishes in their own right, and really don't need to play second fiddle to anything.

Perfect
Chips

*F*orget desiccated wedges, or the pallid crimes of burger joints: proper chips should be thick-cut and defiantly potatoey: golden to the eye, hot and fluffy within. Such perfection is not easily found – particularly since the inexplicable rise of the loathsome Jenga chip – but, with the basics mastered, it's easy enough to achieve at home. Although there are always going to be times when only a vinegary parcel from the Codfather, or a rustling pile of pommes allumettes, will do, a good chip recipe under your belt is surely a friend for life.

The first thing to do is choose the ingredients. As there are only two of them, this should, in theory, be a breeze. I am not the first to make this mistake: 'Unfortunately,' Hertfordshire gastropub chef Paul Bloxham explains bitterly, 'the wrong potato will result in a guaranteed failure.' Spuds divide neatly into two camps: waxy, like Charlotte and Maris Peer, and floury, such as King Edward and Maris Piper. Most recipes call for the latter, but Heston Blumenthal, who has, of course, looked into the matter with a degree of thoroughness I can only dream of, uses Charlotte or Belle de Fontenay for what he describes as 'the best chips I have ever tasted'. Although they produce a handsome golden chip, however, I find them unacceptably dense. Maris Pipers it is. Although it will make your kitchen smell like a chippie for weeks afterwards, Mark Hix, who serves some pretty good fish and chips at his Dorset restaurant, is spot on with his observation that beef dripping gives a crisper and tastier chip than vegetable oil.

Rinsing the chips to wash off the starch, as Hix suggests, is a good idea, but soaking them in cold water, like the Hairy Bikers, makes them soggy. You then need to par-boil them – frying them from raw, as Randall & Aubin chef Ed Baines does, will leave them mahogany by the time they've cooked through – and chill them before the first and second frying. This may seem pointless, but Heston's done his research right – cooking them from cold really does give a crisper result, and what's a few more minutes where the perfect chip's concerned?

200g Maris Pipers per person
Dripping or other animal fat,
    or olive or neutral oil (if you must),
    to cook (enough to half fill
    your pan when melted)

You'll need a cooking thermometer, or an electric deep fat fryer, for this recipe.

1. Peel your potatoes and cut into chips – approximately 1cm for thick-cut chips, half that for thinner ones. Rinse well under cold water, then drain.
2. Put the chips into a pan of cold, salted water and bring to the boil. Turn down the heat, and simmer until just soft to the point of a knife.
3. Drain, pat dry and allow to cool, then put into the fridge until cold.

4. Heat your fat to 120°C, and add the chips. Don't overcrowd the pan. Blanch for about 5 minutes, until cooked through but not coloured.
5. Remove, drain, pat dry, and refrigerate.
6. When you're ready to eat, heat the fat to 160°C and add the chips. Cook until crisp and golden, then remove, drain, season and serve immediately with plenty of salt.

Perfect
Jacket Potatoes

*J*acket potatoes are the ultimate winter convenience food – my modest circle of friends includes both a lady who was sent to school with one wrapped in foil as a hand-warmer-cum-packed-lunch and a triathlete who eschews the pre-race energy bars and powders beloved of his fellow competitors in favour of a simple spud; easier to open, apparently. There's nothing like a foodstuff that comes with its own edible wrapping to make you feel all eco-smug.

Although it has been suggested that the name itself is rather *infra dig*, I reckon a jacket potato suggests a very particular sort of baked spud – any old potato can have a delectably fluffy interior, but it takes real skill to achieve that wonderfully crunchy skin as well. It's not something that can be rushed, which is presumably why most high-street potatoes are such damp squibs: this is a treat best cooked at home.

Floury varieties are a must here – and, as befitting such a humble dish, you don't need much else. Oiling, as suggested by the BBC's food website, gives a better colour, but no other discernible benefit, and brining, an idea from across the pond, is just a waste of good salt; there's only so much sodium chloride one spud can soak up, and the interior tastes disappointingly ordinary. I quite like the idea of brushing the potatoes with butter, or even bacon grease, during cooking, but although the results are good, it's messy work, and cools the oven down too. You can get a crisp skin without them.

A word about the oven while we're on the subject: after years of cooking her potatoes fast and furious, Delia turned her oven down to 190°C in pursuit of the perfect crunch – but I find Nigel Slater's vicious 220°C more effective in my own quest, along with a light dusting of coarse salt for flavour. Always prick your potato before cooking, by the way; it doesn't seem to have any detrimental effect on them, and it's good insurance against an unhappy evening of oven cleaning should a rogue spud go mad and explode while your back's turned. Trust me, you don't want to risk it.

Hearteningly, even Slater admits that sometimes potatoes just do their own thing – at which point you should turn to cheese, and lots of it.

**I floury potato per person
(e.g. Maris Piper, King Edward)
About 20g coarse sea salt**

1. Preheat your oven to 220°C/fan 200°C/gas 7.
2. When the oven is up to temperature, wash the potatoes well, and prick each in a couple of places with a fork. Allow to dry slightly while you tip your salt into a shallow bowl. Roll each potato in the salt to give an even coating, and then place on the middle shelf of the oven, preferably directly on the rack.
3. Cook for around an hour, then give them a quick squeeze – the potato should just give, and the skin should be distinctly crisp. If not, leave them for 10 minutes, and check again – if you overcook them, the insides will be dry, so it's important to be vigilant.

4. Take out of the oven and put whole on to plates: they shouldn't be opened until you're ready to eat, and then preferably by hitting them sharply so they burst, for maximum fluffiness — you can cover your hand with a tea towel to do this if you're feeling wimpy, but remember, sometimes you have to suffer for perfection. Do your thing with butter, and tuck in immediately.

Perfect
Mash

When you're feeling a bit miserable, or sniffly, nothing warms the cockles like a big bowl of steaming mash — not the refined restaurant stuff beloved of the French, who show their ignorance of the true beauty of the dish by using waxy rather than floury potatoes, but the fluffy clouds of comfort that are the British equivalent of congee, or rice and peas, or dal. You know you've been abroad too long when you begin to dream of mash.

In the interests of broad-mindedness, I have, of course, tried using waxy Charlotte potatoes rather than my usual floury Maris Pipers or King Edwards, but although well flavoured, they're too dense for my idea of perfect, whatever Heston prefers. It's important to put the potatoes into cold water and bring it to the boil, rather than dropping them straight into hot water, or they won't cook evenly and you'll end up with soggy, lumpy results.

Butter is of course a must for mash (it's the only addition Marco Pierre White will countenance), but other flavouring ideas abound, from Gruyère and roasted garlic to Dijon mustard. Nigel Slater claims milk is optional, but I like the slight sweetness that it brings to the dish — cream, as favoured by Jamie Oliver, tends to make it too rich for my taste. Not as rich, of course, as Heston's mash, which contains half as much butter as potato, and requires an array of gadgets, including a thermometer for temperature-controlled cooking, and a ricer, to purée it into submission. If you think there's no such thing as too much butter, I urge you to give his recipe a try.

Although a potato ricer, a gadget much favoured by professional chefs, and which looks like an over-sized garlic press, undoubtedly gives a smoother result, I find a traditional potato masher is the secret to the fluffiest mash — take no notice of Delia's advice about using an electric whisk unless you want to repaint your kitchen with starch. You can, of course, leave the skins on if you like, but I'd save that for crushed new potatoes instead — there's a time and a place for wholesomeness, and it's not on a plate of sausage and mash.

Serves 4

900g floury potatoes, peeled
Salt and pepper
100g butter, cut into cubes
50ml milk

1. Cut the potatoes in roughly equal-sized pieces, and put into a large pan of cold, well-salted water. Bring to the boil, then turn down the heat and simmer until tender. Drain well, and put the potatoes back into the hot pan for a couple of minutes to dry off completely.
2. Put the butter into the pan and mash the potato until smooth — you'll need to put a bit of effort in, but you will have earned your mash by the end.

3. Pour in half the milk and beat well with a wooden spoon, then repeat with the rest. Season to taste, and serve immediately — possibly straight out of the pan.

Potato varieties
A spud isn't just a spud. Over eighty varieties are grown for sale in this country — and very few of them, sadly, come with much in the way of labelling, although you can't miss the purple Shetland Black vintage potato (floury, good boiled) or the Pink Fir Apple (waxy, ideal for salads). If you're not familiar with what's on offer, you could end up with entirely the wrong potato for the job. Disintegrating dauphinoise? You'll have an over-floury potato. Chewy chip? Too waxy, mate.

Common floury varieties: ideal for fluffy mash, chips, jacket or roast potatoes: King Edward, Maris Piper

All-rounders: can be used for mashing, but will also hold their shape when boiled: Desiree, Wilja, Estima

Common waxy varieties: dense and flavourful, ideal for potato salads or simply boiling: Charlotte, Maris Peer, Jersey Royal

----

How to store potatoes
Potatoes grow underground. Remember this light-shunning tendency when you unpack your next

bag – leave them out on the counter and they'll turn green, and green potatoes are bad news: bitter, and potentially toxic. Cut out any verdant bits before cooking, and resolve to store them in a dark, cool place in future: a cellar would be ideal, but a well-ventilated cupboard is fine. If you don't have room for them in a cupboard, you can purchase bags with black linings to store your spuds in: never leave them in plastic, because they'll sweat. Buy them unwashed if possible, as they'll keep much better, and it's the work of a mere minute and a stout brush to clean them before cooking.

Perfect
Gratin Dauphinoise

*N*amed after the ancient Alpine province, a gratin dauphinoise is the pinnacle of potato-based glamour. Put a bubbling dish of this on the table, and the meal becomes an occasion as far as I'm concerned.

But, for something so simple – really, it's little more than sliced potatoes, cooked in cream – dauphinoise is fraught with risk for the cook. Soggy spuds – or even worse, semi-raw in unappetizingly curdled cream or no cream at all, the liquid having evaporated into the ether – it's a surprisingly tough one to get right, as I can testify.

Oddly, most recipes seem to use fluffy potatoes such as Maris Piper, which have a tendency to collapse during cooking, making the dish stodgy. Elizabeth David and Raymond Blanc are both with me in preferring a waxier variety, like Charlottes or Maris Peers – much better at keeping their shape, and more importantly, their texture in the oven.

Whichever you happen to prefer, however, it's vital to slice them wafer thin, so they cook through – almost impossible to do with a knife, but the work of a few minutes with a mandoline. They're not expensive, especially in Oriental shops, but please be careful: I sacrificed the top of my finger to the perfect dauphinoise, so there's no need for you to do the same.

Cream is, regrettably, inevitable here – I found Richard Olney's milk and egg version too solid and heavy. That said, Michel Roux Jr's beautifully simple recipe, which just involves tossing the potatoes in double cream and shoving them in the oven, is too sticky and rich to eat in the requisite greedy portions. A mixture of milk and cream, as favoured by Blanc, Nick Nairn and Stevie Parle, gives a more homely, and quite possibly more digestible result.

Giving the potatoes a head start by par-boiling them in the sauce before baking, as Nairn suggests, proves wise insurance against crunchy disappointment, but there's no need to cook them until almost tender, or you risk making them mushy.

Par-boiling also has the benefit of thickening the sauce slightly, as the starch from the spuds leaches out into the liquid – Elizabeth David may be of the view that starch is a very bad thing for a dauphinoise (indeed, she rinses the potato slices before use), but on this occasion, she's wrong. There, I said it.

Nigel Slater writes that 'restraint with the garlic will be rewarded', but I'm of the opinion that potatoes and cream are a combination that can tend dangerously towards the bland – it may be more 'authentic' to rub the dish with a cut clove, but I'm going to crush two and add them to the sauce to give it a bit of Gallic poke.

I don't think infusing the cream with herbs, as Anthony Bourdain suggests, is necessary though – too many flavours can spoil such a simple dish, and a little pinch of sweet nutmeg is a much subtler seasoning. I must admit I do like Bourdain's anchovies though, which add a gorgeously savoury richness: if you're not averse, or afraid of the French, then please, give them a try.

Fish may not be on *Larousse Gastronomique*'s list of permissible additives, but cheese certainly is. They suggest two layers, one on the base, one on top, while Olney stirs his into the cream itself, but I've stuck to a modest amount on top: just enough to melt and brown, in contrast to the creamy starch beneath.

Serves 6

750g waxy potatoes
250ml double cream
100ml whole milk
2 small cloves of garlic, crushed
Nutmeg, to grate
Butter, to grease
50g Gruyère, grated

1. Peel the potatoes and cut them into very thin slices using a food processor or mandoline.
2. Pour the cream and milk into a large saucepan, add the garlic and a liberal grating of nutmeg, and bring just to the boil. Season and add the sliced potatoes, then reduce the heat and simmer them gently for about 10 minutes, until the slices have softened, but not cooked through.
3. Meanwhile, grease a gratin dish with butter, and heat the oven to 180°C/fan 160°C/gas 4.
4. Scoop the potatoes into the buttered dish and spread them out

evenly. Pour over the milk and cream mixture, cover with foil and bake for 30 minutes.

5. Remove the foil, sprinkle the grated cheese on top, and bake the dauphinoise for a further 10–15 minutes, until the cheese has melted into a golden, bubbling sea. Allow to cool slightly before serving.

Perfect
Roast Potatoes

*T*he meat may be the nominal centrepiece of a Sunday roast, but if you get your roast potatoes right, then frankly, you could serve chicken nuggets and most people would still be happy as Larry. There's no big secret to perfection here: you don't need to dust them with semolina, as Nigella does (too grainy), or toss them in seasoned flour, as recommended by *Good Food* magazine. Don't boil them to the point of disintegration like Heston — there's no need, and half of them will fall apart — but do add some of the peelings to the pan when parboiling; they really do improve the flavour (just taste the cooled water for the proof). There's no need to laboriously scrape the spuds with a fork as Jane Grigson suggests: shaking them gently in the pan after boiling and draining should rough up the edges nicely. All you really need is hot fat, and an even hotter oven. And, of course, floury potatoes — waxy ones will never fluff up properly.

That fat is important: beef dripping works well with beef, pork and lamb, olive oil is surprisingly good (although I wouldn't bother with Michael Caine's recipe — the *Italian Job* star revealed on Radio 4's *Desert Island Discs* that the late restaurant critic and erstwhile filmmaker Michael Winner thought he made the best roast potatoes in the world but I found cooking them in a vat of cold extra virgin too greasy: use ordinary olive oil, preheated in the oven, instead) — but goose fat, if you're up for splashing out, gives the best flavour of all, and is ideal with pork and poultry in particular. Make sure you get it sizzling hot before you add the potatoes, and toss them to coat before consigning them to a good hot oven for at least 45 minutes – by the time they're ready, the meat should have rested and been carved.

Serves 6

This recipe also works for 450g of parsnips – blanch for 3 minutes instead, and cook for about 45 minutes.

1.2kg floury potatoes (e.g. King Edward, Maris Piper)
Salt and pepper
2 tablespoons goose or duck fat, or dripping, or 4 tablespoons olive oil

1. Preheat the oven to 210°C/fan 190°C/gas 7. Wash and peel the potatoes, reserving the peel. Cut them into halves or quarters, depending on their size. Put them into a large pan of salted boiling water, along with the peel – it's easiest to retrieve if you use a muslin infusing bag. Parboil for 8 minutes.
2. Meanwhile, put 2 tablespoons of goose or duck fat or dripping, or 4 tablespoons of olive oil, into a roasting tin and put it into the oven to heat. Drain the potatoes and discard the peel, then put them back into the pan and shake gently to rough up the edges. Take the roasting tin out of the oven and put it on the hob over a medium heat. Put the potatoes in one by one – they should sizzle as they hit the pan – and baste all over. Season.
3. Roast for about an hour, until golden and crunchy, keeping an eye on them and basting with more fat if they begin to look dry.

Perfect
Ratatouille

A stalwart of the 1980s dinner party, ratatouille always gave the impression of being an ancient peasant dish one might have picked up from some darling ancient peasant neighbours of Peter Mayle, when in fact, according to Alan Davidson's wonderful *Oxford Companion to Food*, it's a relatively recent creation. The word, which comes from the French *touiller*, to stir, first pops up in 1877, misspelled, in reference to a meat stew. It is not until the 1930s that it becomes associated with a 'ragoût of aubergine with tomatoes, courgettes and sweet pepper'. So authenticity probably isn't something we need to worry about with ratatouille, which is fortunate, given the variety of recipes out there.

A ragoût, of course, suggests something cooked long and slow on the hob — but there is some debate about whether the constituent parts should be cooked together, or separately. Raymond Blanc simmers everything together until tender, which gives a sort of vegetable stew — nice enough, but no more than the sum of its parts. Gui Gedda and Marie-Pierre Moine's *Cooking School Provence* (which promises to teach me to 'shop, cook and eat like a native') demands I char and skin the peppers, blanch and skin the tomatoes, and employ two pans to cook everything separately before combining it into one creamy, but oddly thin stew. Nigel Slater takes the same approach, but sticks the cooked vegetables into the oven instead of simmering them on the hob — which leaves the ratatouille tasty but dry.

In fact, it's a cartoon rat who delivers my ratatouille breakthrough – when making their 2007 film of the same name, the Pixar animation team turned to American chef Thomas Keller, the first American chef to preside over two three-Michelin-starred establishments (New York's Per Se and California's legendary French Laundry), for advice on creating a realistic restaurant kitchen. It's his version of the titular recipe which allows the fictional rat to win over France's toughest restaurant reviewer, and although time-consuming to prepare, it's surprisingly simple: thinly sliced vegetables slow-baked in a pepper, tomato and onion sauce. Although my efforts are not quite as beautiful as the rodent's, I can see why this dish wowed the cartoon critic: the slightly caramelized vegetables on top are earthily sweet, and those beneath meltingly soft from their long, slow steaming, while the sauce is deep and rich, and jammy rather than watery. Much as I hate to admit it, this is one peasant dish which really benefits from tarting up.

Faffing about with Keller's kaleidoscopic vegetable spirals and delicately drizzled vinaigrettes is a step too far for most of us, however: my ratatouille is more homely in style, with slightly chunkier vegetables tossed together on a base of *piperade* with a splash of balsamic vinegar and a pinch of saffron (the last stolen from Joël Robuchon, French restaurant guide Gault Millau's chef of the century – it may have been the last century, but the tip still holds good today). It tastes just as good as the fancy version, and has the benefit of being much quicker to assemble – you can chop the vegetables as the sauce is reducing, chuck it all into the dish, then sit back and enjoy a glass or two of rosé while it's cooking, which seems much more in the spirit of things. It goes without saying that this is a summer dish; you need ripe Mediterranean vegetables for it to work.

Serves 4

2 red peppers
2 tablespoons olive oil, plus
    extra for oiling the tray
1 medium onion, finely diced
4 cloves of garlic, minced
4 ripe tomatoes, peeled, deseeded (page 298)
    and cut into small dice, plus juices
3 sprigs of thyme, plus 1 teaspoon thyme leaves
A pinch of saffron
Salt and pepper
1 teaspoon balsamic vinegar
3 courgettes (a mix of yellow and green
    is good if possible), thinly sliced
1 aubergine, thinly sliced
4 plum tomatoes, thinly sliced
1 tablespoon extra virgin olive oil,
    plus extra to serve

1. Preheat the oven to 230°C/fan 210°C/gas 8. Cut the peppers in half, removing the seeds and pith, and place them cut-side down on a lightly oiled baking tray. Roast for 20 minutes, until the skin has blistered, then remove and leave to cool, turning the oven down to 140°C/fan 120°C/gas 1.

2. Meanwhile, heat the olive oil over a low heat. Add the onion and cook until very soft, but not browned (about 8 minutes), adding three-quarters of the minced garlic 5 minutes in. Stir in the diced tomatoes and juices, and the sprigs of thyme, and simmer until most of the liquid has evaporated.

3. Peel the peppers, cut into small dice and add to the pan with

the saffron. Cook gently for 5 minutes, then remove the thyme sprigs and discard, season to taste, and stir in the vinegar.

4. Spread the sauce on the bottom of an ovenproof dish, and arrange the sliced vegetables on top. Mix the remaining garlic with the extra virgin olive oil and thyme leaves, season and sprinkle over the top. Cover tightly with foil, and put into the oven for 2 hours, until the vegetables are tender to the point of a knife.

5. Remove the foil, and cook for 30 minutes more — if the top starts to brown, cover loosely with the foil again. If there is any liquid left in the dish after cooking, decant it into a small pan, reduce over a medium heat, then stir back in. At this point the dish can be kept for a couple of days.

6. Just before serving, reheat if desired, then put the ratatouille under a hot grill until lightly browned. Serve with extra virgin olive oil and crusty bread.

- -

To salt, or not to salt
Once upon a time, every recipe involving the magnificent glossy aubergine began with the same instruction — salt to draw out the bitter juices, then rinse and pat dry. Such unpalatable flavours have largely been bred out of the modern aubergine, but salting still has its adherents, including Delia Smith, who believes it concentrates the flavour, Hugh Fearnley-Whittingstall, who thinks it stops them soaking up quite so much oil, and Skye Gyngell, who doesn't trouble to explain her reasoning. In fact, as far as I can tell, all it does is season the aubergine, which is no bad thing of course.

Fungi's Dirty Little Secret
Everyone from Gordon Ramsay
to the British Mushroom Bureau
urges you not to wash your
mushrooms before cooking –
fungi absorb water like nobody's
business, they say, and who wants to eat a sponge?
Following a series of rigorous tests, however, food
writer Harold McGee has concluded that soaking
mushrooms for prolonged periods makes so little
difference to their water content that we can spritz
our shiitake and bathe our buttons with a clear
conscience.

How to cook vegetables
Many vegetables need nothing more than a quick
peep at boiling water to turn them into the perfect
foil for a rich, creamy fish pie, or a meaty stew. All
the below should be seasoned and
tossed with a knob of butter, or a
dash of olive oil, before serving,
and, if you're making a real effort,
some chopped herbs. In fact, take
that as a general rule: a sprinkle
of green stuff (or lemon zest or
toasted nuts) is the culinary
equivalent of dressing to impress.

Broccoli: Wash and cut into evenly-sized florets, and chop the stalk into batons. Put into a steamer, and cook for about 8–10 minutes, until tender. The leaves that surround sprouting broccoli stems are perfectly edible, and should be left on unless they're particularly large and tough-looking (leave the stem whole, and serve, like asparagus, with hollandaise or a soft-boiled egg). All broccoli has a particular affinity with anchovies, chilli flakes, lemon zest and garlic.

Cabbage, kale and other leaves: Wash and cut into strips, discarding the woody central core of each cabbage leaf, and put into a steaming basket or colander set over a pan of simmering water. Steam for 4–6 minutes, depending on the vegetable, until soft, but not mushy. All these work extremely well with bacon, chilli and garlic, and chestnuts are also a seasonal possibility.

Carrots: Wash and peel, if necessary (young carrots will not need this), cut into rounds or batons, and steam for about 10 minutes until tender. Carrots can be dressed up with orange zest and hazelnuts, or fresh ginger, chives or parsley, and are even more interesting roasted until soft and caramelized with olive oil and cumin seeds.

Peas and beans: Top and tail runner beans and cut into diagonal pieces if you're feeling fancy, pod peas and broad beans if necessary and peel the beans if they are large – early in the summer season, the skins will be tender enough to eat. Put into a pan of boiling salted water and cook for

2 (peas) to 4 minutes (beans) depending on their
size. As well as the classic fresh mint, peas and
beans pair brilliantly with bacon, smoked fish and
aniseedy tarragon.

Spinach and chard: The big leaves have a better
flavour than the baby salad ones, if you can find
them. Wash well, picking out any grit, then
pat dry and put into a large pan. Cover and
cook over a low heat until they wilt — the water
clinging to the leaves should be enough to keep
them from sticking to the pan. Turn up the heat
and cook, stirring, until the remaining water
has evaporated. As well as the garlic, anchovies
and lemon zest which work so nicely with the
cabbage family, spinach and chard can be made
considerably less healthy, if even more delicious,
with cream or crème fraîche, cheese and nutmeg —
and Jane Grigson recommends stirring in some
Marmite along with the dairy, which gives it an
'unidentifiable, savoury accent'.

Perfect
Aubergine Parmigiana

*I*talian comfort food of the first order, these days there's no real
need to salt aubergines to draw out their bitterness (modern
varieties have had it bred out of them) but I think the practice is still
popular amongst recipe writers because it improves the flavour
immeasurably. The slight salinity that lingers, even after rinsing,
seasons the parmigiana from the inside out.

Peeling the aubergines, as some recipes suggest, is
quite pointless: indeed, the skins offer a pleasing
contrast in texture in a dish which otherwise runs
the risk of verging on the mushy.

Traditionally, the slices (it's easier to build if you cut
long strips, rather than rounds) are fried in generous
quantities of oil before baking, which makes the
whole dish quite ridiculously rich – oil actually spills out of Anna Del
Conte's parmigiana as I slice into it. Though this has the benefit of
also leaving it meltingly tender, if you want to eat more than a sliver,
some compromise is required.

Jamie Oliver chargrills his slices, which looks pretty, but leaves
the dish sadly dry, and *New York Times* writer Ed Schneider bakes
them first, but the best result, surprisingly, comes from Jane
Grigson's blanched aubergines. Used in combination with the
fried variety, they yield a parmigiana that's soft, but not too oily.

I have to disagree with Grigson's caution against colouring the aubergines in the pan, however: they look more attractive in gold, and the slightly caramelized flavour is more interesting too. Breadcrumbs should remain on top, where they can crisp up in the oven.

In an ideal world, of course, we'd be making this dish with obscenely ripe tomatoes, but in this country it's much safer to stick with the tinned variety. If you've got great fresh tomatoes, then enjoy them in a salad instead.

Parmesan is, as Jane Grigson observes, 'the soul' of the dish, but I like the milky blandness of mozzarella in parmigiana too – lifting a slab, stringy with melted cheese, is a pleasure quite beyond measure. No need to splash out though: good buffalo stuff is too wet, and the sharp flavour is lost in the oven: ordinary, rubbery cheese, of the kind used to top pizzas, is actually preferable.

One last thing: if it's cold outside, by all means tuck in right away, but in more clement weather, heed Ed Schneider's advice when he says that the key to parmigiana, 'as to many other Italian things, is not to serve it hot, though it's hard to wait sometimes'. Let it rest for a few minutes – it'll be even more delicious.

Serves 4–6 (main course/side dish)

   1.5kg aubergines
   Fine salt
   2 tablespoons olive oil
   3 cloves of garlic, crushed
   800g good tinned tomatoes

150ml red wine
A pinch of sugar
½ teaspoon dried oregano
Oil, to fry
200g mozzarella, thinly sliced
125g Parmesan, grated
50g breadcrumbs
A handful of basil leaves

1. Cut the aubergines lengthways into 5mm thick slices, sprinkle lightly with salt and leave in a colander to drain for half an hour.
2. Meanwhile, heat the olive oil in a medium pan over a medium-high heat and add the crushed garlic. Fry for a minute, stirring, then pour in the tinned tomatoes and wine. Bring this to the boil, mashing the tomatoes roughly as you do, then turn down the heat slightly. Add a pinch of sugar, some salt and pepper and the oregano, and simmer the sauce gently for 45 minutes, stirring occasionally. Purée with a hand blender until smooth, and taste for seasoning.
3. Preheat the oven to 200°C/fan 180°C/gas 6. Put a large pan of water on to boil if you feel like being relatively healthy. Rinse the aubergines well to get rid of the salt, and dry each slice thoroughly with kitchen paper. Pour enough oil into a frying pan to coat the bottom and put this on a high heat.
4. Fry half (healthy) or all (not) the aubergine slices in this pan until golden brown on both sides, working in batches. Put the cooked slices on paper towel to drain. Blanch the other half, for the more virtuous version, in the boiling water for 2 minutes, then drain well and pat dry with more paper.
5. Lightly grease a baking dish with oil and spread the bottom with a thin layer of tomato sauce, followed by a single layer of

aubergines (packing them tightly, and mixing blanched and fried versions together), a layer of mozzarella and a layer of Parmesan, seasoning all but the Parmesan. Add another layer of aubergines, followed by tomato sauce, the cheeses and seasoning. Repeat this order until you've used up all the aubergine, finishing the dish with a layer of sauce (NB: You may not need all the sauce) – but keep a little Parmesan back for the top.

6. Toss the breadcrumbs with a little olive oil and the remaining Parmesan and sprinkle on top, then bake for about 30 minutes, until the top is bubbling and browned. Allow to cool slightly, and sprinkle with torn basil just before serving.

Perfect
Cauliflower Cheese

Ah, cauliflower cheese. Floury sauce, mushy vegetables, stringy cheese — this is one comfort food I'd often rather swap for a salad. It has to be made with care: the top should be slightly crunchy, the cauliflower tender, but not to the point of disintegration, and the sauce agreeably piquant.

Saying that, you can get too fancy — I don't think the dish requires a béchamel base, as specified by Simon Hopkinson and Lindsey Bareham; that sauce's onion and bay leaf flavours just confuse the issue. Neither do I think the cook needs to fuss about with double cream, in fact, better to use a plain white sauce for such a nursery classic. Tom Norrington-Davies has the right idea, co-opting this basic as the vehicle for vast amounts of cheese. Lancashire, as it happens, which gives the dish a pleasant saltiness; Cheddar, as suggested by Nigel Slater, is more strident. Cauliflower cheese is a quiet dish by nature — although a pinch of mustard powder, in homage to Clarissa Dickson Wright, adds a touch of understated spice to proceedings.

Clarissa also gives instructions for baking an entire cauliflower — which looks majestic, but is, in practice, quite difficult to get right. I'm sticking with florets — topped with Simon and Lindsey's breadcrumbs, which provide that all-important crunch that separates cauliflower cheese from rather dreary invalid food.

Serves 4

50g unsalted butter
25g plain flour
300ml milk
½ teaspoon salt
1 teaspoon English mustard powder
100g Lancashire cheese, grated
1 medium cauliflower, leaves removed, broken into evenly-
 sized florets
30g breadcrumbs

1. Preheat the oven to 220°C/fan 200°C/gas 7. Melt the butter in a medium pan, and stir in the flour to make a roux. Cook on a low heat for a couple of minutes, stirring occasionally, but do not allow to colour.

2. Pour a little of the milk into the roux, and whisk to combine, then gradually add the rest in the same manner until you have a smooth liquid. Cook, stirring regularly, until it has thickened enough to coat the back of a wooden spoon. Remove from the heat, add the salt, mustard powder and half the cheese, and set aside.

3. Meanwhile, cook the cauliflower in a pan of salted, boiling water for 3 minutes, until softened, but not cooked through.

4. Drain the cauliflower and put into a buttered baking dish. Tip over the sauce, then mix together the breadcrumbs and the rest of the cheese and scatter over the top. Bake for about 30 minutes, or until golden and bubbling.

Perfect
Dal

Sometimes – often at dinner parties when conversation flags – I'm asked if I have a 'signature dish'. Truly, *Masterchef* has a lot to answer for. Sometimes I say my brownies (see page 335), which I really, without wishing to seem boastful, believe to be the best in the world. Sometimes I say garlic bread (see page 58), because it's the only reason certain people come to my parties. But, if I'm being truthful, I say dal.

Signature may be the wrong word, because it's rarely the kind of thing I make for guests, but, comforting and requiring little in the way of shopping, it's a Sunday night staple in my house. I'm not alone: Madhur Jaffrey writes evocatively of the 'deep satisfaction' of the dish in her *Curry Bible*, describing dal as 'the core of [an Indian] meal'.

Technically dal means a split pulse, but the word has come to describe all dried peas and beans, as well as dishes in which they're the main ingredient. This allows for a dizzying array of options, but the one I cook the most often is mung dal, according to Madhur the most digestible, eaten 'with equal relish by toothless toddlers, husky farmers and effete urban snobs'.

You don't need to soak the dal before cooking – this was traditionally done to save fuel, but I think you get a better result from long slow cooking, as advocated by Jaffrey herself. The aim is to break it down into a silky soup, and this requires patience.

Although some western recipes cook the dal in stock, this is completely unnecessary: not only does a good dal contain quite enough spice as it is, but the contrast between these spices and the creamy blandness of the pulses is a key part of the dish's charm.

The secret of a great dal is the finishing tarka (sometimes called the baghaar or chownk): a mixture of sizzling spices folded through the creamy pulses just before serving. Thinly sliced shallots, as recommended by *Riverford Farm Cook Book*, supply sweetness, Madhur Jaffrey's cumin seeds spice, and mustard seeds and chilli flakes colour and heat, all fried in rich ghee, although oil would no doubt be the healthier option. Some recipes also add a squeeze of lemon juice for freshness, but I find sharpness unwelcome in my comfort blanket dish of choice.

The consistency is up to you, it can be as soupy or as thick as you like – indeed dals are endlessly versatile, taking just about any spice you'll throw at them. Cooked gently and patiently, and with a sizzling, aromatic garnish, it's the dish that never disappoints.

Serves 4

> 400g mung dal (skinned yellow split mung beans)
> 4 cloves of garlic, peeled and crushed
> A 4cm piece of fresh ginger, peeled and cut into 4
> 1 tablespoon turmeric
> 4 small green chillies, 2 finely chopped, 2 left whole
> 2 tablespoons ghee or groundnut oil

2 shallots, finely sliced
1 tablespoon cumin seeds
1 teaspoon mustard seeds
1 teaspoon crushed chilli
Fresh coriander, chopped, to serve

1. Wash the dal in cold water until the water runs clear, then drain and put into a large saucepan. Cover with 2 litres of cold water, bring to the boil and use a slotted spoon to skim off any scum that rises to the top.
2. Add the garlic, ginger, turmeric and chopped chillies to the pan along with a pinch of salt, then turn down the heat, partially cover, and simmer the dal very gently for about 1½ hours, stirring occasionally, until it's soft and creamy in texture.
3. Add boiling water if you prefer a soupy dal, or reduce it further by turning up the heat if you'd like it to be thicker (bear in mind it'll reduce slightly during the final simmer, so don't make it too dry at this point), season to taste, then add the whole chillies and simmer very gently for 15 minutes.
4. Meanwhile, heat the ghee or oil in a frying pan over a medium-high heat and fry the shallots until golden and beginning to crisp. Add the dried spices and cook for a couple of minutes, stirring regularly, until you hear the mustard seeds beginning to pop.
5. Stir the tarka, oil and all, into the dal, and top with chopped coriander. Serve with plain rice or flatbreads.

An old wives' tale suggests salting any pulses during cooking will make them tough — it doesn't seem to, but with any such lengthy simmering, it's better to add most of the salt at the end, or you risk misjudging the amount and spoiling the end result.

Perfect
Aloo Gobi

'The most common and basic vegetable curry you will find anywhere in India' according to chef Vivek Singh, and, in consequence, one with a million variations across the subcontinent. Cheap, filling and vegan-friendly, it's a very useful recipe to master.

Not that it takes much. Ideally, I'd use waxy potatoes, as Kaushy Patel of Bradford restaurant Prashad recommends, but if floury are good enough for Sumayya Usmani's Nani, then they're good enough for me if they're what I happen to have in the house. They'll give a softer, fluffier result, but on the flipside, are more prone to falling apart in the pan.

Both the spuds and the cauliflower benefit from a brief dance in some hot oil to help bring out their subtle flavour. Do bear in mind that, as Singh suggests in his book *Curry: Classic and Contemporary*, if you cut the florets 'slightly bigger than the potatoes, they will cook in roughly the same time, rather than overcooking and disintegrating before the potatoes are done'.

Tomatoes act as the lubricant in this dish – fresh in its homelands, but the tinned sort are a safer bet in the UK, plus a dollop of purée as well, as Usmani recommends in her book *Summers Under the Tamarind Tree*, 'for colour'. Her sauce is rich and flavourful, which I suspect is because she takes the time to cook off the excess liquid from the

tomatoes, simmering the curry 'until the oil rises', the classic sign of
a well-cooked curry, and a useful detail missing from some of the
other recipes.

The onion should be cooked until soft and golden (or pink, if you
prefer the red variety), along with the customary ginger and garlic,
and some whole green chillies, which will give a gentler heat than the
chopped variety. Spice-wise, earthy cumin and zesty coriander pair
beautifully with cauliflower, and turmeric adds colour. I love the
savoury hit of Usmani's nigella seeds, and the bitter herbaceousness
of her dried fenugreek leaves, balanced by the sweetness of
homemade garam masala – though you can use ready-mixed stuff if
you're in a hurry. Add the chilli powder to taste; aloo gobi should be
a very homely pleasure, and one person's comforting warmth is
another's sweaty nightmare.

A squeeze of lime juice, as Singh suggests, adds an acidic element
lacking in tinned tomatoes in particular, and a handful of coriander
adds freshness; both welcome in a carb-rich dish that can tend towards
the heavy. If you prefer it that way, however, then you might enjoy
Patel's finishing touch: a big dollop of butter – which may go some
way to explaining why Indian restaurant food always tastes so good.

Serves 4

   4 tablespoons neutral oil
   1 teaspoon cumin seeds
   ½ teaspoon nigella seeds
   350g waxy potatoes, cut into rough 2.5cm dice
   1 medium cauliflower, cut into florets and chunks of stalk
      slightly larger than the potato

1 yellow onion, finely sliced

4 garlic cloves, crushed

1 tablespoon grated ginger

1 x 400g tin of plum tomatoes, roughly chopped, or 5 chopped
    fresh tomatoes and 1 tablespoon tomato purée

2 teaspoons coriander seeds, toasted in a dry pan and ground

½–1 teaspoon medium chilli powder

½ teaspoon turmeric

2–4 small green chillies, slit along their length

1 teaspoon salt

1 tablespoon methi (dried fenugreek leaves)

1 teaspoon garam masala

Juice of ½ a lime

A small bunch of fresh coriander, chopped

1. Heat the oil in a wide, lidded pan over a medium-high heat; add
   the cumin and nigella seeds and cook for a few seconds until
   they pop, then tip in the potatoes and sauté until golden,
   stirring to make sure they don't stick. Scoop out with a slotted
   spoon and repeat with the cauliflower, then scoop this out into a
   separate bowl.

2. Turn the heat down to medium-low, add a little more oil to the
   pan if necessary, and fry the onion until soft and golden, then
   stir in the garlic and ginger and cook for a couple of minutes,
   stirring regularly. Mix in the tomatoes and ground spices and
   simmer, stirring regularly, until the oil begins to pool around
   the side of the pan.

3. Add the potatoes back to the pan along with the fresh chillies and
   salt, bring to a simmer, turn down the heat, cover and cook for
   5 minutes. Add the cauliflower along with a good splash of
   water, cover and cook until both vegetables are tender, shaking

the pan occasionally to make sure they don't stick, and adding a splash more water if necessary.

4. Take off the heat, stir in the methi and garam masala, cover and leave to sit for 10 minutes. Sprinkle over the lime juice and fresh coriander before serving – Usmani recommends pairing it with 'plain basmati, naan, paratha or brioche buns, and a pickle or chutney'.

Perfect
Nut Roast

*T*hough veggies may have reason to be grateful for Yotam Ottolenghi, that's no reason to neglect the classics — this is one of those vegetarian options that they'll have to fight the omnivores for. I know: I put it on the table with a roast chicken, and the bird lost.

I think the mistake many nut roast recipes make is to forget just how energy dense the main ingredient is — unless you lighten the load with some sort of carbohydrate, you'll end up with something so dry and heavy you'd be better off selling it in bars to mountaineers.

Breadcrumbs are the most popular choice, used by the likes of Rose Elliot and Mary Berry, but they can make for rather a bland dish — instead, I've bound my roast with fluffy mashed parsnips, which lend a festive flavour for a dish that, after all, should be the centrepiece of the meal, adding just a handful of wholemeal breadcrumbs for lightness.

The flavours are deliberately chosen to pair with the traditional trimmings of a roast — so no Mediterranean aubergine (Mary Berry), or goat's cheese (Annie Bell) here. Instead mushrooms act as the savoury element, while chestnuts work well with the sweetness of the parsnips, and the sage and onion are a nod to the classic roast stuffing.

As this feels like a very wintery dish to me, I've also added crumbled Stilton for richness, although you could substitute any full-flavoured vegetarian-friendly cheese — or, indeed, if you'd prefer, a teaspoon of Marmite instead, a tip I picked up from a friendly vegan on Twitter.

Tasting good, though important, isn't quite enough for a ceremonial dish like a roast — a boring brown loaf lacks the visual impact of a bronzed bird, or a rare joint of beef, so I've wrapped it in blanched cabbage leaves to add a little colour to the table. Good with cranberry sauce or redcurrant jelly — and, of course, bread sauce and the inevitable roast potatoes. Cooked in olive oil, naturally.

Serves 6 *(with accompaniments)*

2 large parsnips
Salt and pepper
Oil, to grease
1 small Savoy cabbage, 4–6 outer leaves only
150g hazelnuts
40g butter
1 red onion, finely chopped
150g chestnut mushrooms, finely chopped
100g cooked chestnuts, roughly chopped
100g Stilton, crumbled (or other vegetarian-friendly cheese of your choice)
100g brown breadcrumbs
2 tablespoons chopped fresh sage
1 free-range egg, beaten

1. Peel the parsnips, cut them into quarters (or halves if small) and cook in boiling, salted water until tender. Drain thoroughly, then mash until smooth.

2. Meanwhile, grease a loaf tin approximately 20cm x 10cm x 7cm with oil, then line it with foil, and grease this generously too. Blanch 6 Savoy cabbage leaves in boiling, salted water for 2 minutes until just softened: you'll need enough to line the tin with overlapping leaves, but exactly how many depends on the size of your cabbage, so make sure you have enough before you tip away the water. Once softened, immediately plunge the leaves into iced water to cool, which will keep them a nice, vibrant green colour.

3. Toast the hazelnuts in a dry frying pan over a high heat until starting to colour, then scoop out and set aside. Turn the heat down to medium, add the butter and chopped onion and cook for 5 minutes, then add the chopped mushrooms and cook for about another 7 minutes, until the mixture is thoroughly softened.

4. Roughly chop the hazelnuts and put them into a large bowl with the chopped chestnuts, crumbled Stilton, breadcrumbs and chopped sage. Add the mashed parsnip, onions and mushrooms, followed by the beaten egg. Season and stir together well so everything is thoroughly combined. Preheat the oven to 200°C/ fan 180°C/gas 6.

5. Pat the cabbage leaves dry and use to line the prepared tin, leaving any excess leaf hanging over the sides. Spoon in the mixture, pressing it down well, and fold any overhanging cabbage back over the top to cover. Cover the tin tightly with foil and bake for 45 minutes. (Alternatively, you can keep it in the fridge for a day or so at this point before baking.)

6. Remove the foil from the top, put the loaf back into the oven for

another 15 minutes, until the top is golden, then remove and allow to cool slightly.

7. Put a large serving plate over the top of the tin. Holding the tin securely with oven gloves, turn the plate over so the loaf inverts on to it. Carefully peel off the foil and cut the loaf into slices to serve.

Perfect
Yorkshire Puddings*

*Y*ou can't beat a Yorkshire pud — in fact, everyone loves them so much I suspect that, with a decent gravy (see page 281), they could be revived as a thrifty way to pad out the joint in these straitened times. After all, who can keep their mind on meat if there's a crisp piece of billowing batter coming down the table in their direction?

I used to think you could only make a good Yorkshire if you'd got northern blood, but it turns out that's just plain daft. In fact, the only secret is heat, and lots of it — you need a smoking hot pan, and a blisteringly hot oven. That said, there's a few things you can do to make your puddings even prouder. For a start, use a metal, rather than a silicone tray; that way you can keep it warm on the stovetop while you ladle the batter in, and it also seems to help get those bottoms nice and crunchy.

If all this talk of crunch is puzzling, you probably hail from below the Watford Gap — according to the *Oxford Companion to Food*, us softie southerners prefer our batter puddings . . . well, a bit softer. However, up north they like their puddings to be crisp on the outside, and tender within, which is why I use Delia's mixture of milk and water for ultimate crunch, rather than celebrity chef James Martin's milk-only recipe, which gives a slightly sweeter, softer result (some Yorkshireman he is).

---

* A wildcard in a chapter devoted to vegetables, pasta and rice admittedly, but how could I leave them out?

Allowing the mixture to rest before cooking seems to give a more satisfactory result, although I couldn't see any benefit in adding the flour at the last minute, as the winner of the 1970 Great Yorkshire Pudding Contest apparently did. I reckon the real secret of his success was the number of eggs in his recipe, recorded for posterity by Jane Grigson in *English Food*.

Traditionally, Yorkshire puddings would have been cooked using the drippings from the roast – and, despite experimenting with Hugh's olive oil, and goose fat, as per the Hairy Bikers, I still think beef dripping gives the best flavour. It should be so hot that the batter sizzles as it hits the pan – put them straight into the oven, and don't open it for at least twenty minutes, because they're not quite as amenable as soufflés.

Once the puddings are cooked, serve them as soon as possible; you can put them in a low oven for a while if the rest of the meal isn't quite ready, but don't leave them sitting in a draught, or you'll have to pass them off as Staffordshire oatcakes. Canadian Susan Sampson reckons you should pierce the puddings as they leave the oven to let the steam out, but this doesn't seem to do anything but make them a bit cold. Oh, and the name of the chef who won that competition? Mr Tin Sung Chan of Hong Kong. Turns out you really don't have to hail from God's own county to make a right fine pudding.

Makes 1 large pudding or 12 individual ones

250g plain flour
Salt and pepper
4 large free-range eggs

150ml whole milk

2 tablespoons beef dripping or sunflower oil

1. Sift the flour into a mixing bowl with a generous pinch of salt, then make a well in the middle and crack in the eggs. Mix the milk with 150ml of cold water, then pour a little in with the eggs and whisk in the flour to a smooth batter. Mix in the rest of the liquid; you should have a consistency much like that of single cream. Leave at room temperature for at least 15 minutes.

2. Once the meat has come out of the oven, turn it up to 230°C/ fan 210°C/gas 8 (this is probably the point where your roast potatoes should be just about done, so make sure they aren't going to burn in the next 20 minutes). Put a large roasting tray, or a muffin tin, with a couple of tablespoons of dripping in the bottom, on to a high shelf – there should be enough fat to grease, but the puddings shouldn't be swimming in them, so don't go overboard. Leave for 10 minutes to heat up.

3. Take the tin out of the oven and keep warm on the hob, if possible, while you ladle in the batter, which should sizzle as it hits the fat. Put back into the oven and cook for 15–20 minutes, until magnificently puffed up and golden. Keep an eye on the pudding or puddings towards the end, but don't be tempted to open the oven door until they're seriously bronzed, and you're just about to eat, as they will sink as they cool.

- -

Toad in the Hole

To turn your Yorkshire pudding into that underrated school dinner favourite, toad in the hole, set the oven to 230°C/fan 210°C/gas 8 and

make your batter
while it heats. Put
6 sausages into a
greased roasting tin
large enough to hold the pudding and cook for 15
minutes, then take out of the oven and put on the
hob over a medium heat — the sausages should have
released some fat, but if the tin looks dry, add 1
tablespoon of vegetable oil. When it's beginning to
sizzle, add the batter, then return the tin to the oven
and cook for 25 minutes. Serve with onion gravy.

Perfect
Pasta

Garibaldi relied on the power of macaroni to unite Italy, Sophia Loren famously claimed she owed her voluptuous figure to spaghetti – and the chef Giorgio Locatelli reckons every Italian is two-thirds pasta. Despite a lingering fondness for 'hoops', even Britain has embraced proper pasta in recent years. These days we know our pappardelle from our penne; and we're beginning to get the concept of different shapes for different sauces, but most of us still don't see the point of making our own.

Dried pasta and fresh egg pasta are two different beasts. You wouldn't use a waxy potato for baking, for the same reason an Italian wouldn't serve dried spaghetti with a game ragù – it doesn't work. Fresh egg pasta gets its 'bite' from egg proteins, and is traditionally served with the butter, cream and rich meat dishes of the north, while dried pasta generally pairs better with the olive oil and tomato recipes of the south.

Good dried pasta is widely available these days, as long as you're prepared to spend a bit more than you would on the budget varieties, and, with a little practice, you can produce your own fresh stuff which will knock the socks off anything from the supermarket – a product which, as Locatelli says, has 'real personality'.

You need a mixture of plain flour — preferably finely milled (or 'OO' grade, as you might find it labelled by Italian brands) for a really silky texture — and semolina for pasta; if you just use 'OO', as in the River Café recipe, it won't be as interesting, and the sauce won't cling to the strands in the same way. The more eggs you mix with the flour, the crisper the result — but if you go overboard with the yolks, you'll get a pasta that's so rich it will compete with any sauce you put with it. Adding olive oil to the dough, as the part-Italian Michelin-starred chef Angela Hartnett does, seems to be gilding the linguine lily; you can't taste it, and it's out of keeping with the northern, butter-based sauces you should be pairing it with.

Real nonnas scorn pasta machines, and roll their dough out on a board using an enormous pin, but for amateurs and Brits, they're a useful tool. If you don't have one, however, cut your dough into quarters, and roll each one out as thinly as possible before cutting it into strips — you can find videos showing the process online.

Folding the dough back on itself during the rolling-out process may seem like an unnecessary faff, but it does, as Angela observes, give a more elastic, uniform result in the end: you can't rush great ravioli.

When it comes to cooking your pasta, never, ever add oil to the water — not only does it not stop it sticking together in the pan (using a large pan, and agitating the pasta, should see to that), but it will make it more difficult for the sauce to cling to the pasta later. Tossing it together in the pan, rather than dolloping the sauce on top at the table, will also help with this. Don't skimp on the salt, though; a cavalier attitude to health is one of the reasons that pasta always tastes better in Italy.

Makes around 750g (enough for 6–8)

340g '00' flour
160g fine semolina flour
½ teaspoon fine sea salt
4 large free-range eggs and 2 egg
   yolks, at room temperature,
   lightly beaten

1. Mix the flours and the salt and shape into a volcano on the work surface, or a wooden board. Make a well in the middle, and pour in two-thirds of the eggs.

2. Using your fingertips in a circular motion, gradually stir in the flour until you have a dough you can bring together into a ball, adding more egg if necessary. Knead for about 10 minutes, until it is smooth and springs back when poked, wetting your hands with cold water if necessary.

3. Divide the dough in two and wrap in a damp cloth. Allow to rest for about an hour in a cool place.

4. With a rolling pin, roll out the first ball of dough on a lightly floured surface until it is about 1cm thick and will go through the widest setting of your pasta machine comfortably. Put it through a couple of times on the widest setting, folding it back on itself each time and using a small amount of flour to prevent it sticking. Roll through the pasta on the next setting down, then back up to the widest setting. Repeat this whole process a couple more times; this will work the dough and help it become more silky in texture. Then start working your way down, from the widest setting to the second narrowest. Cut the dough in half when it becomes too long to handle and finish one piece at a time, using small amounts of flour dredged over the dough to prevent sticking.

5. When the pasta has a good sheen to it, and is thin enough for your liking – pappardelle and tagliatelle should be cut on the second narrowest gauge, filled pastas such as ravioli on the narrowest – cut using a knife, or the cutter on your pasta machine. Curl into portion-sized nests and leave on a floured surface, under a damp cloth, while you repeat with the rest of the dough. Freeze any you're not going to use immediately – or leave it out on the counter overnight, under a tea towel, until completely dry, then store in an airtight container as you would any dried pasta.

6. Bring a large pan of well-salted water to the boil, add the pasta, in batches if necessary, and cook for a couple of minutes, stirring occasionally to keep it moving. Serve immediately.

Perfect
Spaghetti Carbonara

*F*ew dishes make me happier than spaghetti carbonara – rich with eggs, savoury with bacon, and festooned with salty cheese.

It's a dish with an interesting history: although almost everyone agrees that it probably originated in the Roman region, the supposed creators range from Apennine charcoal burners (carbonari) to the American GIs who asked local street vendors to prepare their bacon and egg rations for them over their charcoal braziers. Most plausible, in my opinion, is the theory that the name simply refers to the copious amounts of black pepper the dish is usually seasoned with – like tiny specks of charcoal, but infinitely tastier.

The spaghetti is there for good reason. One of the principal pleasures of this dish is slurping up the egg-slick strands, which is impossible with anything other than long pasta.

Cream and butter, purists claim, are recent additions to the recipe – introduced by restaurants because they're easier to control, and somewhat safer than a sauce of barely set egg. That said, they have some heavyweights on their side: Simon Hopkinson and Lindsey Bareham, and Nigella Lawson, use double cream, Ursula Ferrigno crème fraîche, and the River Café and Anna Del Conte butter. All, in my opinion, are mistaken: cream dilutes the delicate flavour of the egg yolk, and the richness of the butter competes with the richness of the pork fat. There's no need for such an excess of sauce in any case; there should be just enough there to coat the pasta and no more.

It's the egg yolk that adds the flavour, but using just the yolk, as the River Café and Simon and Lindsey suggest, makes the dish rather cloying, and exhibits a tendency to clump together amongst the strands of pasta. Whole eggs, as used by Nigella, Elizabeth David, *The Silver Spoon* and Ursula Ferrigno, give a looser sauce – but, as this is hardly everyday fare, I've sneaked in one extra yolk for extra eggy richness.

Back bacon, as favoured by my dad, won't cut the mustard here: you need pancetta, or a good dry-cured slab of streaky, cut into chunky little cubes, and cooked, as Nigella suggests, until 'crispy but not crunchy'. Make sure it's unsmoked, or you'll be faced with an umami overload – because this isn't a dish where you can get away with a delicate sprinkle of Parmesan. No, cheese plays a major part – preferably a half-and-half mix of salty Parmesan and the slightly fresher, more lactic pecorino romano, a salty ewe's milk cheese popular in central Italy.

Garlic, in subtle quantities, is a welcome addition, though I'd whip it out before adding the other ingredients, or it can dominate. You don't need parsley if you've got enough pepper, but I do love Nigella's final grating of nutmeg, which, although it will no doubt make Romans throw up their hands in horror, always pairs beautifully with egg.

The devil, when cooking carbonara, is in the detail – namely how to add raw eggs to a hot pan of pasta without ending up with egg-fried spaghetti. Having learned from the master, Rachel Roddy, I'd advise the briefest of encounters between eggs and heat, so they thicken to a creamy consistency, without solidifying.

The secret is to work quickly, tossing the cooked pasta in the oily pancetta until every strand is greased, then remove from the heat, toss briefly with the eggs and cheese — with a little cooking water just to loosen — and serve immediately. There's an art to it, but, like art in general, once you get it, it's a thing of rare beauty.

Serves 2

> 1 tablespoon olive oil
> 1 clove of garlic, sliced
> 75g pancetta, cubed
> 250g dried spaghetti
> 2 eggs and 1 egg yolk
> 25g pecorino romano, finely grated
> 25g Parmesan, finely grated
> Freshly ground black pepper
> Nutmeg, optional

1. Put two bowls into a low oven to keep warm, or boil a kettle and half fill them with hot water. Heat the oil in a large frying pan on a medium heat, then add the sliced garlic and cook, stirring, until well-coloured but not burnt. Remove from the pan with a slotted spoon and discard. Add the pancetta to the garlicky oil and cook until translucent and golden, but not brown.
2. Meanwhile, cook the spaghetti in a large pan of boiling, salted water until al dente. Beat together the eggs and the extra yolk,

then stir in the pecorino and most of the Parmesan, reserving a little as a garnish. Grind in plenty of black pepper and set the mixture next to the hob.

3. Scoop out a small cupful of the pasta cooking water and set aside next to the hob, then drain the pasta thoroughly. Tip it into the frying pan and toss vigorously so it's well coated with the pancetta fat.

4. Remove the pan from the heat and tip in the egg mixture, tossing the pasta furiously, then, once it's begun to thicken, add a dash of cooking water to loosen the sauce.

5. Toss again, and divide it between the warm bowls, finishing off with a light grating of nutmeg, if using, more black pepper and a little more Parmesan. Eat immediately.

Perfect
Macaroni Cheese

I must confess, I've come to macaroni cheese pretty late in life. Despite it containing two of my favourite ingredients, namely cheese and pasta, I just didn't get it. And then – then, well, I just did.

That's not to say I've embraced the outrageously rich, cheesy versions that seem to have become popular recently – although I try recipes using double cream, and Parmesan (that from Mrs Beeton, no less!), garlic (I'm looking at you, Jamie Oliver) and Lancashire cheese, in the end, I keep coming back to Tom Norrington-Davies' simple version, with its plain white sauce and modest Cheddar content. Creamy, rather than oppressively rich, and savoury, not cheesy, it's almost the dictionary definition of nursery food.

That said, Parmesan is rather nice on top, along with Martha Stewart's crunchy golden breadcrumbs, which offer a welcome contrast in texture, while a few caramelized tomatoes add a touch of sweetness. English mustard powder, a less acidic version of the mustard used in many recipes, supplies a subtle heat without any accompanying sourness.

Giving credence to every cliché going about Victorian cooking, Mrs Beeton boils the pasta for 1½ to 1¾ hours until 'quite tender' – I only managed an hour before it started to disintegrate, so perhaps stoves were less efficient in those days. More helpful is Martha's tip about rinsing the pasta before adding to the dish, so it doesn't clump together in a gluey mess.

Simon Hopkinson and Lindsey Bareham suggest using penne instead, on the grounds that 'the cheese sauce is better able to flow inside this larger-sized pasta', but I disagree – it's the small size of macaroni, perfect for scooping up in greedy spoonfuls, which sets the dish apart from a pasta bake in my opinion. I quite like their leeks though – softened in a little butter, they're a useful optional extra, especially if you're serving this as a stand-alone supper.

Otherwise, however, this is a dish that epitomizes modest simplicity – to add strong flavours, or fancy ingredients, is to miss the point. It should be subtle, creamy and soft; perfect for eating on the sofa in your pyjamas.

Serves 2

200g macaroni
35g butter, plus extra for greasing
25g plain flour
450ml whole milk
A grating of nutmeg
½ teaspoon English mustard powder
50g mature Cheddar, grated
1 slice of white bread, made into crumbs
1 tablespoon grated Parmesan
2 tomatoes, halved

1. Bring a large pan of salted water to the boil, tip in the pasta, stir and cook until tender. Drain well and rinse under cold running water.

2. Meanwhile, melt 25g of the butter in a pan, and, once it's melted, stir in the flour to make a paste. Cook, stirring, for a couple of minutes, then gradually whisk in the milk until it becomes a smooth sauce. Simmer this, stirring all the time, for a few minutes until it thickens, then add a grating of nutmeg, the mustard powder and grated cheese and stir until smooth. Take off the heat, and season to taste.

3. Preheat the grill. Grease a baking dish with butter, then tip the drained pasta into the cheese sauce and pour it all into the baking dish. (You can make it ahead up to this point, in which case you'll need to reheat it in the oven until warm through before going on to step 4.)

4. Melt the remaining butter and mix it with the breadcrumbs and the Parmesan. Spread the mixture over the top of the pasta, then arrange the tomatoes, cut side up, on top.

5. Grill for about 10 minutes, until the top is golden and the tomatoes charred. Allow to stand for 5 minutes before serving.

Perfect
Rice

*G*iven that it's the world's second most popular grain (pub quizzers: maize comes in at number one), and one that's been eaten in this country since medieval times, we're strangely content to be bad at cooking rice. Either it's served up in dry, claggy clumps, or – and perhaps worse – sliding sloppily across the plate in a trail of cooking water. Ugh.

Theories abound as to the best way to cook rice. Having never enjoyed much success with the microwave (watching food spin has  limited appeal, hence I always end up cleaning up rice from the inside afterwards), and lacking the room for a dedicated rice cooker, it's the hob for me. The recipe below is for basmati, or other long-grain rices, the kind you might eat with a curry or make into a pilaff; short-grain and sticky rices will need rather different treatment.

Although the rice we buy in this country doesn't tend to need much washing, Madhur Jaffrey, the actress turned food writer who introduced many Britons to the idea of Indian home cooking in the 1960s and 70s, calls for it to be soaked before cooking. Annoying as this is when you remember it at the last minute, I've found it does help the grains stay separate, although if you don't have the time, it's not a disaster.

It's important to get the ratio of water to rice right, rather than just chucking your 200g into an enormous pan of water and hoping for the best. Madhur Jaffrey helpfully gives a ratio of 1 part dry rice to 1½ parts water, which is simple enough to work out for any quantity of rice you might happen to be cooking, though you won't go far wrong placing a fingertip on top of the rice in the pan, then adding cold water up to the first knuckle either.

Sri Owen, author of *The Rice Book*, recommends bringing it to the boil, stirring once, then leaving it to simmer until all the water has been absorbed. So far so good – but the next stage, in which the rice is covered and cooked for another ten minutes over a very low heat, leaves me with distinctly sticky results, and a hard job washing up (her tip, which I read belatedly, about putting the pan on a wet tea towel after cooking is a useful one, however. It stops the rice sticking to the bottom of the pan).

Jamie Oliver claims his method for light and fluffy rice is foolproof – he boils it briefly, then transfers the rice to a colander and steams it over the pan of boiling water until it's cooked through. Personally, I think you'd be a fool to let yourself in for so much unnecessary washing up for something so simple.

Step forward Madhur, a woman who has some practice in making exotic foodstuffs simple for British cooks. She brings rice to the boil, then immediately turns down the heat and covers the pan. It's nerve-racking stuff – you can't take the lid off to peep before the twenty-five minutes are up, or you'll let the steam out – but as long as you get the measurements right, I guarantee it will work perfectly, leaving you plenty of time to get on with making the rest of the dinner. And if something does go wrong, console yourself with the knowledge that in rice-eating cultures around the world, from Iran to Korea, that 'burnt' crust at the bottom of the pan is eagerly fought over as a delicacy – in fact, in Puerto Rico, there are even a number of popular *merengue* songs devoted to singing its praises. Remember that as you're doing the washing up.

Serves 6

450g basmati rice
A pinch of salt

1. Toss the rice under running water for a minute and then put it into a large pan and cover with cold water. Leave for at least half an hour.
2. Drain the rice and discard the soaking water. Put it into a large pan on a medium heat with 585ml of fresh cold water and a generous pinch of salt.
3. Bring to the boil, and give it a good stir. Cover tightly and turn the heat down very low. Cook for 25 minutes, then take off the heat – don't take the lid off! – and place on a wet tea towel. Leave for 5 minutes, then fork through to fluff up.

Different kinds of rice
We tend to speak of rice as a single ingredient when in fact there are hundreds of varieties in use around the world. However, once you've discounted the parboiled parvenus peddled by a certain elderly

uncle, which are an affront to taste and decency, you'll be lucky to find more than a handful in your local shop — which is fine, as long as you know what to use them for.

Long-grain: Slim and pointy, these varieties are best for when you want fluffy rice to serve as a side dish, or separate grains for fried rice. Basmati, which hails from the foothills of the Himalayas, is the most prized kind — put your nose inside the packet to find out why. Jasmine rice, popular in Thailand, is another slightly stickier and less aromatic example.

Short-grain: Also known as pudding rice, this is used in Britain to denote a round, white rice which, when cooked, gives a sticky, starchy result, perfect for rice puddings. Obviously.

Risotto rice: Plump, starchy varieties such as Arborio, Carnaroli and Vialone Nano are essential for a really creamy risotto. You can also use them in a rice pudding, but the result will be slightly denser.

Sticky rice: Short-grained Asian rices which become sticky when cooked; often misleadingly known as glutinous rice, which simply refers to their glue-like consistency, as all rice is gluten-free. Also sold as sushi rice. Particularly popular in South-East Asia.

Brown rice: Minimally processed rice that retains more fibre, vitamins and minerals than polished white varieties, but which also takes longer to cook, and spoils faster. Any kind of rice may be sold as brown rice, but in this country it tends to denote long-grain.

Paella rice: Round-grained Spanish varieties such as Bomba and Calasparra. If you can't find them, substitute risotto rice instead.

Wild rice: The joker in the pack, wild rice is actually a grass, rather than a rice. It has a pleasant nutty flavour, and combines well with basmati.

Perfect
Risotto

Risotto recipes are always advertised as perfect for an 'easy, quick midweek supper' – a spurious claim that will only end in tears in the vast majority of cases. If you find yourself still miserably pushing around crunchy rice when you expected to be sitting down to eat, then it's easy to become disheartened and fry the bejeezus out of it instead. In fact, I've never had one on the table within half an hour, but if I can be so bold as to claim I finally understand the risotto, at least now I know why – which is much more satisfying.

First up, ingredients. Carnaroli rice is best – it's the least stodgy of the three main varieties, although if you can't find it, then either Arborio or Vialone Nano will be absolutely fine, and the last is particularly prized for seafood. The stock you use to cook it must be genuinely tasty – after all, it's going to be the predominant flavour of the dish – so this is a great midweek dish for using up the stock you've made from Sunday's roast chicken (see page 173). You also need a generous hand with the dairy at the end, because it's the *mantecare*, or beating in the butter and cheese, which gives the risotto that essential richness. As Nigella's favourite cookery writer, and the author of the wonderful 'memoir with food' *Risotto with Nettles*, Anna Del Conte, so wisely says, if you don't want butter, eat something else. The finished risotto should ripple obligingly across the plate, instead of sitting in one grim, sticky lump.

The traditional way to make risotto is to toast the rice first, and then cook it in hot stock, adding just a little at a time, until you achieve the right texture. Constant stirring is also essential, as it releases the starches in the rice that give risotto its characteristic creamy consistency. All in all, it's a pretty labour-intensive process. Although I've experimented with various quick fixes, including food writer Richard Ehrlich's hands-off approach, which involves tipping in a good glug of stock and then leaving the dish to its own devices for a bit while you grate the cheese, or make a salad, and Parisian chef Toni Vianello's oven-cooked risotto (as recommended by no less a person than Simon Hopkinson), which relies on the *mantecare* for its creaminess, I find you can't beat the traditional method. Sadly. (That said, check out Gabriele Ferron's very decent no-stir recipe online.)

Temperature is vital here: the onions should be cooked gently, so they soften without colouring, but it's crucial that the rice is hot when you add the wine, so turn up the heat to toast it unless you want to be at the stove all evening. The stock must also be hot for the same reason – whatever anyone says about finding stirring a risotto therapeutic, it gets very boring indeed after half an hour.

Once you've mastered the basic technique, you can play around with flavourings as you wish: Giorgio Locatelli's *Made in Italy* has the best collection of recipes I've found (*River Café Cook Book Two* also comes highly recommended in this department), but generally speaking, any ingredients you might think of pairing with pasta will sit happily in a risotto – delicate flavours work best though.

Serves 4

 2 litres good stock – chicken,
   vegetable or fish, depending
   on your flavourings
 1 onion, finely chopped
 100g butter
 400g Carnaroli rice
 125ml dry white wine
 Flavourings of your choice,
   e.g. 400g sautéd mushrooms; a
   bunch of steamed asparagus, chopped;
   1kg mixed cooked seafood
 100g Parmesan, finely grated
 Salt and pepper

1. Bring the stock to the boil in a large pan (if you're using ready-made stuff, bear in mind it's often very salty, so taste and water it down if necessary). Keep at a simmer.

2. Soften the onion with a knob of the butter for 15 minutes over a lowish heat in a heavy-bottomed, straight-sided pan, then add the rice. Turn up the heat, and stir to coat the grains with butter. When they are hot (about 2 minutes), add the wine, and keep stirring until this has evaporated. To make sure the pan is hot enough start by adding a drop of wine – if it doesn't sizzle, turn up the heat before you pour in the rest.

3. Start adding the stock, a ladleful at a time. Stir until each ladleful has nearly all been absorbed – the rice should always be sloppy, rather than dry – and then add another, and so on. Add any extra ingredients at some point during this time, depending on how robust they are – usually about 10 minutes in, but if you

have something which will break up or overcook easily, such as seafood, stir it through a few minutes before serving.

4. When the rice starts to soften, begin pouring in the stock in smaller amounts, and testing it regularly, for 20 minutes or until it is cooked to your liking. Then add the rest of the butter, and most of the grated cheese, and beat in with gusto until the risotto is rich and creamy. Check the seasoning, and serve immediately with the remaining cheese, or leave to stand for a couple of minutes if you prefer a thicker texture.

Perfect
Paella

*P*aella is one of those dishes which is a victim of its own popularity —
a little too tasty, and a little too easygoing for its own good, it's
bravely put up with every indignity the modern world can throw at it,
from 'quick-cook rice' to Thai green curry fusion versions.

The Spaniards themselves can't agree upon the best thing
to put in a paella, whether chicken, or rabbit or snails
— indeed, according to Valencian chef Llorenç
Millo, 'paella has as many recipes as there are
villages, and nearly as many as there are cooks'.

Actually, the garnishes are all but irrelevant — as Colman Andrews
explains, 'paella is above all a rice dish — and it is ultimately good
rice, not good seafood (or whatever) that makes a paella great'. So,
just how do you cook that rice?

First off, it needs to be a short-grained variety, which absorbs
liquid easily and doesn't dry out — and stirring is absolutely
forbidden. With a paella, unlike a risotto, the aim is to keep the
grains separate, rather than beating them into creamy submission.
Alberto Herráiz, author of the book *Paella*, and thus, one suspects,
something of an authority, claims that Japanese sushi rice, or
Italian risotto rice, will do as well as Spanish bomba (often sold
under its geographic indication, Calasparra), and indeed, Arborio
works just fine.

Whatever the variety, the rice should be cooked in stock — jazzing up a bought version with shellfish heads, as Herráiz suggests, is a nice touch, giving a greater depth of flavour with very little more work.

The aromatic sofrito — gently sautéd onions, garlic and tomato — is a cornerstone of many Spanish classics and paella is no exception. You can spend an hour simmering it, but I find José Pizarro's version, made in the pan itself before adding the rice, gives as good a result in half the time — especially with tinned tomatoes, which are more reliable than the fresh sort in this country.

The seafood is largely a matter of choice: firm white fish, like monkfish, work best, and I like the smooth chewiness of squid and the sweetness of prawns and mussels, but feel free to experiment, both here and with the vegetables. My broad beans are a nod to the fresh white lima beans that would traditionally be included in its homeland, but peas would work just as well if you prefer. Copious amounts of olive oil are, however, non-negotiable.

You also, ideally, need a wide flat paella pan to achieve the proper contrast between the crunchy caramelized crust on the bottom, and the moist, fluffy top layer — but there's no truth whatsoever in the old lore that a good paella can only be prepared by a man, in the open air, at midday — 'preferably under the shade of an old vine or fig tree'. Although, if you happen to have one knocking around . . .

Serves 2—4, depending on hunger

- 4 raw, unshelled large prawns or
  langoustines
- 90ml olive oil
- 3 cloves of garlic, finely chopped
- 500ml good-quality fish stock
- Salt and pepper
- 150g sustainable monkfish, cut into chunks
- 1 onion, finely diced
- 1 teaspoon smoked paprika
- 200g chopped tomatoes
- 50ml dry white wine
- 150g baby squid, cut into rings
- 150g broad beans
- 200g Calasparra or other short-grain rice
- A pinch of saffron, soaked in 1 tablespoon hot water
- 150g mussels, scrubbed
- A handful of flat-leaf parsley, roughly chopped, to garnish
- ½ a lemon, cut into wedges

1. Remove the shells from the prawns and, keeping the shells, put the meat aside for later. Heat 1 tablespoon of olive oil in a wide pan and sauté a third of the garlic over a medium heat for a couple of minutes. Add the prawn shells and fry, stirring to break them up, for about 3 minutes, until pink. Pour in the stock and leave to simmer gently for 30 minutes, then strain, discarding the shells, season to taste and keep warm.

2. Heat the remaining oil in a 26cm paella or other wide, thin-based pan and add the chunks of monkfish. Sauté for 5 minutes, until slightly browned, then take out of the pan and set aside.

3. Add the onion and remaining garlic to the pan and cook until softened, then stir in the paprika and cook for a further minute. Add the tomatoes and wine, turn up the heat and simmer for 10 minutes. Add the squid and beans, and fry for 30 seconds.

4. Tip the rice into the pan and stir to coat with the liquid already there, then arrange it into an even layer. Pour in 400ml of the warm stock and the saffron and its soaking water. Simmer vigorously, without stirring, for 10 minutes, then arrange the monkfish, mussels and prawns on the top of the dish, pushing them well into the rice but not otherwise disturbing it.

5. Cook for about 8 minutes – if the dish starts to looks very dry before the rice has finished cooking, add the rest of the stock, bearing in mind paella shouldn't be at all soupy.

6. Take the pan off the heat, cover with foil and allow to rest for 10 minutes. Garnish with flat-leaf parsley and wedges of lemon to serve.

Perfect
Egg-fried Rice

According to Ken Hom, no one actually eats the fried rice at a Chinese banquet — it's served late, to allow guests to appreciate their host's generosity in encouraging them to fill up on meat and fish first. Should anyone ever invite me to such a bash, I'll be sure to save space, however, because, simple as it may be, there's little I enjoy more than a bowl of egg-fried rice. Even pickled sea cucumber.

It's actually a surprisingly difficult dish to get right, however. First of all, you need cold rice. Merely room temperature rice will give a mushy result, and hot rice will, as Delia explains, leave you with a hot mess. Whatever you happen to have left over will be fine, but jasmine is ideal — its slightly glutinous nature will keep it moist in the heat of the wok, which would kill a more delicate long-grain like basmati.

Fried rice will happily absorb most other leftovers you happen to have lying around, but egg should be mandatory, gifting a delicious richness to the dish. Hom's method of adding beaten egg to the rice, then stirring it all together, gives a better result than scrambling the eggs separately and mixing them in once cooked, as Ching-He Huang, Rose Prince and Allegra McEvedy suggest. Their recipes have too many large, dry flakes of egg for my liking, while Hom's rice is moist and richly golden all the way through.

McEvedy does offer some good advice on the heat front, however — it should be stir-fried over a high flame, until the rice 'smells good and is beginning to get nice little brown crunchy bits', and, I think, in a neutral oil. Many recipes add a little sesame oil, but I find the nutty flavour completely overpowering — add it, along with soy sauce, at the table if you like.

Garlic has no place here as far as I'm concerned, but the fresh, green flavour of a few finely chopped spring onions cuts through the richness of the eggy rice nicely. Add peas or pork or prawns if you must, but this is all I need for a solitary banquet.

Serves 2, generously

3 tablespoons groundnut oil
500g cooked jasmine rice,
   at fridge temperature (about 175g raw rice)
2 eggs, beaten with ½ teaspoon salt
2 spring onions, finely chopped

1. Heat the oil in a wok or large frying pan over a high heat until it begins to smoke, then add the rice. Working quickly, spread out the rice so it heats evenly, then toss it until every grain is well coated with oil.
2. Pour in the eggs while stirring furiously, so most of the egg is absorbed into the rice. Continue to stir-fry for a couple of minutes until some grains have just begun to caramelize and turn golden.
3. Sprinkle with the chopped spring onions and serve immediately.

Sauces

As the cornerstone of classical French cuisine, the mere mention of sauces, ketchup aside, can put the fear of God into most plain British cooks. Ever practical, Len Deighton brings them down to earth with a bang: 'a sauce', he announces matter-of-factly, 'is a thickened liquid'. And if you bear that in mind, and remember that gravy's a sauce — and any self-respecting granny can knock that up while listening to *The Archers* and keeping half her brain on the crossword — they become a little less scary.

Even Julia Child, the woman who introduced American home cooks to French cuisine, and who wasn't entirely immune to its grandeur herself, admits there is nothing 'secret or mysterious' about sauces — once you know how to make a few basic 'mother sauces', such as mayonnaise, you're equipped to produce 'the whole towering edifice'. If they didn't have such intimidating names, I reckon we'd all be happily making hollandaise for eggs Benedict every Sunday morning without a second thought.

For the most part, the great sauces of the traditional kitchen –
hollandaise, béarnaise, mayonnaise – require nerve and know-how,
rather than any great skill. If you *know* that an unpromising-looking
bowl of egg yolk and oil will eventually thicken into something that
will knock anything Mr Hellmann has to offer into a cocked hat, as
long as you stick at it, then success becomes just a question of
patience – and faith. The problem with sauces as far as I'm
concerned is that once you've tasted a homemade pesto, or
guacamole, the shop-bought kind will never seem quite as good
again. Ignorance is bliss, as they say.

Perfect
Hollandaise

*T*he secret of hollandaise is, I think, confidence. You need to show this sauce who's boss from the start – no mollycoddling it with a bain-marie, Mr Slater, or fiddling about with a blender in its honour, à la Delia Smith. As long as you have a heavy-based pan, and a strong backbone, you can make it straight in the pan.

Although hollandaise is one of the classic sauces of the French kitchen, there is some debate about whether to use clarified or whole butter to thicken it, and if lemon juice or vinegar is better for flavouring. Gary Rhodes, Gordon Ramsay and Michel Roux all come down in the clarified camp, which means melting the butter and skimming off the milk solids from the top, to leave just the butterfat, before whisking it into the sauce. It's not hard to do, but it is fiddly, and I find that I prefer the flavour of the whole butter, even if the end result isn't quite so thick. (The solids also contain water, so leaving them in will give a thinner sauce.)

The great Escoffier used vinegar in his sauce, but I think that takes this a little bit close to the béarnaise below – lemon keeps things fresh, and is particularly nice with vegetables like asparagus, which is, of course, hollandaise's dream date in early summer.

Serve with grilled fish, steamed vegetables, or, best of all, as the star attraction of eggs Benedict, that heavenly breakfast dish of toasted muffins, poached eggs and ham.

Makes 300ml

4 large free-range egg yolks
1 tablespoon white wine vinegar
250g cold unsalted butter, diced
¼ of a lemon
Salt and pepper

1. Put the yolks, vinegar, butter and 2 tablespoons of water into a pan and heat very gently, whisking all the time. As the butter melts, the sauce will begin to thicken – don't be tempted to hurry things along by turning the heat up; the sides of the saucepan should be cool enough to touch at all points. Do not leave your station at the pan under any circumstances, imminent danger excepted.

2. Once the butter has melted, turn up the heat to medium-low and whisk vigorously until the sauce thickens – if it begins to steam, take it off the heat, but do not stop whisking.

3. When the sauce is thickened to your taste, stir in 1 tablespoon of lemon juice and some seasoning. Taste and adjust if necessary. Serve immediately, or store in a warm place or even a thermos flask until needed – hollandaise does not reheat very well.

Perfect
Béarnaise

*T*he difference between these two great sauces, to those unschooled in classical French cookery, is basically one of flavour — while most hollandaises are finished with the barest squeeze of lemon to cut through the butter and egg, béarnaise is much more of a big hitter in the taste stakes, with vinegar, shallots and herbs all putting in an appearance. I've given a more classic method for this sauce — you can also use this for the hollandaise, disregarding the first step, if you run into problems.

Larousse adds chervil, and John Burton Race parsley, but I think all béarnaise needs is a generous amount of tarragon — one of the more underrated herbs, and one that should be allowed to shine here. Serve with steak (see page 109), or any grilled meat or fish.

Makes 300ml

2 shallots, finely chopped
½ a bay leaf
A small bunch of tarragon,
    separated into leaves and stalks
4 tablespoons white wine vinegar
4 large free-range egg yolks
250g cold unsalted butter, diced
Salt and pepper

1. Put the shallots, bay leaf, tarragon stalks and vinegar into a small pan. Bring to the boil, then simmer until almost all the liquid has evaporated. Take off the heat, add a tablespoon of water, allow to cool slightly, then strain through a fine sieve and discard the solids.

2. Put the egg yolks into a heavy-based pan over a very low heat and whisk in the vinegar reduction. Add the butter piece by piece, adding another as soon as one melts, and whisking well all the time. The sauce will gradually start to thicken.

3. If it becomes too thick, or begins to look like scrambled eggs, take off the heat immediately and add up to 1 tablespoon of cold water, a little at a time. Stir in the finely chopped tarragon leaves and season to taste before serving.

—aise doctor

If your hollandaise or béarnaise begins to split, it probably means it's got too hot. Take the pan off the heat and stand it in a bowl of cold water (it's useful to have one of these by the hob just in case), whisking as you go. Add a tablespoon of cold water and whisk vigorously; it should come back.

Any leftovers will solidify in the fridge. Take a tip from *Toronto Star* food editor Susan Sampson and put the hollandaise or béarnaise in a small metal bowl inside a larger bowl. Half fill the outer bowl with hot, but not boiling water, and leave the sauce for 5 minutes before stirring; if you keep doing this, you should eventually be able to coax it back to life. If it curdles, however, follow the advice above.

Perfect
Mayonnaise

*S*hop-bought mayonnaise is one of those things that's so different from its homemade counterpart that, like instant coffee, or oven chips, it ought to come with a warning prefix – whether you like the pale, wobbly mass-produced stuff or not, you have to agree that even the very best (by which I obviously mean the most expensive) versions bear little resemblance to the rich, yellow sauce which slips so silkily over a side of poached salmon in the déjeuner sur l'herbe of your dreams.

The jar I have in front of me, the own-brand of a terribly respectable supermarket, lists ten ingredients, including wheat-glucose-fructose syrup and colouring. Classical mayonnaise requires just three: egg yolks, oil and vinegar, and as Michel Roux points out in the first episode of the excellent late 80s television series *The Roux Brothers* (available online), it's very easy to make at home – although it might take you longer to separate the eggs than it takes them to whip up a batch and some new potatoes to go with it.

Mayonnaise is a simple emulsion of oil in water, egg yolks being half water. As any cookbook will tell you, it's important to dribble in the oil very gradually, or you will overwhelm the yolk, and end up with an egg yolk in oil mixture, rather than the other way around – and this will curdle. The Roux brothers add theirs with cavalier speed, and in theory, according to Harold McGee, the oil can be added in doses of up to a third of the volume of the yolk at a time, but after a few disasters, I decide to stick to Delia's drop-by-drop method. If you have a stick blender, however, put all the ingredients into a container just larger than the head of the blender, adding the oil last, then plunge the blender to the bottom, turn on and hold it there for about a minute, until you begin to see the emulsified mayonnaise emerging from the side. Very slowly raise the blender to the top of the mixture and you should have mayonnaise in under 5 minutes (I'd recommend watching a video of the process online before you start).

Add salt at the beginning, to help thicken the yolk, but leave the vinegar to the end – I've tried out Julia Child's recipe from *Mastering the Art of French Cooking*, which begins with the acid, but this seems to give a thinner result. I have picked up one useful tip from the 'American Elizabeth David', however: beating the yolks 'until thick and sticky' before adding the oil. This makes them, according to Child, 'ready to receive the oil' – which makes sense if, as McGee suggests, the more solid the yolks, the easier they are to mix with the oil.

Now we've established the method, it's time to turn to ingredients. There's a tendency these days to assume that olive oil, with its healthy reputation and biblical heritage, is always the best choice, and it has its devotees in Elizabeth David and Theo Randall, but I notice that Michel Roux suggests using groundnut oil instead, although, he says, you can add a little extra virgin olive oil at the end if you like, just for flavour. I have tried an all-olive mayonnaise with an oil which declared itself to be light, but found the flavour harsh and overpowering. Add a dash or two of your favourite extra virgin at the end instead if you want that peculiarly green flavour.

Michel Roux also suggests two different acids: warm wine vinegar, or cold lemon juice. McGee debunks the idea that the temperature of any liquid you add at the end will make a difference to its texture, but it will, he says, help thin the mixture, as well as, in the case of the acids, helping to stabilize it. Whether you, like Michel, like lemon juice, or side with Albert and his vinegar, is up to you, just as the kind of mustard you put in (I use Dijon), and whether you want to add garlic, is a matter for personal preference: I think lemon goes better with olive oil and with fish, whereas the vinegar matches well with salads.

Really, however, once you've achieved the sacred mayonnaise, you can add whatever you like: grapefruit, truffles — even soy sauce, although please not when I'm coming to dinner. Or, of course, you can just sit there and stare in wonderment at the amazing thing you've created.

Makes 300ml

> 1 large free-range egg yolk
> A generous pinch of salt
> 250ml groundnut or sunflower oil
> 25ml extra virgin olive, walnut or rapeseed oil
> 1 teaspoon white wine vinegar or lemon juice
> 1 teaspoon mustard of your choice (or 1 teaspoon mustard powder)

1. Make sure all the ingredients are at room temperature before starting. Place a damp tea towel beneath a large mixing bowl, and add the egg yolks. Beat well with an electric whisk for a minute

or so — you can do it by hand with a balloon whisk, but bear in mind it will take a lot longer.

2. Add the salt and continue to beat well for 30 seconds, until the yolk is thick and sticky. Begin to add the neutral oil, a tablespoon at a time, beating all the while, and making sure each is incorporated before adding the next — don't be tempted to rush this, or your mayonnaise will split. You can begin to add the oil in slightly larger amounts once you've mixed in about half. If the mayonnaise becomes too thick, and hard to beat, add 1 tablespoon of warm water to the mixture and whisk it in before adding any more oil.

3. Once you've incorporated all the neutral oil, switch to the olive oil and add it in the same way. Once it is all incorporated, beat the mayonnaise for another 30 seconds until thick and glossy, then add the vinegar or lemon juice, and the mustard, and mix in.

4. Stir in any further ingredients, such as chopped herbs or anchovy essence, then cover and keep refrigerated until you are ready to eat.

Marvellous mayonnaise
Crushed garlic may be the most obvious tweak that springs to mind here (aïoli is delicious with fish, cold chicken and crudités), but mayonnaise is a master of reinvention.

Anchovy mayonnaise: Puréed anchovies (serve with vegetable fritters — it goes particularly well with cauliflower ones — fried mushrooms or calamari)

Dijonnaise: Dijon mustard (cold meats, particularly pork)

Rémoulade: Dijon mustard, garlic and pepper (folded through shredded raw celeriac or carrot to make the classic French salad)

Tartare: Chopped gherkins, capers, tarragon and parsley (usually served with fried foods, particularly fish; it would be ideal with the fishcakes on page 180)

Watercress: Finely chopped watercress (cold fish, especially poached salmon)

Perfect
Gravy

*T*here's no French translation for gravy. Their nearest equivalents don't really cut the mustard – you can hardly imagine an effete *jus* powering any sort of train, or everything coming up all *sauce brune*. In Britain, gravy is more than just a condiment; it's liquid comfort. Think of the warm, meaty embrace of every-mother Lynda Bellingham in the Oxo adverts of yesteryear, or that self-satisfied 'ahh, Bisto' slogan which perfectly encapsulated a nation's feelings about a piping jug of gravy – even if we've since realized that making your own is just as easy.

It brings together a Sunday roast like a cup of tea brings together a group of strangers – bestowing a soothing, savoury homeliness on  everything it touches. And, like many traditional favourites, every cook has their own method. As Hugh Fearnley-Whittingstall wisely points out in his *River Cottage Meat Book*, 'there is no recipe for gravy, nor should there be'. There are, however, various ways to make sure you do your patriotic duty by the scrapings in the pan.

First of all, I firmly believe that gravy should be thick – perhaps not quite thick enough to stand a spoon up in, but certainly more robust than a *jus*. For this, you need a roux, and the easiest way to do this is to tip the juices out, make it in the pan with all the lovely crusty bits, then whisk the juices back in. Far quicker than doing it the other way round, and you're much less likely to end up with lumpy gravy.

Michel Roux Jr may know a thing or two about French food, but I am less than convinced by his suggestion about mashing tin-roasted vegetables into the gravy – mushy carrots don't taste any better in liquid form, so if you're going to use what Jamie Oliver describes as a 'vegetable trivet', discard it before you begin making the gravy. I'm equally sceptical about the Royal Society of Chemists' conclusions regarding cabbage cooking water during their investigation into the chemistry of the perfect gravy. I like a nice Savoy as much as the next person, but it's not a flavour I want to find in a sauce.

More surprisingly, wine isn't an altogether welcome presence either, which is a revelation – most of us add it out of habit, but once you've tried it without, it can't be denied that this makes it taste more like a red wine sauce than an honest British condiment. Perhaps John Torode is right: wine's for drinking with a roast, not for tipping into it. The scientists also suggest adding dark soy sauce to bring out the umami flavours of the meat. Now, I'm happy to add Bovril or Marmite to meat dishes when required, but tipping in such a distinctively Oriental ingredient goes against the grain – particularly when you can taste it in the finished gravy. If your gravy isn't quite up to scratch, I'd recommend using Marmite, or a little stock instead. Alternatively, if you use homemade stock instead of water, you're unlikely to have the problem in the first place. But that's why they're chemists, and not cooks.

Hugh Fearnley-Whittingstall provides a long list of sweeteners, seasonings and aromatizers for gravy, but one he doesn't mention is English mustard, which is my favoured choice for beef. Mix a teaspoon in at the end and you've got all your sauces in one boat – and the same goes for horseradish. This recipe can be used for other meats, so adjust the condiment as desired: redcurrant jelly for lamb, apple juice for pork, etc.

For perfect gravy, you need good-quality meat, good-quality stock – and that's it. It really is as easy as (meat) pie.

1 tablespoon plain flour
600ml hot good-quality stock,
preferably homemade (see page 169)
Salt and pepper
Flavourings of your choice (see above)

1. Make the gravy in a flameproof roasting tin while the joint is resting elsewhere. Pour off most of the fat (you can put it through a gravy separating jug if you like), leaving about a tablespoon, as well as the meat juices, and put the tin over a medium heat. Sprinkle over the flour and stir into the fat, scraping to loosen any bits on the bottom of the tin. Cook, stirring, for a couple of minutes, until the flour is slightly browned, being careful not to burn it.
2. Add a ladle of stock to the tin and stir to incorporate. Add the rest of the stock and bring to the boil, stirring. Simmer, stirring regularly, until the gravy has reached your preferred thickness, then season to taste. If you want to add any other flavourings, do so now, then heat through to serve.

Perfect
Vinaigrette

*O*n a recent trip to Paris, I was reminded of why, for all their
fondness for le Big Mac and enormous hypermarkets, the French
can still teach us a thing or two about good food. My epiphany came
in the form of a side salad, a simple dish of lamb's lettuce – no
micro herbs, or heirloom radishes – dressed with the most perfect
of vinaigrettes. It clung lightly to every tiny leaf, a delicate essay in
culinary restraint – the kick of the vinegar, the heat of the mustard,
the seasoning – all finely balanced so as to complement, but not
overpower, the dish.

In his *Bouchon* cookbook, the Californian chef
Thomas Keller prefaces a recipe for
vinaigrette with the arresting thought that it
might even be 'the perfect sauce'. Hang on a
minute, you might think – it's up against some
pretty stiff competition. But whereas a
béchamel, or a velouté, repel creative
customization, the good-natured vinaigrette
positively encourages it. Plus, it can be put together
in under five minutes, which is not something you can say for
anything involving a roux.

As the vinaigrette, or *sauce ravigote*, also goes by the name 'French
dressing' (although, like the unappetizing-sounding 'French stick',
this seems to have fallen from favour in recent years), it makes sense

to consult the original Gallic cookery Bible, *Larousse Gastronomique*, for a definitive recipe.

'Dissolve a little salt in 1 tablespoon vinegar,' it counsels. 'Add 3 tablespoons oil and some pepper.' That's it – unless you want to get creative with mustard and the like. But it's this basic recipe which interests me. A 3:1 ratio of oil and vinegar seems a good one – 2:1, which I have seen elsewhere as 'sacred for the best and thickest vinaigrette', is too thin and acidic, and any more oil is difficult to incorporate properly.

I like the vegetable oil suggested by *Larousse*; I used to use extra virgin olive oil, but their vinaigrette has a much lighter, silkier feel, and tastes fresher without the slightly overpowering flavour of extra virgin. It also seems to mix more easily, and takes longer to separate. But it seems a shame to use such a bland oil in one of the few recipes in which the stuff really shines, so I suggest a compromise: a 2:1 vegetable/extra virgin olive oil mix, which combines a light texture with just a hint of peppery greenness.

Vinaigrette is what is known in the trade as an unstable emulsion – two liquids (water, in the form of vinegar, and oil) that, in the words of the great Harold McGee, 'can't mix evenly with each other', and which will eventually separate back into their original forms. You can slow this process down by adding an emulsifier, which will act as a bond between the two ingredients. Many commercial dressings use a fatty substance called lecithin, but at home it's much easier, and tastier, to add a flavouring that will do the same job.

Although wisdom has it that you can use everything from egg yolk (which, in my opinion, starts to stray dangerously into mayonnaise territory) to cold mashed potato to stabilize your dressing, the most popular choices are things which actively complement the existing ingredients — miso paste for a Japanese-style vinaigrette with rice vinegar, for example, or tahini if you're feeling a bit Middle Eastern. For a more classic flavour, I generally use mustard — because it's already emulsified, ready-made mustard gives a thicker, more mustardy finish than powder.

Whisked into a vinaigrette at the end, mustard adds heat, but has very little effect on how long the dressing holds together. Stir it into the vinegar along with the salt before you add the oil, however, and your sauce should be good for quarter of an hour or so. Honey rounds out the flavour nicely.

Although a whisk makes a perfectly decent dressing, if I'm making large amounts I take a tip from Thomas Keller and use a blender to start my vinaigrette off — if you do it all in there, it will become unpalatably gloopy. The blender smashes the oil and water molecules up so finely that it takes them ages to reassemble and subsequently separate, and it lasts days in the fridge. Normally, however, you can't beat a simple jar — very little washing up, and after all, a dressing only needs to stay together for as long as it takes you to eat the salad.

So, as long as you stick to the ratio of oil and vinegar that suits your taste (different vinegars, in particular, vary in strength, so be careful with anything new), and keep a balance of flavours in mind, the world's best sauce is now your playground. You can even make it with bacon fat if you've got some going spare.

A pinch of salt
A generous ½ teaspoon Dijon mustard
A generous ½ teaspoon honey
1 tablespoon red wine vinegar
2 tablespoons vegetable oil
1 tablespoon extra virgin olive oil

1. Put the salt, mustard and honey into a jar, and mix together into a paste. Add the vinegar, and stir well to combine.
2. Pour in the oils, screw the lid on tightly, and shake until you have an emulsion. Store in the fridge.

How to dress a salad

First, make sure your leaves are completely dry, or they'll repel the dressing. Second, I find it helpful to pour some of the vinaigrette into the base of the serving bowl before adding the salad, and then toss it through the leaves — it seems to give more even coverage. And third, don't dress a green salad until you're ready to eat it — the oil in the dressing will make your leaves look all sad and wilted.

Perfect
Salsa

Salsa is a dish that relies so heavily on freshness that it's impossible to capture it in a jar – especially this simple tomato and chilli version, which is versatile enough to pair with grilled meat, rice and beans, scrambled eggs or a big bowl of salty tortilla chips. Make it once, and you'll never pay a visit to Old El Paso again.

It stands or falls on its tomatoes, which according to Chicago chef and Obama favourite Rick Bayless, who's devoted his career to spreading the word about authentic Mexican food north of the border, are 'a critical ingredient in Mexican cuisine, second only to chillies'. I try a number of different approaches, simmering them with onion and garlic until 'well thickened' like Elisabeth Lambert Ortiz in her *Complete Book of Mexican Cooking*, which yields a rich flavour, but not the punchy fruitiness I'm after, roasting them like Thomasina Miers, which gives a lovely smokiness, but doesn't feel fresh enough, and using them raw, like Bayless. This, the simplest method, is also, happily, the most delicious: along with the lime juice, they give just the acid hit I'm looking for. (Vinegar is often suggested as a substitute, but, though wine vinegar is fine at a pinch, you really can't beat the citrussy zing of lime.)

Bayless suggests using either plum or round tomatoes; unless it's high summer, I find it difficult to source either with a sufficiently intense flavour, so instead I decide to use the sweet little cherries which seem to taste better all year round.

Making a fresh tomato salsa rules out most of the almost infinite array of dried chillies deployed in Mexican cuisine, essentially reducing me to a choice between jalapeños, which Lambert Ortiz describes as 'very flavourful as well as hot', and serranos which, according to Bayless, have a 'pure and simple' heat. (See glossary below for a bit more info about different types of chillies you might come across in this country.)

I prefer the herbaceous quality of the jalapeño, but those available in this country tend to be unpredictable in terms of heat, so don't worry too much – if all the examples you can find are bland and watery, swap in a Scotch bonnet or a bird's-eye instead. (Don't be tempted to substitute pickled jalapeños, however – they'll muddy the flavour here. Save them for your nachos.)

Onions add a different sort of heat – a white onion, which, as Bayless notes, is a quite different beast from the yellow ones we get over here, would be most authentic, but given the difficulties in sourcing them, I'm forced to try other options. The fresh green tang of spring onions works wonderfully, though, as this makes ideal party food, I'm going to marinate them briefly in lime juice to soften their bite.

You can use a pestle and mortar, as Miers does – though even Bayless concedes that careful pulsing in a food processor can produce a 'decent salsa' – but actually, if your tomatoes are sufficiently ripe, simple chopping produces the most satisfying texture for scooping.

Note that the quantities below are all to my taste, and will vary according to yours, and the ingredients you have to hand, so do play around until you're happy – at which point you can call it your perfect salsa.

Makes 500ml

3 spring onions
Juice of 1 lime
500g ripe cherry tomatoes
1–2 jalapeño or other green chillies,
    depending on taste
A small bunch of coriander
¼ teaspoon salt

1. Finely chop the spring onions right up to the part where the green separates its leaves and put them into a serving bowl. Stir in the juice of half the lime. Chop the tomatoes into rough 5mm dice, and deseed and finely chop the chilli.
2. Add these to the bowl along with the roughly chopped coriander – you might want to add the chilli gradually and keep on tasting as you do so, until you achieve your ideal level of heat, especially as they vary so much according to provenance and season.
3. Season the salsa to taste with salt, leave to sit for half an hour, then serve, with a spritz more lime juice if you think it needs it – it should be fresh and punchy, so don't be tempted to make it too far ahead.

Chillies: a field guide
The range of chillies available in supermarkets has improved greatly in the last few years, although some

areas are still better than others. For obscure varieties you'll still need to visit specialist suppliers, or look online (southdevonchillifarm.co.uk is a good source), but you might well find this lot more easily:

Bird's-eye: these pointy, diminutive red and green chillies, popular in South-East Asian cookery, are viciously hot.

Jalapeño: sold either green (unripe, with a herbaceous flavour) or red (ripe and sweeter), these bulbous carrot-shaped chillies vary wildly in heat, but most of the ones in British supermarkets tend towards the milder end of the spectrum. You'll also find them pickled for topping nachos and the like, and once dried and smoked, they're known as chipotle, a spice widely used in Mexican cookery.

Habanero: pumpkin-shaped orange or red chillies with a fiery, fruity flavour, these, like Caribbean Scotch bonnets, should be treated with caution and, preferably, rubber gloves.

Serrano: similar in appearance to the jalapeño, serranos have a hotter, sharper flavour, and are usually used in an underripe, green state.

Perfect
Guacamole

Guacamole and I did not get off to a good start. We first met in the context of a home-assembly fajita kit — marinated chicken in a little cellophane pouch, sachets of soured cream and salsa, a few doughy tortillas and something distinctly unappetizing-looking in a small plastic pot. In those innocent pre-pesto and wasabi days, green food was a bit of a novelty outside the salad aisle, and the colour unnerved me until I realized the contents were, in reality, little more than double cream with a soupçon of avocado paying lip service to the original recipe. How sophisticated I felt, rolling my own dinner.

Now, this was 1994. Leggings and Take That were hot stuff. What puzzles me is why, nearly twenty-five years later, when both these things have fallen from grace at least twice, the same awful guacamole is still in fashion. It's not as if Mexican food is a novelty; why, these days you can even find restaurants that manage to make money without the help of a hat-stand of amusing headgear and fifteen types of tequila slammer. But somehow the pea green sludge, heavy with dairy and low on flavour, still lurks alongside the hummus and the taramasalata in the chilled aisle.

As I discovered some years later, guacamole should be zingy with lime, to cut through the creamy richness of the ripe avocado. Rick Bayless, one of the finest Mexican chefs north of the Rio Grande, and an award-winning writer on the subject, describes it in his *Mexican Kitchen* cookbook as 'a verdant, thick-textured bowl of festivity, ripe with the elusive flavour of avocado. Mash in a little lime, raw onion, coriander, chilli, perhaps tomato, and the avocado comes fully alive.' I have tried a version with soured cream, but find it bland and heavy.

According to *Bon Appetit* magazine, down Mexico way, 'some cooks coarsely mash avocados, season them with salt — maybe a little garlic — and call the result "guacamole"'. Their point, I think, is that there is no definitive recipe, which means you don't have to worry too much about 'authenticity' — although, after experimentation, I can confirm there is no room for *Bon Appetit*'s aggressive garlic or Bayless' acrid onion in my guacamole; spring onion is about as far as I'm prepared to go down that road.

I'm surprised to discover that Thomasina Miers, founder of Mexican chain Wahaca, doesn't include tomato in the perfect guacamole recipe she supplied to *The Times*, although I notice they do feature in the stuff served in her restaurants. Thank goodness for that, because for me they're a must: the sauce seems sadly one-dimensional without their acidic fruitiness. Bayless made a version of his house guacamole with sun-dried fruits for an Obama victory party (Michelle was apparently a big fan of his Chicago restaurant, Topolobampo, before she took off for DC); I prefer to use fresh ones if possible, but it's a good substitute to bear in mind for winter months, when our tomatoes will be watery and thin on flavour. Fresh chillies are also a must for a really sharp guacamole, although smoky chipotles are an interesting variation, particularly if you're serving it with meat, and in an avocado-based emergency, I have used chilli flakes with no ill effect. Aromatic coriander and zingy lime are also non-negotiable: they bring out the flavour of all the other ingredients. If you don't like coriander, I will grudgingly accept flat-leaf parsley as a substitute, but it won't be quite as aromatic.

Guacamole should be made by hand, rather than in a machine – you're not aiming for a purée, but a chunky, creamy salsa. A pestle and mortar is good, but if you don't have one of those big Mexican sort hewn from volcanic rock, a large bowl and a fork or potato masher will do just as well. And, lastly, forget anything you've read about avocado stones keeping it greener for longer – lime juice helps, but the only way to stop avocados turning brown is to keep them away from air, which means pressing clingfilm into the surface until you're ready to serve.

Guacamole is one of those dishes which is happy to be played around with according to taste. The only golden rule is – use ripe avocados!

Makes 500g

> 1–3 fresh green chillies, depending
>   on heat and your taste (1 will give
>   a very mild result, 3 an extremely
>   spicy one), finely chopped
> 2 spring onions, thinly sliced
> A handful of fresh coriander, roughly chopped
> Sea salt
> 3 ripe avocados (Hass, the knobbly
>   brown ones, tend to be the creamiest
>   and most flavoursome)
> 1 ripe medium tomato, cut into 3cm dice
> Juice of 1 lime

1. Put a teaspoon each of the chilli, onion and coriander into a pestle and mortar, along with a pinch of sea salt, and grind to a paste.
2. Cut the avocados in half and remove the stones with a teaspoon.

Scoop out the insides, cut into rough cubes, then put into a serving bowl and mash to a chunky paste, leaving some pieces intact.

3. Stir the chilli paste into the avocado, then gently fold in the tomatoes and the rest of the onions, chilli and coriander. Add lime juice and salt to taste. Serve immediately, or cover the surface with clingfilm and refrigerate.

Rolling citrus fruit firmly along the kitchen counter before cutting them open and squeezing them helps to release the juice and makes the job much quicker – if you don't have a citrus reaming tool to help with juicing, use a fork to squeeze the juice out. If a recipe calls for zest as well, always do this before cutting them in half, as it's far easier to zest whole fruit.

The searing truth
Recipes will often urge you to deseed a chilli for a milder result – this isn't, as many people suppose, because the seeds themselves are particularly hot, but because the innocuous white membrane that attaches them to the fruit contains a capsaicin hit hefty enough to blow your head off. Try the pith of a Scotch bonnet and weep – literally. Good ways to soothe the pain include milk, yoghurt, plain rice and bread. Contrary to popular belief, however, mockery does not help one little bit.

Perfect
Tomato Sauce

*T*omato sauce is one of the cornerstones of the modern kitchen –
handy for a thousand things, from quick pasta dishes to curry bases
– so it makes sense to find a recipe you like, and make up a big batch
to freeze. After all, you can cook all the Heston recipes you like, but
if someone opens your fridge to find a jar of overpriced ready-made
stuff you're rumbled.

In Italy, spiritual if not ancestral home of the
tomato, such sauces are made with both fresh
and tinned tomatoes, depending on the season.
They're wise enough to realize there's little
point in trying to force flavour out of the thin
fruits of the winter months – and, unless you have
a glut of overripe ones on your hands, I'd be inclined
to stick with the tinned sort all year round in this country,
and enjoy any truly excellent tomatoes you might come across in
a salad instead.

Giorgio Locatelli uses a mixture of fresh and tinned tomatoes in the
sauce at his London restaurant, which he says is best in summer
– but, probably because his suppliers are better than mine, I find his
recipe rather acidic. The River Café's rich tomato sauce calls for
Italian peeled plum tomatoes packed in their own juice, slow cooked
with onions and garlic, which gives a much fuller flavour – but it's
Angela Hartnett's tip about adding a little sugar that makes all the

difference. A dash of tomato purée makes the sauce even richer, and flavourful enough to need nothing but a drizzle of olive oil, or a sprinkling of basil leaves, to make a winning pasta dish.

If you prefer your sauce even sweeter, however, consider using a red onion instead, as the River Café does — you shouldn't see the bits, because it will melt into the sauce as it cooks, but it will give a jammier result. I think leaving the herbs until serving makes the finished sauce more versatile, and slightly fresher tasting, but you can add thyme, oregano or even chilli along with the onion if you prefer.

Serves 4

5 tablespoons olive oil
I small onion, very finely sliced
I clove of garlic, very finely sliced
A pinch of salt
A pinch of sugar
I teaspoon tomato purée
2 x 400g tins of Italian plum tomatoes in juice

1. Put the olive oil into a deep heavy-based frying pan over a lowish heat. Add the onion and cook very gently until completely softened, but not browned — this should take at least 10 minutes. Add the garlic and cook for another 5 minutes.
2. Stir in a generous pinch of salt and sugar and the tomato purée, then tip in the plum tomatoes and roughly break up with a wooden spoon. Cook, stirring occasionally, for about 35 minutes, until thick and jammy. Taste, and add a little more sugar or salt if necessary.

How to skin and deseed a tomato
Cut a small cross in the base, then plunge the
tomato into boiling water for 20 seconds. Remove
into a bowl of ice-cold water to cool down — the skin
should then just peel off.

Cut the tomato into quarters, and scoop out the
seeds with a teaspoon — most of the flavour is in the
seeds and the jelly that surrounds them, however, so
do this over a bowl to catch the juices and add these
to whatever you're making along with the flesh.

Never keep tomatoes in the fridge
They don't like the cold, and will become tasteless
and woolly. Keep them at room temperature
instead.

Perfect
Pesto

*F*rom sophisticated Italian saucepot to 'middle-class ketchup' in a single generation, pesto has suffered more than most foodstuffs at the hands of the British mania for gastronomic appropriation. In the greedy heat of passion, we've spawned pesto crisps, pesto hummus (shudder) and even pesto oatcakes, but oddly enough, we eat very little of what might be described as 'proper pesto'. The long-life stuff is undoubtedly a useful thing to have in the cupboard for emergencies, but don't kid yourself that it's the authentic taste of the Cinque Terre.

To clarify, we're talking classic pesto, of the kind that was being made in north-west Italy and south-east France long before the Romans and their fermented fish sauce – not 'Japanese pesto', or sun-dried tomato pesto, or anything involving rocket. The backbone of this is, of course, basil: Giorgio Locatelli recommends the smaller, sweeter leaves for the fullest flavour and smoothest texture, but then he also has these leaves flown over specially from Prà, the epicentre of Ligurian pesto production, so he's what might be described as a details man. As long as the herb is fresh, and vibrant in colour, you'll probably be OK.

I'd laboured for years under the misapprehension that cheese, garlic and pine nuts were also non-negotiable, but the nice man at

Borough Market set me straight when I went to buy my cheese there. 'Every pesto is personal,' he told me. 'As long as it has basil, cheese and olive oil, it is pesto.' So, after experimentation, I discover that my particular pesto lacks garlic, like the one in *The Silver Spoon* (raw garlic is a bully – without it, the basil and pine nuts shine all the brighter), and also takes its cue from that book for its cheese, using a mix of fresh, delicate pecorino, and salty, savoury Parmesan. Locatelli just uses pecorino, but I find its more delicate flavour gets lost. Pine nuts are vital for thickening the sauce, and toasting them, as the great chef suggests, really helps to bring out their sweetly nutty flavour.

Even Locatelli admits that if you have to make large quantities of pesto, it's easier to use a food processor, as Marcus Wareing does, but I find that smashing up the basil seems to affect the flavour; a theory confirmed by Harold McGee, who has concluded after experimentation that the larger the pieces of leaf, the slower they are to discolour. Making it in a pestle and mortar may seem time-consuming, but the flavour speaks for itself – just try and imagine you're on a sun-dappled terrace on the Ligurian coast, rather than in your kitchen, and the minutes will fly by. (That said, a food processor will still give decent, if not perfect, results.)

Pesto, as we've discovered, is a very amenable condiment, but the traditional way to serve it in Italy is with linguine, green beans and potatoes. Add a little of the pasta cooking water to the pesto to thin it before tossing them together, so it coats the strands better.

Makes 200g

2 tablespoons pine nuts
A pinch of salt
125g fresh basil leaves (pick off as
    much of the stalk as you can, as this
    discolours faster than the leaves)
15g Parmesan, grated
15g pecorino, grated
125ml extra virgin olive oil

1. Toast the pine nuts in a dry pan on a moderate heat, stirring
    regularly and being careful not to let them burn, and then allow
    to cool completely. Lightly crush in a pestle and mortar, along
    with a pinch of salt.
2. Add the basil leaves a few at a time, and, working as quickly as
    possible, pound them into the mixture until you have a thickish
    paste.
3. Work in the cheese, then gradually incorporate the oil, reserving
    a little for the top.
4. Spoon the pesto into a jar, and cover the top with oil.
    Refrigerate until use.

Baking

*P*erhaps my favourite chapter in any cookbook – because, unless
you're looking at this with wild eyes at 11 p.m. the night before a
school cake sale or surprise birthday party, this is the kind of cooking
that's pure pleasure. Let's be honest, no one needs a piece of
chocolate cake, or a gingerbread man; the truly hungry would be
better off turning to page 78 for a wholesome chicken soup, or
cooking up the nice dal on page 228.

No, baking is all about indulgence – and thank God for that. We're
bombarded with 'wicked' brownies and 'naughty' cream horns, and
frankly I'm bored with it all: the recipes in this chapter aren't designed
to be guiltily gorged on, but shared with friends and loved ones in
joyous greed. And, OK, if there happens to be a slice left over
afterwards . . . well, wasting food, there's a real sin if ever there was one.

It's a special sort of alchemy, to turn flour and sugar and butter and
eggs and their ilk into something so happy – and whether you end

up with a fancy tarte au citron or a homely ginger cake, when it comes out of the oven you're never sorry you bothered.

Although baking does demand a certain pedantry (leaving out half the eggs in a cake recipe because your boyfriend ate them for breakfast is likely to end in disaster), it also has one of the best effort to results ratio of any branch of cookery. There's very little in the way of finicky chopping or patient reducing, and, as long as you've followed the recipe, the results are guaranteed to please.

Equipment-wise, a good pair of scales is invaluable, and, if you bake a lot, an electric mixer of some kind – a stand one that sits on the counter is great, but if, like me, you have limited space, and an even more limited budget, it's helpful to know I get a lot more use out of my hand-held version. For about £25, you can take all the elbow grease out of the process and still have your cake and eat it.

A silicone spatula is useful for getting every last bit of mixture out of the bowl (though you can still save the last bit for licking), and a few variously sized mixing bowls, preferably stainless steel or ceramic, will also come in handy: pound shops are a good source of them, though, as with everything else in there, they generally cost more than the name suggests.

Measuring spoons, though not essential, are an inexpensive way of ensuring your teaspoon of baking powder really is 5ml, and I've recently discovered reusable baking mats, which make lining tins and trays much less of a faff.

Lastly, with all these recipes, check you've got roughly the right-sized tin before switching the oven on: there's little more frustrating than making the mixture, and then realizing you've got nowhere to put it, and your proud 7 inch cake will actually be more of a 9 inch pancake. I speak from experience.

Perfect
Brown Bread

*B*aking your own bread is apparently a dangerous pastime. 'Beware of making that first loaf,' cautions the late, great cookery writer Margaret Costa. 'Unless you are quite exceptionally lucky in your baker, and/or have a very easy-going family, you will find it difficult to go back to shop bread again.'

Perhaps bread has improved since those lines were written in the 1970s, but I'm a proud regular at my local loaf pushers — proper bakers deserve our support, after all. You can't beat the thrill of producing your own on occasion, though, and this nutty brown loaf is simple enough to be a weekend staple.

After testing several methods, including the unconventional approach of award-winning baker Richard Bertinet, Brittany-born author of the fabulous *Dough* (and a 'bread guru' according to the *Sunday Times*), and a more traditional technique from *Leiths Baking Bible*, as well as an overnight rise, as suggested by Delia, and Margaret Costa's no-knead loaf, I've settled upon Dan Lepard's intermittent knead technique as giving the lightest texture. (Lepard dismisses the idea that kneading develops gluten — it's all down to time apparently, which is good news, as you don't have to spend hours pummelling away.) His secret weapon? Some vitamin C, which apparently counteracts the chemical that makes so much brown bread unpalatably heavy.

A little melted butter boosts the flavour, while a proportion of white flour, as suggested by the Ballymaloe Cookery School, gives the bread a more open texture without spoiling the illusion of health. The result? A light, deliciously savoury loaf that requires very little actual work – ideal for a lazy Sunday morning.

400g strong wholemeal bread flour
50g strong white flour
2 teaspoons easy-bake yeast
  (a 7g sachet)
½ a 500mg vitamin C tablet,
  crushed to a powder
2 teaspoons salt
3 teaspoons brown sugar
400ml warm water
50g melted butter, plus a little for greasing

1. Tip the flours, yeast, vitamin powder, salt and sugar into a bowl and mix well. Add 300ml of water and stir in, then pour in the butter and work in well. You should have a soft, sticky dough: if not, add a little more water. Cover and leave for 10 minutes.

2. Tip out on to a lightly oiled work surface and knead for 10 seconds, then put back into the bowl and cover. Repeat twice more at intervals of 10 minutes, then leave the dough to rest for 15 minutes.

3. Flatten the dough into a rough rectangle about the length of your baking tin, then roll up tightly and put into a greased 1kg loaf tin, with the join facing downwards. Cover and leave to rest in a warm place until it has doubled in height (at least 1½ hours).

4. Preheat the oven to 220°C/fan 200°C/gas 7. Bake the bread for 20 minutes, then turn the temperature down to 200°C/ fan 180°C/gas 6 and cook for a further 15–20 minutes, until the crust is a deep brown, and the loaf sounds hollow when tapped. Turn out on to a cooling rack: don't be tempted to cut into it straight away. It may smell good, but hot bread is very difficult to digest!

How to knead
Lightly oil the work surface – this makes it much easier to clean than flour, and also prevents the dough from absorbing too much more flour and drying out. Place the ball of dough in front of you and push it away from you with the heel of your hand, shifting your weight from one side to the other as you do so. Flip the dough over with your fingertips as you bring it back towards you. Give it a quarter turn and repeat. A dough scraper is a useful tool if you make bread regularly – you can use it to pick up and portion dough, and it makes cleaning the work surface an awful lot easier.

How to store bread
Bread is best kept wrapped in paper at room temperature: plastic traps moisture and makes the crust soft, while refrigeration will dry it out.

Perfect
Soda Bread

*T*he great Elizabeth David once wrote that 'everyone who cooks, in however limited a way, should know how to make a loaf of soda bread' – and, as with so much else, she's right. Even if you live next door to the world's best bakery, or frankly you rather like your supermarket sliced white, there's no denying the satisfaction of a loaf that can be in the oven in less time than it takes to brew a pot of tea, and is ready to eat by the time you get out of the shower.

The first time I saw soda bread made – at Pierce and Valerie McAuliffe's cookery school in the grounds of Dunbrody Abbey, County Wexford – I was astonished that baking could be so easy. No need for proving or kneading – the simplicity of these chemically raised breads made them popular throughout the British Isles in the late nineteenth century, but they were particularly eagerly adopted in rural Ireland, where the available equipment tended to run to a pot oven and a peat fire.

Ireland remains the heartland of soda bread today. Filling and wholesome, it pops up at almost every meal, and is so universal that the more common wholemeal version is generally known simply as brown or wheaten bread. It goes with everything from salty butter to soup, and creates very little in the way of washing-up. Seriously, can you afford not to have a recipe for soda bread in your life?

Though brown soda bread is my favourite, it can also be made with white flour, or a mixture of the two (don't bother paying extra for bread flour: the cakey texture is the whole point). But for me, the darker and chewier the bread the better: ideally use the coarsest ground wholemeal you can find, with a few oats thrown in for good measure.

You'll also need buttermilk, not these days generally a by-product of butter-making, but artificially soured milk, though you can also use milk and lemon juice or vinegar if that's what you have to hand. Either way, the acid will react with the bicarbonate of soda that takes the place of yeast in these breads, to make the dough rise in the oven: some people like the bitter tang of the latter, and add more for flavour, but a teaspoon is quite sufficient for raising purposes.

Salt and sugar aren't so essential, but they will of course make a better-tasting loaf: I like a combination of treacle and honey because I always have both on hand, but one or the other will do just fine — as will brown sugar, or indeed, almost anything sweet.

Happily, there's no need to knead here, and you don't even have to bother greasing a loaf tin, though you can make it in one if you prefer: I like the rustic appearance of a free-form loaf, slashed to bake more quickly/let the fairies out as you prefer, and brushed with melted butter to soften the crust. More butter is my serving suggestion.

Makes 1 loaf

450g coarse wholemeal flour
50g rolled oats
1 teaspoon salt

1 level teaspoon bicarbonate of soda
1 tablespoon treacle
1 tablespoon honey
450ml buttermilk (or sour milk, or milk with 1 tablespoon
    lemon juice)
1 tablespoon melted butter, to finish

1. Heat the oven to 200°C/fan 180°C/gas 6 and lightly grease a
   baking sheet.
2. Once the oven has come to temperature, put all the dry
   ingredients into a large mixing bowl and whisk together. Make a
   well in the middle. Stir the treacle and honey into the buttermilk
   until combined, then pour this into the well and, very quickly,
   stir together with your hands until you have a soft, sticky dough.
3. Form the dough into a round on your baking sheet and cut a
   deep cross in the top. Bake for 50 minutes to 1 hour, keeping an
   eye on it, until the crust is golden and the loaf sounds hollow
   when tapped underneath.
4. Brush with melted butter and leave to cool before tearing into it.
   Eat as soon as possible, as it doesn't keep very well.

Perfect
Hot Cross Buns

As someone who relishes an annual rant on the impropriety of purchasing hot cross buns before Good Friday, I have mixed feelings about including this recipe here.

There is a real risk, I suppose, that it could be used in February, or on a picnic in July — or even, God forbid, during a dull moment on Boxing Day. But then, surely a homemade bun at any time of year beats a thousand dry old mass-produced versions at Easter.

I've tried an old, old recipe included in Dorothy Hartley's masterful survey, *Food in England*, which uses lard and beaten egg and, though I missed the currants (apparently replaced by yellow candied peel for Eastertide), I found the results beautifully light and fluffy. I preferred the slightly denser butter, milk and egg version favoured by Nigella Lawson, however: soft and moist, it tastes like a real treat — and is much quicker and easier than the pre-ferments favoured by serious bakers online. It also seems in the celebratory spirit of the season.

Variations on the classic hot cross bun abound — Dan Lepard uses milk stout for a dark and malty result, but this doesn't taste like a hot cross bun to me, and I'm not keen on his tea-soaked fruit either, which seems almost obscenely juicy. Not very godly.

Nothing is as outrageous, however, as the American suggestions of piping the traditional cross on in icing or 'cream cheese frosting'.

No, the defining feature of the hot cross bun should be formed from muscularly plain dough, seasoned with a pinch of salt to contrast with the sweetness of the rest.

At all other times of the year, you can leave it off – or, of course, shape it into any old shape you like. Just do me a favour: please don't call it a hot cross bun.

Makes 16

200ml milk, plus a little more for glazing
3 cardamom pods, bruised
1 cinnamon stick
2 cloves
¼ teaspoon grated nutmeg
A pinch of saffron
20g fresh yeast
50g golden caster sugar, plus extra to glaze
450g strong white flour
100g cold butter
½ teaspoon salt
½ teaspoon ground ginger
3 eggs
150g currants
50g mixed peel
3 tablespoons plain flour

1. Gently heat 200ml milk in a pan along with the cardamom, cinnamon, cloves, nutmeg and saffron until threatening to boil, then turn off the heat and leave the mixture to infuse for 1 hour.

2. Strain and discard the spices, then bring the milk back up to blood temperature (warm, but not hot) and mix it with the yeast and 1 teaspoon of sugar.

3. Sift the flour into a large mixing bowl and grate over the butter. Rub this in with your fingertips, or in a food mixer, until well combined, then add the remaining sugar and the salt and ground ginger. Beat together 2 of the eggs.

4. Make a well in the middle of the flour, and pour in the beaten eggs and the milk/yeast mixture. Stir in to make a soft dough – it shouldn't look at all dry. Knead for 10 minutes, until smooth and elastic, then put the dough into a lightly greased bowl, cover and leave in a warm place until doubled in size – this will probably take a couple of hours.

5. Tip the dough out on to a lightly greased work surface and knead for about a minute, then flatten it out and scatter the fruit and peel over the top. Knead again to spread the fruit out evenly, then divide the dough into 16 equal pieces.

6. Roll these into bun shapes. Put them on to lined baking trays and score a cross into the top of each, then cover loosely and put in a warm place to prove until doubled in size.

7. Preheat the oven to 220°C/fan 200°C/gas 7 and beat together the last egg with a little milk. Mix the plain flour with a pinch of salt and just enough cold water to make a stiff paste. Paint the top of each bun with the eggwash, and then, using a piping bag or a steady hand and a teaspoon, draw a thick cross on the top of each. Put them into the oven and bake for about 25 minutes, until golden.

8. While they're baking, mix 1 tablespoon of caster sugar with 1 tablespoon of boiling water. When the buns come out of the oven, brush each with this glaze before transferring to a rack to cool. Eat with lots of butter – they're pretty good the next day too, toasted carefully under the grill until golden and crisp.

Perfect
Pizza

*E*veryone – absolutely everyone – likes pizza. It's surely the
epitome of the American dream, imported to the States by dirt-
poor Italian immigrants, transformed into enormous pies loaded
with an embarrassment of toppings, then re-exported around the
world in a glorious multitude of forms and styles.

But it's the Neapolitan version that's still held up as a model
of pizza perfection. Not as crisp as the Roman variety, or
as doughy as a Chicago pie, the base should be
soft and light, yet charred and chewy around
the edges, and topped with the bare
minimum – tomatoes, garlic and olive oil,
with perhaps mozzarella if you're feeling really indulgent.

Cooking an authentic pizza requires a blisteringly hot, wood-fired
oven – somewhere around the 485°C mark – but as most of us aren't
lucky enough to have one of those in the garden, this is the best
version you can make in a domestic kitchen.

Certainly far better than the takeaway variety; as Giorgio Locatelli
explains in *Made in Italy*, pizza has to be eaten 'within 5–6 minutes of
it coming out of the oven or it will be soggy and spoilt'. Hence, he
claims, in Italy 'not even if they threatened you with six years in
prison, would you eat a . . . pizza delivered on a motorbike'.

There are a few things you can do to help your oven out: turning it on to heat for an hour beforehand (pizza may be cheap, but the fuel to cook it is sadly not), and cooking the pizza on a hot pizza stone, or a terracotta tile, so it crisps on the bottom.

If you can find strong '00' flour, that's the best thing to use: the double zero indicates it's been finely milled, which will give you a softer result, with just a hint of chewiness thanks to the higher gluten content. Dusting the pizza base with semolina not only makes it easier to slide in and out of the oven, but gives it a bit of extra crunch.

If you're really patient, you can ape Heston Blumenthal and make a small batch of dough the day before: the longer fermentation gives it a tangier flavour, which works well with milky mozzarella. Indeed, the longer the ferment, the more complex the base will taste. Four hours seems like a good compromise: long enough to be interesting, but not so long that the base starts to compete with the toppings for your attention.

The Associazione Vera Pizza Napoletana permits only four ingredients in a pizza base: flour, water, yeast and salt, which rules out Locatelli's extra virgin olive oil, or the River Café's milk, or indeed Heston's malt extract (which apparently helps the dough to brown). Fortuitously, I find all of them also make the dough more difficult to work with, so I'm going to kowtow to the Neapolitans and keep mine simple: you can always add olive oil on top. Indeed, I'd go so far as to suggest you must.

Add the toppings just before you slide the pizza into the oven, or they'll make the base soggy, especially if you're using mozzarella, and slide it in as quickly as possible so you don't let too much heat out. Then all you can do is wait, pray . . . and get out the napkins.

Makes 6–8, depending on size

10g fresh yeast (or 7g instant dried, made up as on the packet)
½ teaspoon sugar
320ml warm water
500g pizza flour (or half '00' flour and half strong white flour), plus extra to dust
1 teaspoon salt
Olive oil and semolina/cornmeal/polenta, to serve
Your chosen toppings (see below)

1. Mash together the yeast and sugar in a small bowl and leave for 1 minute. Stir this mixture into the warm water. Put the flour in a food processor, add the yeast mixture and mix on the lowest speed for about 4 minutes, until it comes together into a soft dough. Tip in the salt, turn the speed up slightly and mix for another 4 minutes. Alternatively, mix the yeast mixture and flour together with a wooden spoon, then turn the dough out on to a lightly floured work surface, add the salt, and knead for 10 minutes until springy.

2. Put the dough into a large, lightly greased bowl, and turn until coated in oil. Cover the bowl with a damp cloth, shower cap or clingfilm, and leave it in a warm place for 4 hours.

3. Divide the dough into satsuma-sized bits and use the palm of your hand to roll these into balls on the work surface. Place, well

spaced out, on a lightly oiled baking tray, then cover and store somewhere cool until you're ready to cook (if you don't want to use it all, the leftover dough should keep at this point for about 2 weeks in a sealed container; in this case, don't divide it up until just before use).

4. Meanwhile, turn the oven to its highest setting, and put your seasoned (a new stone should come with seasoning instructions) pizza stone, terracotta tile or heavy baking tray on a high shelf. Allow the oven to heat for about an hour to make sure there are absolutely no cold spots.

5. Dust a work surface lightly with flour and put a ball of dough on to it. Flatten the ball with the heel of your hand, then use your fingertips to knock the air out of it. Lift it up on to your fingertips and rotate it, stretching it out as you do so, until the dough is as thin as possible, leaving a slightly thicker rim of dough around the edge.

6. Slide the base on to a rimless baking tray, chopping board, or pizza paddle dusted with semolina, then add the toppings and a drizzle of olive oil.

7. Working as quickly as possible, slide the base on to the hot stone, tile or baking tray and bake for about 8 minutes, keeping an eye on it, until crisp and golden. Devour immediately.

Some toppings
CLASSIC

- Torn mozzarella, roughly chopped cherry tomatoes, basil leaves to finish
- Tomato sauce, anchovies, capers, oregano
- Tomato sauce, torn mozzarella, baked ham, roasted artichokes in oil, mushrooms, egg
- Caramelized onions, anchovies, black olives

NEAPOLITANS LOOK AWAY

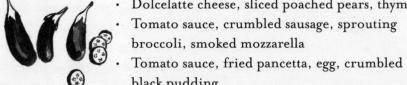

- Tomato sauce, roasted aubergine slices in oil, ricotta, mint to finish
- Dolcelatte cheese, sliced poached pears, thyme
- Tomato sauce, crumbled sausage, sprouting broccoli, smoked mozzarella
- Tomato sauce, fried pancetta, egg, crumbled black pudding

Perfect
Oatcakes

Oatcakes, our native version of the rye crispbread, popular in
northern regions where the climate is too damp and cold to favour
wheat production, have gone global – these days you can even find
them as far south as Staffordshire, where they're threatening to
eclipse the local sort. (If you're not familiar with the wonderful soft,
pancake-like oatcakes of the Potteries, I urge you to go online,
purchase some, and eat them stuffed with bacon and brown sauce.)

But back to the Scottish biscuit, once a long-lasting alternative to
bread, now a favourite accompaniment to cheese, and infinitely
more delicious homemade. The main ingredient is, unsurprisingly,
oats: Orkney-born F. Marian McNeill, whose *The Scots Kitchen* was
published in 1929, uses medium oatmeal alone, while everyone else
combines it with something else; oat flour, in Rose Prince's *Pocket
Bakery* book, porridge oats in a recipe given to Hugh Fearnley-
Whittingstall by Bill Cowie, island manager of Rona, white flour in
the Macroom oatmeal biscuits in Mark Hix's *British Regional Food*, and
coarse pinhead oatmeal and porridge oats in Sue Lawrence's *Scottish
Baking*.

I discover that I like my oatcakes, like my porridge, to have a bit
about them in the way of texture. A mixture of medium oatmeal, to
act as a binder, and pinhead oatmeal, to make them pleasingly
chewy, with just a handful of porridge oats for interest, will do
nicely. There's no need to add any raising agent: we want them solid

enough to hold a hearty wedge of cheese, but toasting the oats before use will help bring out their flavour.

You can use olive oil if you'd prefer to keep things vegan-friendly (in which case, forget I said the thing about the bacon), but I like the flavour of butter, both on and in the biscuits, with some extra hot water to bind the dough together.

Flavour-wise you can add just about any dry ingredient you like: black pepper or seaweed flakes are popular choices, though I'd also recommend a pinch of brown sugar as well as the obligatory salt. Traditionally they would have been cooked on a cast-iron girdle over the fire, but it's far easier for amateurs to use the oven and season with imaginary peat smoke instead.

Makes about 10 depending on size

200g medium oatmeal, plus extra for
  dusting
50g pinhead oatmeal
25g porridge oats
¼ teaspoon salt
¼ teaspoon brown sugar
75g butter, diced
75ml boiling water

1. Heat the oven to 200°C/fan 180°C/gas 6. Spread the oatmeals and oats out on a lined baking tray and bake for about 15 minutes, shaking occasionally, until they smell toasty.
2. Tip into a mixing bowl, keeping the oven on, and whisk in the

salt and sugar. Melt the butter in the boiling water, and then stir this into the oats to make a damp dough; if it's too wet to hold together, add a little more of the medium oatmeal, but don't overdo it; it should still be sticky.

3. Dust a clean surface with a little medium oatmeal and tip the dough on top, in a ball. Flatten until it's about 5mm thick (hands are easiest, but you can use a well-floured rolling pin if you prefer), then cut out rounds of your chosen size.

4. Use a palette knife to carefully lift each on to the lined baking sheet, keeping them in the cutter, as they will be fragile. Re-roll any scraps until all the dough is used up.

5. Bake for 20 minutes, then very carefully turn them over and bake for about 10 more minutes until they feel hard and dry on both sides. Gently transfer to a wire rack to cool, then store in an airtight tin.

Perfect
Scones

Ah, the Great British scone. Such an innocuous-looking little thing – plain really, in comparison with the monstrous American muffin, or the gaudy macaron – yet how much more precious than these more fashionable baked goods. The honest scone has no sugary icing or exotically perfumed ganache to hide behind – it stands or falls on its absolute freshness, which is why it's impossible to purchase a good example on the high street. You will never get a better scone than a homemade scone.

Every scone maker aspires to the towering triumphs of the soufflé – the miraculous transformation of lumpen flour and fat into a billowing cloud of fluffy dough – but all too often ends up with stubbornly flat biscuits instead. The secret, learnt from the unnervingly wholesome Irish celebrity chef Rachel Allen, is using a raising agent (bicarbonate of soda and cream of tartar) and super-fine flour. Both Rachel and Marcus Wareing put eggs in their scones, but I find this makes them rather rich and cakey – being of

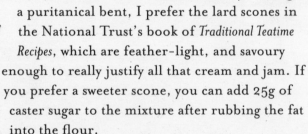

a puritanical bent, I prefer the lard scones in the National Trust's book of *Traditional Teatime Recipes*, which are feather-light, and savoury enough to really justify all that cream and jam. If you prefer a sweeter scone, you can add 25g of caster sugar to the mixture after rubbing the fat into the flour.

River Cottage baker Dan Stevens cautions against overworking the dough, and Delia believes success lies in pushing, rather than twisting the cutter — both tips that seem to help give a slightly better rise. If you really want billowing scones, gently pat the dough down, rather than rolling it out — it gives slightly unruly, wild-looking results, but at least no one will be in any doubt that they're homemade. Top with rich, salty West Country butter, a slick of ruby red jam and a thick dollop of clotted cream, in whatever order takes your fancy — just make sure there's plenty of them!

Makes 6

350g super-fine '00' flour,
   plus extra to dust
1 heaped teaspoon
   bicarbonate of soda
2 heaped teaspoons cream of tartar
A pinch of salt
50g chilled butter, plus extra to grease
50g chilled lard (or double the
   quantity of butter above)
130ml milk, plus 1 tablespoon to glaze

1. Preheat the oven to 210°C/fan 190°C/gas 7. Sift the flour, bicarbonate of soda and cream of tartar into a large bowl with a pinch of salt and add the butter and lard. Rub the fat into the flour as quickly as possible, until the mixture resembles breadcrumbs.
2. Gradually add enough milk to create a soft dough, and bring together into a ball. Very gently roll or press out on a floured

surface until about 2.5cm thick, then cut into rounds using a 7cm cutter lightly dusted with flour, being careful not to twist the cutter. Bring any remaining dough together and repeat the process until it is all used up.

3. Place on a lightly buttered baking tray, and brush the tops with milk. Bake for about 15 minutes, until well risen and golden on top, then cool slightly on a wire rack and eat as soon as possible.

Perfect
Banana Bread

Not really a bread, if I'm honest – more of a loaf-shaped cake, but the name lends it a spuriously wholesome air, allowing it to be included on breakfast menus in the States without a blush. And, like many cakes, it's not hard to see why it's so popular, the fruit lending a natural sweetness, and delectable gooeyness, to what's otherwise a fairly standard recipe.

Contrary to popular opinion, you don't need bananas so ripe they're almost black, although this is certainly a good way to use up fruit on its way out – the overripe versions are somewhat easier to mash, but surprisingly, they don't seem to give the cake a more intense banana flavour. However, if you are using really ripe specimens in the recipe below, you may want to reduce the amount of sugar slightly, depending on taste.

However ripe they are, there's no need to purée the bananas, as Charles Campion does in *Fifty Recipes to Stake Your Life On*: though it gives the whole loaf a great flavour, I miss the chunks of whole fruit that are such a highlight of the America's Test Kitchen version. A mixture of well-mashed (bananas aren't worth washing up a blender for) and coarsely chopped seems to offer the best of both worlds.

A little squidginess is good but I like my banana bread to have a certain fluffiness, so I use baking powder, like pastry chef Claire

Clark, whose cake is the lightest I try. If you'd prefer to keep it dairy free, as she does, you can use vegetable oil, but I'm a sucker for the richness and softness you can only get from butter.

The caramel flavour of light brown sugar, as used by the Hummingbird Bakery, goes wonderfully with the bananas (just think of banoffee pie), but I've left out their spices – after trying vanilla, cinnamon and ginger, I decided the sweet fruit needed no such help.

I have added walnuts, though: I love the contrast between the soft, sweet crumb and their slightly bitter crunchiness, but feel free to leave them out, or indeed substitute some other nut if you're not a fan.

Nigella Lawson also adds bourbon-soaked sultanas to her rather louche loaf, but, though delicious, I think my bread is moist enough not to require any extra juiciness. In any case, such outrageous decadence has no place in a good, wholesome bread, as I'm sure you'll agree.

Makes 1 x 21cm loaf

350g ripe bananas (peeled weight)
180g plain flour, plus extra for the tin
2½ teaspoons baking powder
4 tablespoons melted butter,
   slightly cooled, plus extra to grease
160g soft light brown sugar
2 eggs, beaten
50g walnuts, roughly chopped

1. Preheat the oven to 190°C/fan 170°C/gas 5. Put two-thirds of the peeled bananas into a bowl and mash them with a fork or potato masher until smooth. Roughly mash the remainder, and stir in gently.

2. Sift the flour and baking powder into a bowl with a generous pinch of salt, and grease and lightly flour a 21cm loaf tin.

3. Put the sugar, eggs and melted butter into a large mixing bowl and use an electric mixer or a whisk to beat them together until the mix is pale and slightly increased in volume. Gently fold in the banana and the dry ingredients until there are no more streaks of flour, then fold in the walnuts and make sure they're evenly distributed.

4. Spoon the mixture into the tin and bake it for about an hour, until a skewer inserted into the middle comes out clean. Allow to cool in the tin for 10 minutes before turning out on to a wire rack to cool completely.

Perfect
Chocolate Chip Cookies

*J*ust before writing this recipe, I heard on the radio that the British are one of the world's biggest spenders when it comes to biscuits. This made me pretty proud, I can tell you – we've created some fine examples in our time, but even I have to admit that our supremacy on the teatime seas is seriously challenged by the American chocolate chip cookie.

It's that combination of crunch and chew, dough and chocolate that makes them so damn addictive – and a good CCC ought to be a bit chewy. British imitations often give them the texture of shortbread: another fine biscuit, but quite beside the point here.

The original Toll House cookie, invented in Whitman, Massachusetts, in the 1930s, is incredibly buttery and sweet, with a crisp, sugary shell – addictive, but too one-dimensional to be quite perfect. I do approve of their choice of sweeteners though: a mix of granulated sugar for crunch, and light brown sugar for flavour.

Chewiness is a virtue, then, but you want a bit of crunch too, which is why I've plumped for plain flour instead of the strong bread flour recommended by Marcus Wareing and American culinary celebrity Alton Brown, which gives a tougher, puffier result. I've deployed bicarbonate of soda for the same reason: Wareing's baking powder makes the cookies too cakey.

Fat-wise, butter is an essential: my old school friend Alex's mum Charlotte (a real live American) has an incredible recipe using margarine, which gives a crisp, moist result but, in a side-by-side tasting, I miss the richness of the butter.

In the pioneer spirit, you can chuck in just about anything you like along with the chocolate (having experimented with dark and milk, I've chosen the bitterness of the former to contrast with the sweetness of the cookie itself, but would note that a mixture is preferred by a discerning younger audience) – nuts would be nice, dried fruit if you must, even spices if you're feeling exotic. Chopping your own chocolate may seem like a faff, but it gives a more interesting result than evenly-sized chips.

Resting the dough before baking may seem like an odd idea for a biscuit, but in fact, although it's not mentioned in many modern versions of the recipe, the 1953 *Toll House Cook Book* notes that, at the inn, they refrigerated the dough overnight.

Baking batches at 12, 24, 36 and 48 hours reveals they're at their best between 12 and 24 hours: still doughy in the middle, but dry and crunchy without. But if you really must have cookies immediately, all is not lost – these may get better with time, but bear in mind they're starting from delicious.

Makes 15

120g salted butter, at room temperature
75g light brown sugar
75g granulated sugar

½ teaspoon vanilla extract

1 egg, beaten

240g plain flour

½ teaspoon bicarbonate of soda

170g dark or milk chocolate, roughly chopped

Sea salt flakes (optional – but if not using,
   add a pinch of fine salt to the dough along with the sugars)

1. Using a wooden spoon, or (and even better) a food mixer, beat together the butter and both sugars until just combined. Add the vanilla extract, then the egg, and beat in well.

2. Sift the flour and bicarbonate of soda into the bowl, and stir in until it just comes together into a dough. Mix in the chocolate pieces until evenly distributed, then, if you've got time, chill the mixture overnight, or for up to 72 hours.

3. Preheat the oven to 200°C/fan 180°C/gas 6. Line two baking trays with greaseproof paper, and divide the mixture into golf-ball sized spheres, spacing them well apart on the tray, so they don't melt into each other as they cook. Bake the cookies for about 15 minutes, until golden, but not browned.

4. Sprinkle them lightly with sea salt, if using, and allow to cool on the tray for a couple of minutes, before moving to a wire rack to cool completely – or alternatively, sampling immediately.

Perfect
Gingerbread Biscuits (and men, and women, and children, dinosaurs and assorted animals)

*I*f any recipe sums up the joy of cooking with, and for, children, it's this one – everyone remembers the slightly cannibalistic joy of biting off a fat little leg, or tenderly saving the head until last (just so the poor fellow had time to really appreciate his predicament), and the beauty of these robust biscuits is that they're very easy to shape into whatever takes your fancy. Policeman, princess, pirate: all you need is the right cutter, and some artistic flair with the icing.

Medieval gingerbread was made from stale bread, and sweetened with honey and spices, making it more like a sticky flapjack than anything we'd recognize today – and Mrs Beeton's Victorian version is heavy on the treacle and cayenne pepper, giving it a rather dour, serious flavour. Even the famous Grasmere gingerbread isn't fit for shaping – made with oatmeal, the dough is so crumbly we end up with quite a few stray limbs.

I turn to the Germans, kings of festive lebkuchen biscuits, for help – after all, their version is so solid you can build houses out of them.

James Beard's recipe involves heating honey, sugar, water and butter together before mixing in flour, bicarbonate of soda and spices to make a tacky dough that's easy to roll out and shape. So far, so promising, but the flavour just isn't right: it tastes of Christmas markets and glühwein, not picnics and currant eyes.

In the end, I decide to adapt a recipe from Leiths Cookery School, which uses baking powder for a slightly lighter texture — I find the flavour of the original too meek and mild, so I've swapped the caster sugar for the caramelly soft brown sort, and increased the levels of spice, so they have a definite kick.

And, because you can never have enough ginger in a ginger biscuit, I've added the crystallized sort for a more interesting texture: admittedly, it will give your little people a rather pock-marked complexion, but that's nothing a little icing can't conceal. (It also strikes me that such a warty appearance might be a positive boon to a gingerbread stegosaurus or similar.)

I've provided a recipe for a simple white icing, in case you just want to make pretty shapes, rather than people or animals — they do make good decorations, so follow the instructions for poking a hole in each for hanging if that's their destiny.

Makes about 30 small biscuits or about 20 gingerbread people

340g plain flour
½ teaspoon baking powder
½ teaspoon salt
1½ teaspoons grated nutmeg

1½ teaspoons ground cloves
2 teaspoons ground cinnamon
3 teaspoons ground ginger
225g unsalted butter, softened, plus extra to grease
340g soft brown sugar
1 egg, beaten
75g crystallized ginger, finely chopped (optional)
Currants (optional)
225g icing sugar (optional)
Hundreds and thousands (optional)

1. Sift the flour, baking powder, salt and spices together into a mixing bowl.
2. Beat together the butter and sugar with a hand mixer or wooden spoon until fluffy, and then add the egg very gradually, so the mixture doesn't curdle.
3. Stir this into the flour to make a dough, then mix in the crystallized ginger, if using, making sure it's evenly distributed throughout.
4. Put the dough between two sheets of clingfilm and roll it out to the thickness of a £1 coin. Chill for half an hour. Preheat the oven to 200°C/fan 180°C/gas 6, and grease and line two baking trays.
5. Cut out the biscuits to your preferred shape, and arrange, well spaced out, on the lined trays. If you're going to add currant eyes and buttons, do so now, poking them firmly into the dough.
6. Bake for about 10 minutes, then, if you're going to hang them, poke a hole in each straight from the oven (a skewer is the best thing to use) and leave to cool completely on a wire rack before threading a ribbon through.

7. Decorate with writing icing, or, if you prefer, sift the icing sugar, then mix to a stiff consistency with boiling water (add it gradually, because you'll need less than you think). Brush the icing over the cooled biscuits, and decorate with hundreds and thousands while still wet.

Perfect
Chocolate Brownies

Confronted by these all-American delights, the human soul crumbles into fudgey defeat, and a million eyes widen into heart-shaped pools of chocolate goo. But the dearly beloved brownie is not without its problems for the cook. For a start, there's the divisive issue of cakey versus fudgey.

The two opposing schools of thought are represented neatly by the twin deities of Nigel (Slater) and Nigella (Lawson) – the former's method is designed to incorporate as much air as possible into the batter, giving a surprisingly light, but divinely dark result, whereas the domestic goddess concentrates on cramming as much butter as possible into her brownies, in order to ensure something quite obscenely rich and gooey. At the risk of prompting Nigella's many fans to toss away this book in disgust, her brownies are just too much for my taste – designed more for smearing saucily around the place than actually eating, perhaps.

Replacing some of the chocolate with cocoa powder, as Nigel does, ensures a rich flavour without weighing the brownies down with too much fat, and vigorous whipping of the batter helps to give them a lovely crisp crust. Plunging them straight into cold water as soon as they leave the oven, as recommended by the American First Lady of Chocolate, Alice Medrich, stops them from continuing to cook – so they stay gorgeously moist. But definitely not gooey.

250g chocolate (70% cocoa)
250g unsalted butter, softened
300g golden caster sugar
3 large free-range eggs,
    plus 1 extra egg yolk, lightly beaten
60g plain flour
½ teaspoon baking powder
A pinch of salt
60g good-quality cocoa powder
100g walnuts (optional)

1. Preheat the oven to 200°C/fan 180°C/gas 6, and line the base
   and sides of a 23 x 23cm baking tin (a loose-bottomed one won't
   work here) with baking parchment, cutting slits in the corners to
   help it fit better.
2. Set a bowl over, but not touching, a pan of simmering water, and
   add 200g of the chocolate, broken into pieces. Allow to melt,
   stirring occasionally, then remove from the heat immediately.
3. Meanwhile, beat the butter and sugar together until light and
   fluffy, and break the rest of the chocolate into chips.
4. With the mixer still running, gradually add the eggs, beating well
   between each addition to ensure it's thoroughly incorporated
   before pouring in any more. Leave it mixing on a high speed for
   5 minutes, until the batter has a silky sheen and has increased
   in volume. Sift the flour, baking powder, salt and cocoa powder
   into a large bowl and mix well.
5. Remove the bowl from the mixer and gently fold in the melted
   chocolate and chocolate chips with a metal spoon, followed by
   the dry ingredients and walnuts.
6. Spoon the mixture into the tin, and bake for 30 minutes. Test
   with a skewer; it should come out sticky, but not coated with raw

mixture. If it does, put it back into the oven for another 3 minutes, then test again. Prepare a roasting tin of iced water.

7. When the brownies are ready, remove the tin from the oven and place in the cold water bath. Allow to cool for an hour before cutting into squares, and leave the tin in the water bath until cooled completely. Store in an airtight container: they're even better the next day.

How to melt chocolate
Chocolate is very sensitive to heat, and burns easily, so it's important to take care when melting it. You can microwave chunks of chocolate, stirring every 30 seconds until fully melted, but I find it safer to break it into a heatproof glass bowl set over a pan of simmering water, so I can keep an eye on it, and stir regularly. Don't allow the bowl to touch the water, and be careful not to drip any liquids into the chocolate or it will solidify.

Things to add to the brownies instead of walnuts
100g of pistachio nuts and the bruised seeds of 10 cardamom pods
100g of chopped toffee and 50g of roughly chopped pecans
100g of mini marshmallows
100g of fresh or frozen raspberries and 50g of white chocolate chips
125g of dried fruit – sour cherries or dried apricots are my favourites

Perfect
Fairy Cakes

(By which I mean the dainty, native sort, rather than the overgrown and brazenly blowsy cupcake which has rampaged its way across the Atlantic and into British bakeries in recent years, like some sort of garishly iced grey squirrel.)

Lightness is key with these diminutive treats – hence the addition of some extra baking powder to the self-raising flour. Make sure you beat the mixture until you can see air bubbles popping in it – the idea is to get as much air into it as possible.

Good Food magazine suggests adding some ground almonds to the batter, which helps keep the cakes nice and moist as they bake – because of their large surface area, fairy cakes are prone to dry out during cooking. Too much will make them greasy and heavy, however, so don't be tempted to increase the amount too much. I sometimes like to use a little ground rice instead, as in the *Leiths Baking Bible* recipe, which gives them a surprisingly crunchy texture.

If you're a stickler for appearances, don't fill the cases right up to the top, and allow the batter to rest for half an hour before going into the oven – this should help give you a flatter top, which is easier to decorate. According to baking expert Mich Turner, who has made cakes for everyone from the Queen to David Beckham and written

several books on the subject, fairy cakes should be topped with a
simple glacé icing rather than the great swirls of lurid, luscious
buttercream that graces their transatlantic cousins. But I won't tell if
you don't . . .

Makes 12 small cakes or 6 larger, cupcake-sized ones

85g unsalted butter, softened
85g golden caster sugar
1 medium free-range egg, at
   room temperature, beaten
100g self-raising flour, sifted
40g ground almonds
¼ teaspoon baking powder
100ml milk
150g icing sugar
Decorations such as hundreds and
   thousands or silver balls (optional)

1. Preheat the oven to 200°C/fan 180°C/gas 6, and line a fairy
   cake or muffin tin with cases.
2. Cream the butter and sugar together until very light and fluffy –
   if you do this by hand you'll need a very strong arm, so if you've
   got one use a food mixer on its fastest setting. It will take at least
   5 minutes.
3. While continuing to mix, drizzle the egg in gradually, adding a
   tablespoon of flour if the mixture looks like it's about to curdle.
4. Combine the flour, almonds and baking powder, then gently
   fold into the mixture. Add the milk to bring the mix to a
   dropping consistency (i.e. it drops easily from a spoon).

5. Divide the mixture between the cases and bake for 20 minutes (25 for larger cupcake-sized cakes), then turn out on to a rack to cool.

6. Mix the icing sugar with a few drops of boiling water to make a thick paste, then smooth over the cooled cakes and add decorations before it sets. Eat quickly – fairy cakes don't keep!

Perfect
Victoria Sandwich

*T*his queen of the tea table can, in my opinion, never be toppled by any chocolate-flavoured pretender – and Hugh Fearnley-Whittingstall, who's won first prize for his Victoria sandwich in his local village fête, agrees, calling it one of the finest cakes ever to grace a plate. Although it's often spoken of as such, strictly speaking, it's not a sponge at all – according to Mary Berry, a true sponge is a whisked mixture of eggs, sugar and flour; the kind of thing one would make a Swiss roll from in fact, rather than an honest British doorstop of a cake.

It wasn't until the development of baking powder in the 1840s that butter could be added to cake mixtures without weighing them down in the oven. This fabulous new invention was celebrated with an appropriately patriotic cake – although anyone making Mrs Beeton's first recipe would have been left scratching their heads, as the original domestic goddess (more recently revealed as a remarkably astute plagiarist in Kathryn Hughes' biography) forgot to include the eggs.

The same general principles apply as with the fairy cakes above, but you can afford to be a little more generous with the eggs, and dispense with the ground almonds, as bigger cakes are less prone to drying out during cooking. I'm with Hugh on insisting on raspberry jam in my sandwich – it's something about the gritty texture of the seeds — but if you're feeling particularly decadent, you can add clotted cream, or butter cream (a mixture of softened butter and icing sugar) as well. Just don't forget the eggs.

3 large eggs, weighed in their shells
The same weight of softened butter,
   caster sugar and self-raising flour
I teaspoon baking powder
2 tablespoons milk
3 tablespoons raspberry jam, to serve

1. Preheat the oven to 200°C/fan 180°C/gas 6. Grease two 20cm sandwich tins with butter and line the bases with baking parchment.

2. Cream the butter and sugar together in a mixing bowl or food mixer until light and very fluffy. Very gradually add the eggs, beating well between each addition, so the mixture doesn't curdle — if it threatens to do so, fold in a tablespoon of flour before adding the rest of the egg.

3. Sift the flour and baking powder together, then fold the flour and milk into the creamed mixture to give a batter loose enough to fall from the spoon when you give it a sharp shake. Divide the mixture evenly between the two tins, smooth the tops with the back of a spoon, and put them into the oven for about 20 minutes, until they're well risen and golden, and the edges have started to shrink away from the sides — keep an eye on them for the last 5 minutes of cooking.

4. Allow to cool in the tins for a few minutes, then run a table knife round the edges to loosen them and gently tip the cakes on to a wire rack. Leave to cool completely — if you add jam when the cakes are warm, it will melt.

5. Choose the flatter of the two sponges, and top with a thick layer of jam. If it's annoyingly pointy, you can cheat and cut a little bit off so the two will stick together better. Sandwich the two cakes together, and dust the top with caster sugar.

Perfect
Christmas Fruit Cake

As the very first real cake I ever baked, Christmas cake occupies a special place in my heart. Admittedly, the result, cruelly dubbed 'the rock of ages' by my ever-doting dad, was still going strong long after Easter eggs were old news, but practice makes perfect, and now I'd like to think I'm a bit of a dab hand (these days I make two, just to be sure of having some left to come back to for the rest of the year. It really does keep that well).

Although fruit cakes are fair game from the moment they emerge from the oven, as with many truly great foodstuffs they actually improve with age, especially if they're drip-fed booze as they mature. Hence the tradition of Stir-up Sunday, the last before Advent, and as such, the proper time to mix up the holy trinity of festive dried fruit goodies: mincemeat, Christmas pudding and Christmas cake. (The keenest, of course, pooh-pooh such last-minute arrangements – I know some smug sorts who make their puddings a year in advance.)

Whenever you get round to baking it, however, one thing you must do ahead of time is soak the fruit in liquid overnight: you could go for tea, apple juice or beer, but a spirit like rum, brandy or (my own favourite) whisky will make the most impact.

And there's a lot to compete with: dark muscovado sugar for its treacley sweetness, dried fruit (I'll leave the specifics up to you, as long as you keep the weight the same, but if you've never tried figs in a fruit cake, I'd highly recommend them), candied peel – and nuts. All the best fruit cakes, by which I mostly mean mine, have nuts in them.

Don't be alarmed by the relatively brief baking time: it works, I promise.

Makes 1 x 20cm cake

250g currants
250g sultanas
100g dried figs, roughly chopped
100g glacé cherries, cut in half
100g mixed peel
125ml whisky, or spirit of your choice, plus extra to feed
125g butter, softened
125g muscovado sugar
4 eggs, beaten
130g plain flour
½ teaspoon baking powder
1 teaspoon mixed spice
50g ground almonds
Grated zest of 1 lemon
50g whole almonds, chopped
25g crystallized ginger, chopped

1. Put the dried fruit and peel into a bowl with the whisky, cover and leave to soak overnight. Stir well before use. Grease a 20cm cake tin and line with two layers of baking parchment.

2. Preheat the oven to 160°C/fan 140°C/gas 3. Cream together the butter and sugar until light and fluffy, then gradually add the eggs, beating well after each addition so the mixture doesn't curdle.

3. Mix together the sifted flour, baking powder, spice, ground almonds and a pinch of salt and fold this into the butter and sugar mixture. Add the soaked fruits, and any remaining whisky, the lemon zest, chopped almonds and ginger, and stir to combine.

4. Tip the mixture into your prepared tin and smooth the surface, scooping out a small hollow in the middle to prevent a doming effect.

5. Put the cake into the oven for about an hour, then cover with foil and bake for another 30 minutes, then check the cake. It's done when a skewer inserted into the middle comes out clean – check every 10 minutes until it's cooked.

6. Leave to cool in the tin, then use the skewer to poke a few holes almost all the way through the cake, and brush them with more whisky. With the baking parchment still attached, wrap well in greaseproof paper and store in an airtight tin or a layer of foil, repeating the feeding every week or so until you're ready to ice just before Christmas.

Perfect
Carrot Cake

*F*or many years in this country, carrot cake was seen as the teatime choice of the sandal-wearing *Guardian*-ista – until its American cousin came visiting. Then the humble health food suddenly supersized, with a topping of sugary cream cheese icing – and, surprise surprise, went mainstream.

Carrot cake actually has quite a long history here: Britons have been using such root vegetables as a canny substitute for pricier imported dried fruits and sugars since the Middle Ages, and the idea was revived by the wartime Ministry of Food.

A recipe with such a past is never going to be neat and tidy, and indeed I try two very unusual carrot cakes in my quest for perfection. Nigella Lawson's version, which originated in the Venetian Jewish community, is made with ground almonds, eggs, olive oil and pine nuts. It's flat as a pancake, but deliciously moist and nutty – not quite what I'm after here, but as it's both gluten and lactose free, it's a good one to remember. Jane Grigson, meanwhile, offers a fatless sponge that's light as a cloud – even the carrots are finely shredded – but far too delicate for my liking.

As a nod to its hippy heritage, I've decided to make my more conventional carrot cake with wholemeal flour, like Delia Smith and Claire Clark – theirs are heavier than those made with white flour, but they have a defiantly wholesome texture which seems apt. Carrot cake, like muesli, shouldn't melt in the mouth.

I've rejected white sugar for the same reason; Geraldene Holt's unrefined light sugar gives the cake a lovely toffee flavour, without taking over like Delia's dark muscovado. Holt's butter also gets the thumbs up: although it may have been the enemy back in the marge-happy 1970s, it's definitely the wholesome choice nowadays, and more importantly, it gives the cake a wonderful richness.

I've loaded the cake with dried fruit and nuts – pecans are my nod to its popularity in the States, but you could substitute walnuts if you wanted to keep things British. Sweet spices go brilliantly with carrot, as does Holt's orange zest, though her coriander seems a step too far. Save that for the soup.

If you're determined to be healthy, you can leave the cake at that, but I've warmed to the cream cheese icing over the years. I've gone for a very classic version – no butter, as used by Claire Clark, or mascarpone, like Nigel Slater's recipe – and in strictly restrained quantities. Lemon zest adds a little freshness, but here, less is definitely more. This is a cake, after all, that's good enough to eat on its own.

Makes 1 x 18–20cm cake

150g butter, melted, plus extra for greasing
150g soft light brown sugar
3 eggs
200g self-raising wholemeal flour
I teaspoon bicarbonate of soda

½ teaspoon salt

1 teaspoon ground cinnamon

½ teaspoon grated nutmeg

Zest of 1 orange

100g sultanas or raisins

200g carrots, peeled and grated

100g pecans, toasted and roughly chopped,
plus extra to decorate

For the icing

150g full-fat cream cheese

50g soft light brown sugar

Zest of ½ a lemon and a squeeze of juice

1. Preheat the oven to 200°C/fan 180°C/gas 6, and grease and line the bases of two 18–20cm sandwich tins with butter.
2. Put the melted butter, sugar and eggs into a large mixing bowl and whisk well, preferably with an electric mixer, until the ingredients are thoroughly combined and the mixture has almost doubled in volume.
3. Sift together the flour, bicarb, salt and spices and fold these very gently into the liquid mixture, being careful to knock as little air out as possible as you do so. Fold in the remaining ingredients with similar care, and divide the mixture between the tins. Bake these for about 30 minutes, until a skewer inserted into the middle comes out clean. Allow to cool in the tins.
4. Meanwhile, beat together the ingredients for the icing and chill to make it easier to spread. When the cakes are cool enough to ice (ideally, room temperature), remove from the tins, and top one with half the icing, and then the other cake. Ice the top of the upper cake, and decorate with the remaining pecans.

Perfect
Lemon Drizzle Cake

*D*rizzle isn't often good news — not on the weather forecast, not on a menu when followed by the words 'balsamic vinegar', and definitely not where the hot water's concerned, but with this cake it makes an honourable exception. Drizzle here means sticky and citrussy and deliciously moist — a deluge would be too much, a sprinkle too little. Here, a drizzle is just right.

The cake itself is a classic Victoria sponge: solid enough to stand up to the drizzle, light and fluffy enough to invite a second slice. Extra indulgence is unnecessary: Raymond Blanc uses double cream and eggs, for example, but this just makes his cake dense and heavy in comparison. I do like the way Nigel Slater's sweet ground almonds point up the sharpness of the lemon, however, as well as creating a more interesting texture.

Blanc does redeem himself slightly by adding lemon zest to the batter — if you stick it in early, before you cream the butter and sugar together, you'll release the citrus oils as you work, creating, as Tonia George explains, 'a much more lemony sponge'. That said, you can overdo it: adding lemon juice at this point, like Gary Rhodes, makes the cake sour (and Blanc's rum, meanwhile, just gets lost. A rare occasion when booze in a cake is a bad idea).

More important than the cake, of course, is the drizzle. I had to disqualify Blanc from the contest at this point, because he uses a lemon-flavoured icing which has no hope of sinking into the sponge. Slater squeezes over some lemon juice, which makes things a little austere for my taste — better is Gary Rhodes' golden syrup and lemon juice combination, which reminds me pleasantly of a steamed pudding, but best of all is the granulated sugar used by Geraldene Holt and Tonia George. It creates a crust so robust it's almost crunchy: a lovely contrast to the soft, fluffy cake beneath.

Adding the syrup while the cake's still warm will help the absorption process, as will poking a few discreet holes in the top — don't worry if there seems to be more liquid than the cake could possibly hold, because by some wondrous miracle, it always disappears.

You can have too much of a good thing, though: George sandwiches her cake with lemon curd and mascarpone too. Sharp and rich, it steals the cake's thunder utterly — this should be a simple sticky pleasure, not a rococo masterpiece of icings and fillings.

Makes 1 cake

175g butter, softened, plus extra to grease
175g caster sugar
2 unwaxed lemons
3 eggs, beaten
100g self-raising flour
75g ground almonds
A little milk
100g demerara sugar

1. Preheat the oven to 200°C/fan 180°C/gas 6, and grease and line a 900g loaf tin with butter and greaseproof paper.
2. Use an electric mixer or a wooden spoon to beat together the butter, caster sugar and the finely grated zest of 1 lemon until well combined, light and fluffy. Add a pinch of salt and the eggs, the latter one at a time, beating until each is thoroughly absorbed before adding the next.
3. Sift the flour over the top and fold in, followed by the ground almonds. Add just enough milk to take the mixture to a dropping consistency (so that it falls easily off the spoon), then spoon it into the prepared tin and smooth out the top. Bake for about 50–55 minutes, until a skewer comes out of the middle dry (a few crumbs clinging to it are fine).
4. While the cake's still hot from the oven, mix together the remaining lemon zest, the juice of both lemons and the demerara sugar, then poke holes all over the top and pour over the drizzle, waiting for the cake to absorb one lot before adding the next.
5. Allow to cool in the tin before turning out.

Perfect
Chocolate Cake

I never, ever order chocolate cake. Not because I don't like
chocolate (well, duh), but because, unless it's the kind you get for
dessert, a cake only in name, and so rich you can only pick at
teeny-tiny morsels with a fork, they always disappoint. They may
look the part, all dark and crumbly, but they rarely deliver on
flavour – they're always too, well, cakey. This one, I'm pleased to
say, will not let you down. It's moist yet fluffy, and packs a proper
cocoa punch.

Most recipes I try actually use cocoa, rather than chocolate – as with
brownies, this supplies all the flavour of chocolate with none of the
fat, creating a lighter crumb. The exceptions are
Margot Henderson's steamed chocolate cake in
You're All Invited, which uses melted chocolate for
a ridiculously rich result, and Florence
White's Really Delicious Chocolate Cake
from the 1920s, which calls for me to
grate the chocolate into the mixture. Not
an experience my knuckles would care to repeat, and thank goodness
I won't have to; it creates a strange mottled effect, although I do like
the interesting pockets of melted chocolate it creates.

I love the intense flavour of Henderson's version, but because I'm
after a lighter cake I've used a mixture of melted chocolate and
cocoa, with a few chocolate chips thrown in as a nod to White.

I've also chosen, like White, to use butter rather than the oil favoured by Nigella Lawson, because I prefer the flavour. A little milk makes the crumb even softer, like a favourite blanket.

Dense, flourless chocolate cakes, good as they are, are outside my remit for this particular recipe (and ground almonds supply too much of a marzipan flavour for my liking), and where there's flour, there must be a raising agent – simple baking powder suffices.

As usual, I've chosen the caramel flavour of light muscovado over boring white or bitter dark sugar; it works particularly well here, adding an extra layer of flavour which is the only extra I'm allowing: vanilla extract, coffee and cinnamon are all a distraction from the main attraction as far as I'm concerned.

That said, there's certainly room for some icing. Making the cake into a sandwich allows for a double whammy of excitement – London baker Lily Vanilli's simple cocoa buttercream supplies the perfect gilding, topped with Annie Bell's crushed Oreos. Though we make some fabulous chocolate biscuits in this country, the slightly bitter cocoa crunch of these American imports makes them the only option, I'm afraid.

Light enough to eat for tea, rich enough to serve for dessert, I really believe this is the ultimate chocolate cake. I'm excessively pleased with it and I hope you will be too.

Makes 1 x 20cm cake

250g butter, at room temperature, plus extra to grease
250g light muscovado sugar
½ teaspoon salt
100g cocoa powder
250g plain flour
2 teaspoons baking powder
3 large eggs
50g dark chocolate, melted and allowed to cool slightly
250ml milk
50g chocolate chips

For the buttercream
140g butter, softened
50g cocoa powder
200g icing sugar
A pinch of salt
2 tablespoons milk

To garnish
5 Oreo cookies

1. Grease and line the bases of two 20cm springform cake tins with
   butter and greaseproof paper. Preheat the oven to 200°C/
   fan 180°C/gas 6. Use a hand or stand mixer, or a wooden
   spoon, to cream together the butter and sugar with ½ teaspoon
   of salt until light and fluffy.
2. Sift together the cocoa, flour and baking powder until well
   combined. Beat the eggs into the butter mixture one at a time,
   then fold in half the flour mixture, followed by the melted

chocolate. Fold in the rest of the flour mixture, followed by just enough milk to give the batter a soft dropping consistency (so it falls off a spoon easily), and finally the chocolate chips. Divide equally between the two tins and bake for about 25–30 minutes, until firm in the centre.

3. Allow the cakes to cool completely on a wire rack, then make the buttercream. Beat the butter in a mixer, or with a wooden spoon, until fluffy, then sift in the cocoa, icing sugar and salt and, if necessary, a little milk to loosen the mixture.

4. Put one of the cakes on a serving plate and spread a third of the icing on top of it, spreading it more thickly around the edge. Place the second cake on top, then spread the rest of the icing over the whole thing, smoothing the sides with a palette knife.

5. Blitz the biscuits to a fine crumb in a food processor, and sprinkle them over the cake.

Perfect
Flapjacks

*F*lapjacks have an oddly wholesome reputation for something that's basically a mixture of butter and refined sugar, with a few oats chucked in to bind them together in an unholy alliance of deliciousness. Still, I'm not complaining — life can't all be macarons and meringues, and it's good to have a few things in your repertoire robust enough to survive being hoisted up a hill in a Barbour pocket.

There are two principal schools of flapjack: the chewy, and the crunchy. I'm firmly in the latter camp, but pleasingly the two can be  made to the same recipe; it's the cooking method that determines the texture. According to Lyle's Golden Syrup, all you need to do to turn a soft flapjack into a tooth-breaker is choose a shallower baking tray and turn the oven up. Lining it with greaseproof paper makes it easier to lift the cooked flapjacks out: all that syrup does have a tendency to be rather sticky.

The National Trust's book of *Traditional Teatime Recipes* suggests adding flour to your flapjacks, but I wouldn't — it makes them grimly stodgy, like something you might buy from a railway buffet. Jumbo oats, as recommended by Delia, give the best texture, but take a nifty tip from the internet, and cut them with easy-cook oats; it stops the finished flapjack falling apart. Pressing the mixture down firmly before baking, and allowing them to cool completely in the tin before lifting them out, also helps keep them from becoming tomorrow night's crumble topping.

Brown sugar is a must for flavour and I use demerara, for crunch; a generous amount of golden syrup helps on this front too. Tom Norrington-Davies gives a 'brilliantly trashy' recipe with cornflakes, in homage to his grandmother, which reminds me of the treats we used to be given at school for tidying our desks. It's unorthodox, and you may prefer to keep up the healthy pretence with seeds or dried fruit instead, but do chuck in a few handfuls one day; they lower the tone, but by golly it's fun down there.

Makes 16

300g butter
75g demerara sugar
120g golden syrup
A pinch of salt
250g jumbo rolled oats
200g quick-cook oats

1. Preheat the oven to 210°C/fan 190°C/gas 7 (170°C/fan 150°C/gas 3 if you prefer them chewy rather than crispy). Line a 30 x 20cm baking tin with baking parchment, cutting slits in each corner so it fits more neatly.
2. Melt the butter in a small pan with the sugar, syrup and a pinch of salt. Stir well to combine, then take off the heat and stir in the oats. Press evenly into the tin and bake for 25 minutes for chewy, 30 minutes for crunchy, until set and golden. Allow to cool completely in the tin, but cut into squares a few minutes after they come out of the oven, before they harden.

Perfect
Shortcrust Pastry

I've never understood why people are so scared of making their own pastry. The ready-made stuff is a useful freezer standby, but if you've got forty-five minutes to spare, nothing beats the satisfaction of creating your own, and shortcrust is very even-tempered, so it's unlikely to go wrong. It's the slightly crumbly, buttery stuff you get round mince pies or under quiches, and can be made with a variety of fats depending on what you're going to use it for.

A lard and butter mixture, as used by Delia Smith, gives a savoury pastry a delectable crispness – I prefer to use all butter for my sweet shortcrust, and add an egg, rather than water, to make it a little bit richer. You can increase the amount of butter in the recipes below – Darina Allen of Ballymaloe Cookery School suggests using up to 175g for the same amount of rich shortcrust – but unless you're serving it with a very plain filling, I think this is overkill. Cold butter, as ever with pastry, is a must – put it in the freezer for fifteen minutes before you start, along with a bowl of water.

Delia pits herself against just about everyone else by recommending you bring the fat to room temperature before making the pastry – this does make it easier to rub in, but I find it more difficult to work with afterwards, so I've stuck with the traditional method here. It freezes well too, so you can make your very own convenience food.

Sweet (for fruit tarts, mince pies and so on)

225g plain white flour
2 tablespoons caster sugar
A pinch of salt
120g cold butter
1 medium free-range egg, beaten
Iced water

1. Sift the flour into a large mixing bowl and add the sugar and salt. Grate in the cold butter, then rub together with your fingertips until it resembles coarse breadcrumbs.
2. Mix the egg with 2 teaspoons of cold water, and sprinkle over the mixture. Mix with a table knife; you're after a coherent but not sticky dough, so add more water very gradually until it comes together.
3. Bring into a ball with your hand, then cover with clingfilm and refrigerate for at least 20 minutes before rolling out – 5mm is the usual thickness.

Savoury (for quiches, meat pies, vegetable tarts and so on)

225g plain white flour
60g cold lard, or twice
   the amount of butter below
60g cold butter
A pinch of salt
Iced water

1. Sift the flour into a large mixing bowl. Grate in the lard and butter, add a pinch of salt, and mix with your fingertips until it resembles coarse breadcrumbs.
2. Sprinkle 2 tablespoons of cold water over the mixture. Mix with a table knife; you're after a coherent but not sticky dough, so add more water very gradually until it comes together.
3. Bring into a ball with your hand, then cover with clingfilm and refrigerate for at least 20 minutes before rolling out — 5mm is the usual thickness.

The mysteries of pastry

Can I ever make pastry with my hot little hands? Although this is one of the few good things to come out of poor circulation, actually, as long as you keep everything else as cold as possible (putting the butter and water into the freezer for 15 minutes before starting is the easiest way to do this), you should achieve success, however warm your mitts are. It's important to keep the fat cold so it doesn't melt too quickly in the oven and cause the pastry to collapse.

What's the point of blind baking? Exciting as this sounds, blind baking simply means the pastry needs to be cooked before the filling is added. You must weight it down with a substitute filling, however, or it will bubble up in the heat or cave in — you can buy special ceramic balls known as baking beans or, more thriftily, you can use dried beans or even rice for the purpose; make sure you keep them in a clearly marked jar between uses though, or someone might be in for a disappointing dinner. Line the pastry with foil (shiny-side down) or baking parchment before adding the weights, or they'll sink in, and you'll have to pick every single one out, which is no fun, particularly if you're using rice (I speak from experience).

How do I know how much pastry to use? According to the baking experts at Leiths Cookery School, to calculate the amount of pastry you'll need for a flan ring, you need to subtract 2 from the ring's diameter in inches. This will give you the amount of flour to use in ounces. For example, an 8 inch/20cm flan ring will need a pastry with 6oz/170g flour, and thus 100g butter. The recipes here should be enough for most dishes, however – leftovers can be frozen, well-wrapped in clingfilm, for a month or so.

How do I stop pastry from sticking to the work surface? You can flour or lightly oil the work surface, or, if you're really having problems (or are averse to clearing up), roll the pastry out between two sheets of greaseproof paper or clingfilm. This also makes it easier to transfer it to the dish – peel one side off, use the other one to help you guide the pastry into place, then chill and carefully peel the rest off before use.

Perfect
Rough Puff Pastry

*L*ife may not be too short to stuff a mushroom (had Shirley Conran never heard of Portobellos?) but it is almost certainly too brief to make your own puff pastry, particularly when this buttery flaky pastry is so much easier. If you want something even lighter, *Leiths Baking Bible* has a very clear explanation about how to attempt your own puff, but personally, my standards just aren't that high.

Rough puff is a layered pastry – which means that, like real puff, it is rolled and folded several times before cooking. It's used on the top of pies, as the vehicle for little nibbly things (cheese straws, for example), or when cooking things 'en croute', which is a fancy way of saying 'in a pastry case'. Every layer traps air, which expands in the oven, forcing the  pastry to rise – so the more folds you put in, the taller your pastry. I've gone for a simple two-stage process, but if you have the time and the inclination, you can add a few more (although beware; at some point, the flour and butter will separate, so don't go too far down this road!).

Although rough puff is a lot quicker, and easier, than proper puff, there are a few rules to be followed – this is baking, after all. Don't over-mix the butter and flour – it isn't shortcrust pastry. You should still be able to see small lumps of butter in the dough when you've finished – and that butter, as usual, should be ice cold, like the water.

Lard, as used by Lindsey Bareham, does make rough puff pastry slightly crisper, but I don't think it's strictly necessary, as I prefer the flavour of butter. Delia, in contrast to most other writers, brings the pastry back up to room temperature before using it, but I'm with Michel Roux and Gordon Ramsay on this one: keeping it cold makes for taller results – and saves time. (She also reckons that strong flour provides more elasticity than ordinary flour, but if it makes a difference, I can't see it, so I stick with the cheaper plain stuff.)

225g plain flour
A pinch of salt
225g very cold butter
150ml iced water

1. Sift the flour and a generous pinch of salt on to a cold surface. Cut the butter into 1cm cubes and stir it in using a table knife, then gently squidge the two together, so the flour combines with the lumps of butter – the aim is not to mix it completely, so it turns into crumbs, but to have small lumps of butter coated with flour. Like the name, it should look quite rough, even unfinished.

2. Sprinkle half the water over the top and stir it in. Add enough water to bring it into a dough (unless your kitchen is very dry, you almost certainly won't need all the water), without overworking the mixture, then cover with clingfilm and refrigerate for 20 minutes.

3. Lightly flour a work surface and shape the dough into a rectangle. Roll it out until 3 times the length.

4. Fold the top third back into the centre, then bring the bottom third up to meet it, so your dough has three layers. Give the dough a quarter turn and roll out again until three times the length, fold again as before, and chill for 20 minutes before using.

Perfect
Cheese Straws

*T*he cheese straw is the sine qua non of party food – easy to eat with one hand, simple to prepare in advance, popular with all ages and, most importantly, just the kind of fatty, salty thing people eat in quantity after a glass or too many of wine. They're the grown-up version of a big bag of Wotsits, and, gratifyingly, rather less likely to stain your hands a tell-tale orange.

Bought versions tend to disappoint, being made in the continental fashion with puff pastry – Michel Roux's homemade puff pastry twists are wonderfully light, but soften quickly as they cool, which is not ideal unless you've got a Michelin-star kitchen at the ready to churn out a fresh batch. Shortcrust, more traditional in this country, is far better: crisp, but dangerously light, especially when made with a mixture of lard and butter, as suggested by Rose Prince. (Use the same weight of butter if you'd like to keep them vegetarian friendly.)

Another feather in the cheese straw's cap is that it will happily accept just about any hard cheese you happen to have hanging around – the older the better, in fact, because as Mark Hix observes, 'to get them thin and thoroughly cheesy the cheese needs to be as strong as you can get it'. If you're buying it new, however, I'd go for Parmesan, as Hix does – Roux's Emmental and Prince's Gruyère are too mild, and most Cheddars too damp. If you'd prefer to use a British cheese, go for a really mature Cheddar, and leave it unwrapped somewhere cool to dry out a little before use.

Cheese straws can, of course, be made with ready-bought pastry, and the cheese folded in in layers, as Hix suggests (sprinkling it on top, as Michel Roux does, means much of it falls off before it even reaches the oven), but one of the advantages of making your own is that you can mix it into the dough itself, which is much easier, and gives a more even distribution.

You could just leave it at that, but as this is party food, I add a little English mustard for heat, a pinch of nutmeg for a festive flavour – and a final scattering of cheese, just to hammer home the point. Smoked paprika or cayenne pepper would also work well.

Finally, a good tip from Ireland's Ballymaloe Cookery School: although cheese straws are best eaten warm from the oven, if you must make them in advance, leave them to crisp up in a cool oven (100°C) before storing in an airtight container – they'll keep better, as long as you don't eat them all in the process.

Makes about 50 straws

    150g cold butter
    150g cold lard
      (or double the weight of butter)
    450g plain flour
    150g Parmesan, finely grated
    ½ teaspoon mustard powder
    A pinch of freshly grated nutmeg
    1 egg, beaten

1. Grate the cold butter and lard into a large mixing bowl, and tip in the flour. Rub the fat into the flour until you have a breadcrumb-like mixture, then stir in all but 2 tablespoons of cheese, plus the mustard powder and grated nutmeg.

2. Add just enough iced water to the mixture (you'll probably need 2–4 tablespoons) to bring it together into a firm dough, then wrap the dough in clingfilm or greaseproof paper and refrigerate for 30 minutes.

3. Preheat the oven to 220°C/fan 200°C/gas 7. Roll out the pastry to 5mm thick, then brush it with beaten egg and sprinkle with the remaining Parmesan. Cut into rectangular strips about 1cm wide and 10cm long, and arrange these on a lightly greased baking tray. (You can cover and refrigerate the dough at this point, until you're ready to cook.)

4. Bake the straws for about 15–20 minutes, until they're golden brown, then cool them briefly on a rack to firm up, and serve. They are best eaten warm from the oven, but if you need to make them ahead, leave them to crisp up in a cool oven (100°C) instead before removing to an airtight container – they're less likely to soften.

Perfect
Sausage Rolls

*T*he sausage roll lives a double life. Borne aloft, hot from the oven, by the hostess of a drinks party, or produced from Tupperware at a picnic, it's the finger food they eat in heaven. Emerging from a plastic wrapper at a service station, however, they're enough to drive you in the direction of an egg and cress sandwich. This is one of those foods which is always better fresh — and unless you have a decent bakery in the vicinity, that means homemade.

Not that this is any great chore: even sausage rolls made with bought pastry and split sausages are pretty good, but to really hit the jackpot, it's worth expending a little extra effort. You can make great sausage rolls with rich, crumbly shortcrust, but Delia's quick flaky pastry, spiced up with a little mustard powder, is a winner in the lightness stakes — even better than the real puff pastry from Simon Hopkinson and Lindsey Bareham's *The Prawn Cocktail Years*, which I find too delicate for the filling, and which droops sadly on cooling. (NB: Shortcrust can work better for picnics, however: it stands up more bravely to transportation.)

Ready-prepared sausagemeat can be rather salty — useful in extremis, but in comparison to Simon and Lindsey's pleasingly rustic-looking filling, made from lean belly pork, lean shoulder, streaky bacon and fat, it lacks texture and substance. Theirs is just more interesting both in texture and taste: it's meatier, and less greasy and salty.

I don't think the filling needs the extra fat, however – good bacon has quite enough of that. Ideally, ask your butcher to mince the meat for you; otherwise, patience and a sharp knife will do the trick.

Herbs and spices are a matter of personal preference, so feel free to muck about as you wish – sage and thyme are traditional partners with pork, as is the sweetness of nutmeg or mace, but the lemon zest is rather more novel. I think it really lifts the flavour of the filling, making the sausage rolls dangerously moreish – which is, of course, just what you want.

Makes about 25 small rolls

For the pastry
225g plain flour, plus extra to dust
A pinch of salt
2 teaspoons English mustard powder
175g very cold butter
ice-cold water
1 egg, beaten with a little water and salt

For the filling
300g pork belly, skin removed, minced or
finely chopped
300g pork shoulder, minced (this can often be
bought ready minced if you don't have a good butcher)
200g smoked streaky bacon, rind removed, finely chopped
Zest of 1 lemon

Nutmeg, to grate
2 tablespoons roughly chopped thyme leaves
8 sage leaves, roughly chopped

1. Sift the flour into a mixing bowl, add the salt and mustard powder and grate in the butter. Stir them all together with a knife, so the strands of butter are well coated with flour – it should look like a rough crumble mixture. Pour in just enough ice-cold water to make a dough that comes away cleanly from the bowl – do this very cautiously though, it shouldn't be at all sticky – and bring it together into a ball. Wrap in clingfilm or greaseproof paper and chill for 30 minutes.

2. Put all the meats into a large bowl and mix them well with your hands. Tip in the rest of the ingredients and mix in, seasoning well with black pepper and a little salt (remember the bacon will be salty, so don't go mad – you can always fry a little of the mixture to check the seasoning if you like). Preheat the oven to 220°C/fan 200°C/gas 7.

3. Roll out the pastry on a floured surface to a thickness of about 5mm, and cut into 3 lengthways. Divide the meat into 3 sausages, as long as your pastry, and place one slightly off-centre down each strip.

4. Brush one edge of each pastry strip with beaten egg and then fold the other side over to enclose the sausagemeat. Press the edge down to seal, and then go along it with the back of a fork to decorate. Brush the top with more eggwash, cut the rolls to the desired size, and prick each one with a fork.

5. Put the rolls on a baking tray and bake for 25 minutes, or until golden brown. Cool on a rack, and serve warm.

Perfect
Mince Pies

I realized a couple of years ago that, after the excitement of the first dozen or so, I didn't really much care for most mince pies. They're oddly sour and gloopy, with the kind of stodgy, sugary pastry that weighs on festive merriment like lead. The beauty of making your own, apart from the fact that it's possibly the very best way to get yourself in the Christmas mood, is that you can customize them to your taste.

Let's tackle the mincemeat first, which is usually a mix of dried vine fruits, mixed peel and apple base. Leiths' mincemeat includes a chopped banana, which adds a surprisingly subtle sweetness to the mix, but means that the mincemeat has to be used immediately, so the flavours don't have a chance to really develop.

Delia's recipe has a similarly unusual addition – fresh cranberries, to add some 'sharp acidity' to the mixture. Rather too much of it, in my opinion – cranberries are indeed very bitter. Her recipe also differs from the rest by gently cooking the mincemeat for 3 hours to melt the suet. This, she says, coats the apple, and stops it fermenting. It does, however, make the mixture look pretty ugly, so unless you're planning on keeping the mincemeat for a few months, it probably isn't worth it.

Mrs Beeton, of course, uses real mince in her mincemeat – lean rump steak, to be precise. It has novelty value, but I can't really see that such a small amount adds much to the pies themselves, apart from making people oddly nervous – and it has to be matured for two weeks, by which time the beef is impossible to distinguish from the rest of the ingredients. Thank God.

The *Ballymaloe Cookery Course* mincemeat, matriarch Myrtle Allen's family recipe, calls for the apple to be baked before it's stirred into the rest of the ingredients. I don't like the smoother texture this gives the mincemeat, or the breakfasty flavour that the marmalade she uses imparts, but whisky is, I have to agree, a much nicer idea than brandy – it has a more assertive booziness which seems appropriate at this time of year. Feel free to tinker with the mix of dried fruit and nuts in the recipe below – if you often find mincemeat too sweet, for example, substitute sour cherries for the glacé ones.

If you've made the mincemeat, then you may as well go the whole hog and knock up some pastry as well – the admiration you'll receive is utterly disproportionate to the actual work involved. Nigella's flaky pastry is too greasy for mince pies, we reckon – crumbly shortcrust works better, particularly if you're not going to scoff them all straight from the oven. Christmas deserves better than workaday plain shortcrust though: instead, replace some of the flour with ground almonds, as Leiths do, and add a little orange flower water, like Nigella, to make the case as tasty as the filling.

Listening to a Radio 4 phone-in while baking one Christmas, I heard mention of a family tradition I rather liked the sound of. The caller filled one mince pie every year with English mustard, turning every teatime over the festive period into a Russian roulette until the rogue pie was discovered — not a game for those with weak hearts, apparently, but a nice way to inject some danger into the cosiest season of the year.

Makes 24 pies (800g mincemeat)

For the mincemeat
50g each sultanas, raisins, currants,
   finely chopped mixed peel
50g each dried figs and glacé
   cherries, finely chopped
1 piece stem ginger, finely chopped,
   plus 1 tablespoon of its syrup
25g each almonds and pecans, finely chopped
200g dark muscovado sugar
½ teaspoon mixed spice
3 tablespoons whisky, rum or brandy
2 tablespoons suet or cold grated butter
Zest of 1 lemon, finely grated
1 small unpeeled cooking apple, coarsely grated

For the pastry
340g plain flour
A pinch of salt
225g cold butter, plus extra to grease
85g ground almonds
100g golden caster sugar
2 egg yolks
1 teaspoon orange blossom water or orange juice
Beaten egg or milk, to glaze
Icing sugar, to dust

1. Mix together the mincemeat ingredients and ideally put into sterilized jars to mature for at least a fortnight or up to a year, shaking occasionally; you can use it immediately, but it will be even better if the flavours are given a chance to blend.

2. To make the pastry, sieve the flour into a mixing bowl with a pinch of salt. Grate in the butter, and rub into the mixture until it resembles coarse breadcrumbs. Stir in the ground almonds and sugar.

3. Mix the egg yolks with the orange blossom water and 1½ tablespoons of ice-cold water. Add enough to the mixture to bring it together into a firm, but not wet dough when stirred with a knife. Shape into a ball by hand, wrap in clingfilm, and chill for half an hour.

4. Preheat the oven to 210°C/fan 190°C/gas 7. Grease your tartlet tins with butter, and roll out half the pastry on a floured surface until about 3mm thick. Using a 7cm round cutter, cut out bases to line the tartlet tins. Fill each three-quarters full with mincemeat, then roll out the other half of the pastry and cut out lids, using a 6cm round cutter. Dampen the edge with a little water or milk, and press down lightly on the pies to seal. Brush the tops with water or beaten egg, and prick the tops with a fork.

5. Bake for about 20 minutes, until golden, then leave to cool in the tins for 5 minutes before lifting out on to a wire rack. Dust with icing sugar to serve.

Fancy pies
If you have the right-shaped cutter, you can top the pies with a pastry star instead of a lid – or one made out of marzipan. You can also adapt

the crumble topping on page 397 to make a more unusual mince pie topping: try adding a couple of tablespoons of flaked almonds, a pinch of cinnamon or the zest of ½ an orange. Minimalists, however, might want to simply set a single glacé cherry, or blanched whole almond, in the middle of the mincemeat in mini mince pies — why, they practically count as a health food.

Perfect
Bakewell Tart

*F*or such a familiar foodstuff, found in every corner shop from
Aberdeen to Aberystwyth, this modest Derbyshire creation has
excited its fair share of controversy – in Bakewell itself, it's known as
a pudding, but truth be told, as Alan Davidson's *Oxford Companion to
Food* observes, 'it's more of a tart', wherever it's baked.

More interesting than this linguistic squabbling I think is the fact that,
although the first recorded recipe dates from 1836, its
medieval precursors came in two forms, both custard
and almond flavoured, and until the mid-twentieth
century it was the former that was usually served up as a
Bakewell tart or pudding. Nowadays, however, the frangipane
is a deal breaker, and I like to think I've created a good one.

My frangipane, like those in Annie Bell and Lily Vanilli's recipes, is
made in much the same way as any cake, by creaming together
ingredients – I find this gives a much fluffier result than Tamasin
Day-Lewis' version with hot butter. Bell also adds baking powder for
an even lighter texture, which I really like, especially with Lily Vanilli's
lemon zest, which stops the filling from being overpoweringly sweet.

I've not added an extra layer of marzipan, as Bell does – very much
almond overkill for me – but instead of the bog-standard jam, I've
followed Vanilli's example and made a compote. This sounds very
fussy, but actually allows you to create a slightly sharp, emphatically
fruity contrast to the sweet topping. (If you're not convinced, I'd

urge you to go for a seedy, low-sugar raspberry number instead of ordinary jam: it's a better match for the almonds than strawberry, or even apricot, which I also try.)

The pastry is almost always shortcrust these days: puff is more traditional, but proves far too flimsy for frangipane. You could add ground almonds to the dough, as Bell does, but I prefer the more savoury plain version deployed by Day-Lewis, blind baked, as Lily Vanilli suggests, so it's extra crunchy. (Vanilli makes individual cupcake sized tarts which are a great idea for a picnic – topped with an almond buttercream and a cherry, they're pretty as a picture.)

I've also gone for the traditional toasted almond topping, to add an extra crunch to every mouthful of your tart. Or pudding, if you prefer – whatever you call it, it will still be delicious.

Makes 1 x 23cm tart

For the pastry
140g plain flour, plus extra to sprinkle
A pinch of salt
85g cold butter, plus extra to grease
Ice-cold water

For the frangipane
110g butter
110g caster sugar
2 eggs, beaten
110g ground almonds
25g plain flour
½ teaspoon baking powder
Zest of ½ a lemon

For the compote (or use 100g low-sugar raspberry jam)

250g raspberries (fresh or frozen)

**25–35g caster sugar, depending on
  sweetness of tooth**

Juice of ½ a lemon

25g flaked almonds, to top

1. First make the pastry by combining the flour and salt in a mixing bowl, then grating in the cold butter. Rub the strands of butter into the flour, then stir in only as much cold water as you need to bring it together into a firm dough; it shouldn't be sticky. Alternatively use a food processor to do all this. Shape the pastry into a disc, wrap in clingfilm or baking parchment and chill for at least an hour.

2. Preheat the oven to 210°C/fan 190°C/gas 7 and grease a 23cm tart tin. Roll out the pastry on a lightly floured surface until it's large enough to line the tin, and about 5mm thick. Use to line the tin, then line the pastry with baking parchment and top with baking beans or dried pulses. Blind bake for about 15 minutes, until golden.

3. Meanwhile, make the compote, if using, by putting the berries into a small pan with the sugar and lemon juice, stirring to dissolve the sugar, and bringing to the boil. Turn down the heat slightly and simmer for about 12 minutes, stirring occasionally, until the mixture has thickened. Allow to cool slightly.

4. For the frangipane, beat together the butter and sugar in a mixing bowl with a stand/hand mixer or a wooden spoon until fluffy, then gradually beat in the eggs. Gently fold in the remaining ingredients.

5. Remove the parchment and beans from the pastry case, and

return to the oven for about 4 minutes, until the top is beginning to colour.

6. Spread the compote, or jam, over the base and spoon the frangipane over the top. Smooth out with a spatula and bake the tart for about 20 minutes, then arrange the almonds on top and bake for another 5–10 minutes, until the frangipane is golden and well risen. Serve warm (but not hot), or at room temperature, with cream.

Perfect
Treacle Tart

*U*nabashedly sweet and sticky, this is a childhood pleasure that never quite leaves you, even if you're 'really more of a fresh fruit person these days'. Though the idea of binding breadcrumbs together with sugar is a far older one, the modern tart dates only from the invention of golden syrup in 1883 – all such by-products of the refining process were known as treacle at that point, despite bearing little resemblance to the bitter black treacle that had gone before. Such thrifty ingredients made them a firm favourite with school cooks – and, unusually, generations of schoolchildren too.

I like the crispness of Simon Hopkinson and Lindsey Bareham's savoury shortcrust in the *Prawn Cocktail Years* recipe rather than anything too sweet or rich – it makes a nice contrast to the outrageous sweetness within. You'll need to blind bake it though, if you're to avoid a sticky, soggy mess.

Bread-haters might be interested to know Mark Hix makes a version with oatmeal, and Annie Bell grated apple, but neither deliver the fluffiness of the traditional recipe, though I will rather daringly be substituting malted brown for the usual white sliced: the flavour is far superior.

Bareham and Hopkinson use a high proportion of crumbs to syrup to give a crunchy, chewy texture quite different to the other wobbly fillings. To get the best of both worlds, I've used a lot of syrup, and almost as many breadcrumbs, pouring the syrup mixture over the crumbs once they're in the pastry case, so the top stays relatively dry, which helps it to crisp up in the oven. I've also added a little black treacle to the mixture, as Hix suggests, for a more rounded sweetness, and a high number of eggs, as in Shaun Rankin's recipe, to give it a custardy quality. (Note this does not mean you can't serve it with custard. Indeed you must, and preferably Bird's.)

Finish it off with a good squeeze of lemon juice, and enjoy in theoretical moderation.

Serves 8–10

For the pastry
200g plain flour, plus extra to dust
A pinch of salt
100g cold butter, cubed, plus extra to grease
3–4 tablespoons ice-cold water
1 egg, beaten with a little water

For the filling
60g butter
400g golden syrup
35g treacle
2 tablespoons double cream
1 egg, beaten with 1 egg yolk
1 tablespoon lemon juice
140g fresh brown breadcrumbs

1. Start with the pastry. Put the flour into a large bowl with a pinch

of salt. Rub in the butter with your fingertips until the mixture forms large crumbs, then add just enough cold water to bring it into a dough. Pat it into a disc, wrap in clingfilm and chill for 30 minutes.

2. Grease a deep, loose-bottomed 23cm tart tin with butter and roll the pastry out on a lightly floured surface to about 5mm thick. Use to line the tin, and prick the base in several places with a fork. Chill for 20 minutes. Meanwhile, heat the oven to 180°C/fan 160°C/gas 4.

3. Put a large sheet of foil in the pastry case, shiny side down, and fill with baking beans, dried pulses or rice. Blind bake for 15 minutes, then remove the foil and beans, brush the base with the beaten egg, and put back into the oven for 5 minutes, until golden.

4. While the shell is baking, melt the butter in a medium pan, stir in the syrup and treacle, and heat until warm and liquid, stirring to combine. Stir in the cream, take off the heat and beat in the egg and yolk, lemon juice and ¼–½ teaspoon salt, to taste.

5. Tip the breadcrumbs into the blind-baked pastry case and spread them out evenly. Pour over the syrup mixture, making sure there are no dry patches to be seen on top, then carefully put back into the oven for 20 minutes.

6. Turn the oven down to 140°C/fan 120°C/gas 1 and bake for another 15–20 minutes, until the pastry is golden brown and the filling set, but still jiggly. Allow to cool before serving.

Perfect
Tarte au Citron

I make no apologies for the name – this isn't some homely thing, generously filled with sticky lemon curd, but a proper piece of Parisian pâtisserie, with all the airs and graces that suggests. Crisp, wafer-thin pastry filled with a wobbly, delicate yellow custard, it's a restaurant classic that's surprisingly easy to recreate at home.

The Roux brothers are said to have popularized the dish in this country, but I find their version, as passed to Marco Pierre White, slightly disappointing: the richness of the lemon custard filling, with its egg yolks, sugar and double cream, seems to mute the pure, sharp flavour of the fruit itself.

Jane Grigson gives a recipe in her *Fruit Book* supplied by the local doctor in the Loire village where she and her husband owned a 'cave-cottage', with an unusual fluffy, ground almond filling. The sweetness of the nuts works well with the sour fruit, but it has a bit too much of a whiff of the Bakewell about it for me.

The 10-minute tart from American blog Smitten Kitchen, which blitzes a whole lemon with butter, sugar, eggs and cornflour, meanwhile, is just a disappointment; bitter, with an off-puttingly floury texture, the lesson I take away is that this isn't a recipe you can rush.

Much more to my taste is the lemon curd used by macaron man Pierre Hermé, made by rubbing together sugar and zest into an unusually fragrant pile of yellow snow, then adding eggs and lemon juice and cooking the lot slowly over a pan of simmering water until it's as thick as Bird's custard. He then beats in a ridiculous amount of butter, but the results are well worth it: silky smooth, and intensely, shockingly citric, it's the kind of dessert best served in elegant slivers. All I had to do to make it perfect was to tone down the sugar slightly, to further accentuate the lemon flavour.

Making your own pastry is a worthwhile enterprise here: you need a crisp, delicate pâte sucrée rather than a bog-standard crumbly shortcrust for this most refined of desserts, and that's not easy to buy in. It's pretty simple to make though — and perfectly complemented by Grigson's topping of candied lemon slices, which are both utterly delicious, and make the tart look even prettier on the table. Almost too good to eat — but not quite.

Serves 8

For the pastry
180g plain flour
90g caster sugar
A pinch of salt
90g unsalted butter, diced,
    plus extra to grease
3 egg yolks and 1 egg white

For the filling
6 unwaxed lemons
275g caster sugar
4 eggs, beaten
300g unsalted butter, diced

1. Start by making the pastry. Put the flour, sugar and a pinch of salt into a food processor and pulse briefly to mix. Add the diced butter and continue to pulse until well combined.

2. With the motor still running, add the egg yolks, and continue to pulse until the mixture comes together into a dough. Remove from the machine, shape into a disc, wrap in clingfilm or baking parchment and chill for about an hour, until it's pliable but not sticky to the touch.

3. Grease a 22cm fluted tart tin. Roll out the pastry on a lightly floured surface until it's about 5mm thick, and use to line the tin. Chill until firm, meanwhile preheating the oven to 190°C/ fan 170°C/gas 5, then line with greaseproof paper and baking beans, and blind bake for about 15 minutes, until the edges are golden. Remove the paper and beans and brush the base with egg white. Return to the oven for another 8 minutes, then remove and set aside to cool.

4. Bring a small pan of water to the boil. Meanwhile, finely zest 5 of the lemons into a heatproof bowl which will sit over, but not touching the water, then add 225g of caster sugar and rub the two together with your fingers: you should be able to smell the zest.

5. Stir the eggs and the juice of 3½ lemons into the sugar, then put the bowl over the pan. Heat, whisking gently but continuously, until the mixture thickens to the consistency of lemon curd: this should take about 20 minutes.

6. Take off the heat, leaving the pan of water where it is, and allow the filling to cool for 10 minutes, then stir in the diced butter and either whiz with a hand blender, or beat with a wooden spoon, until completely smooth. Spoon into the tart case, flatten the top and allow to cool completely.

7. Meanwhile, cut the remaining unzested lemon into delicate slices and remove any pips. Soften them in the pan of simmering

water for 10 minutes. At the same time, put the remaining 50g of sugar into a wide pan with 50ml of water, stir to dissolve, then bring to the boil. Add the drained lemon slices and simmer them for 10 minutes, then remove with a slotted spoon and arrange on top of the cooled tart. Brush the slices with more syrup, and chill to set before serving.

Perfect
Meringues

Meringues have the reputation of being difficult to make, but actually, as long as you follow a few cast-iron commandments, they're a doddle. (I say that as someone who has disregarded these rules in the past, and paid the price. As with so many baking recipes, creativity with the basics will not pay off here.) Egg whites, beaten to stiff peaks, are obviously a must, plus sugar. But here things get surprisingly complicated for a dish containing just two ingredients . . .

One of the golden rules of meringue making is that all of your equipment must be scrupulously clean, without a speck of grease, or it will be much more difficult (although not impossible, as is often claimed, according to the food chemist Hervé This) to produce the desired foam with your ingredients. Marcus Wareing suggests rubbing your mixer bowl with half a lemon before beginning, to eliminate any last specks of fat before you beat the egg whites, which is an excellent idea. (Unless you're in training for Britain's Strongest Man, a food mixer or electric whisk is a must for meringue making.)

Although I've tried a few traditional recipes which whip the egg white into a foam before gradually adding the sugar, I get the best results from Yotam Ottolenghi's half-Italian, half-French meringue, using hot sugar — unsurprising, given that his proudly billowing creations stop pedestrian traffic outside his London cafés.

Using a mix of caster and icing sugar, as Angela Nilsen of *Good Food* magazine does, makes the meringues lighter, but rather one-dimensionally sweet. If I'm making them for eating, rather than showing off, I like to use golden caster sugar — it does make them a bit beige, but the slightly caramelized flavour is gorgeous.

Meringues need clean equipment, good sugar, and, most important of all, a low oven. If you don't have an oven thermometer, and you suspect your oven is too hot, try turning it down to the coolest setting, and leaving the meringues to it. They're too good to hurry.

Makes about 10 large ones

300g caster sugar (golden if you prefer a more caramelized flavour and colour)
5 large free-range eggs, whites only, at room temperature
½ a lemon

1. Preheat the oven to 220°C/fan 200°C/gas 7. Spread the sugar over an oven tray lined with baking parchment and cook until it has just begun to melt at the edges, but not caramelize (about 8 minutes).
2. Meanwhile, crack the eggs, being careful not to drop any yolk into your whites. If you lose any bits of shell, scoop them out with a clean spoon rather than your fingers.
3. Wipe the inside of your mixing bowl, and the whisk, with the cut side of the lemon and add the egg whites. As soon as you spot the sugar beginning to melt at the edges, set the mixer to whisk at high speed while you take the sugar out of the oven, and continue to whisk for 5 minutes.
4. The mixture should be just foamy by the time you add the sugar.

Wearing oven gloves, pick up the baking parchment and tip the hot sugar slowly into the still-whisking mixer. Continue whisking until the mixture has cooled, and is glossy and will hold its shape. Turn the oven down to its lowest setting and open the door for a few minutes to help it cool down more quickly.

5. If you want to fold through any spices or other flavourings, or roll the meringues in nuts or another topping, this is your moment – but they'll be pretty good as they are.

6. Line a baking tray with parchment, and spoon the meringue on in great gorgeous blobs – remember they'll increase in size as they dry out, so leave a good couple of centimetres between each. Put them into the oven and bake for about 3 hours, until they are crisp on the outside, and sound hollow when tapped on the bottom.

7. Turn the oven off and leave the meringues in there with the door closed for 6 hours until it has cooled completely. Then immediately transfer them to an airtight container.

How to tell if your meringues are ready to bake
Properly beaten egg white should hang from the beater in a firm tuft.
You should be able to balance an egg on top.
The egg whites should be shiny, rather than dull, and smooth, rather than grainy. If you've overbeaten them, you can rescue the situation by adding another egg white and beating until just glossy.

FACT: Baked Alaska works because meringue acts as insulation – protecting the ice cream inside from the heat.

Perfect
Fudge

*F*udge is probably the first thing I cooked without supervision, and the washing up that resulted proved a salutary lesson in the tricky business of confectionery — because, although fudge isn't a complex recipe with many steps, it is one that demands the kind of precision and attention to detail lacking in your average thirteen-year-old.

Softer and crumblier than toffee, smoother and richer than its close relative tablet, its dairy content means fudge is associated particularly with the south-west, though shops churning it out in a mind-boggling array of weird and only occasionally wonderful flavours are mandatory in tourist honeypots throughout the British Isles. But before you can hope to achieve bacon-flavoured nirvana, you need a decent basic template.

Almost any sugar can be made into fudge, but I like the subtle caramel flavour of demerara, plus a dollop of golden syrup to smooth out the texture. The second, and most important, ingredient in this glorious health food is fat. Dairy fat to be precise. Clotted cream is popular in the south-west, but in combination with butter, it can feel like too much of a good thing: double cream is (very slightly) less rich, especially when tempered with a generous pinch of salt. Vanilla is the other classic flavouring (and here common or garden extract works better than seeds), but can be swapped out for all sorts of more interesting flavours, from rose water to rum.

This is one recipe where a sugar thermometer will come in useful, as just a couple of degrees can make a real difference to the texture of your fudge. The sooner you take it off the heat, the softer it will be: my preference is for 116°C fudge: firm, yet still melt-in-the-mouth. You'll need to beat it as it cools to help it thicken — at which point you can add any chopped nuts, dried fruit or even bits of crispy bacon you fancy. Don't taste it until it's cool though. Your tongue will thank you.

Makes a 23cm x 23cm tin

100g butter
550g demerara sugar
200g golden syrup
350ml double cream
1 teaspoon vanilla extract
¼–½ teaspoon sea salt flakes

1. Melt the butter, sugar, syrup and cream together in a medium, high-sided heavy-based pan, stirring just until the sugar has dissolved. Line a tin about 23cm x 23cm with greaseproof paper and ready the sugar thermometer.
2. Bring the mixture to a simmer over a medium-low heat without stirring and cook, stirring occasionally, until it reaches 116°C, stirring more regularly after it reaches 100°C and turning down the heat swiftly if it begins to catch.
3. Take off the heat and beat in the vanilla and salt or flavourings of your choice with a wooden spoon, then continue beating until the fudge has thickened and lost its shine. Pour into the tin and leave to set. (Boiling water will help with cleaning the pan.)
4. Once it's firmed up a little, slice into squares and leave to cool completely. Best kept refrigerated.

Perfect
New York Cheesecake

*T*here are two very different types of dessert rejoicing in the name of cheesecake: one baked, and one chilled. This recipe for the classic New York-style baked dessert is therefore bound to disappoint some people, but I'd urge you to give it a try nevertheless.

I've always found the traditional cream cheese and egg variety rather claggy — indeed, that seems to be part of their attraction (Delia has a good recipe if you like your cheesecakes to stick to the roof of your mouth) — but if you cut the mixture with cream you'll get a smoother, lighter result. Nigella whisks in egg whites to make her cheesecake fluffy, but I prefer a wobbly, creamy texture. I use soured cream, which gives a lovely tanginess to the filling, and a little vanilla extract and lemon zest to subtly flavour it; you really don't need anything else, I promise. It should still be slightly undercooked in the middle — if you leave it in the oven to cool, it's less likely to crack on top.

Lindy's, the Broadway deli so famous for its cheesecakes that they get a mention in the classic New York musical *Guys and Dolls*, uses a pastry crust, but a mixture of crumbly digestives and crunchy ginger nuts gives a much more interesting flavour and texture. I also quite like crushed Oreo biscuits, but it's often difficult to leave enough uneaten to work with, so, for a slightly cheaper chocolate hit, add a layer of melted chocolate to the base and allow to cool before adding the topping.

As well as providing flavour, chocolate can also act as a handy barrier between the topping and the base, helping to keep it crunchy – many recipes I've tried suffer from slightly soggy bottoms, which comes as a bit of a let-down, however delicious and creamy the topping. On a non-chocolate cheesecake, however, this can also be rectified by pre-baking the base in a hot oven, and then brushing it with egg white, which will set to form a film – a bit fiddly, but well worth it.

Cheesecakes are surprisingly fragile things at the best of times, so make life easier for yourself by investing in a springform tin – one of the ones with a separate upper, which is fastened with a spring – or you'll be hard-pressed to get the thing out in one piece.

60g digestive biscuits (4 biscuits)
60g ginger nuts (6 biscuits)
50g butter
A pinch of salt
600g full-fat cream cheese,
    at room temperature
200g soured cream
4 tablespoons cornflour
150g caster sugar
Zest of ½ a lemon, finely grated
1 teaspoon vanilla extract
4 large free-range eggs, at room
    temperature, plus 1 egg white

1. Preheat the oven to 200°C/fan 180°C/gas 6 and put a baking sheet on the middle shelf. Crush the biscuits by putting them into a freezer bag and hitting them with a rolling pin – you want to

leave some larger chunks in there, so this is better than using a food processor. Melt the butter in a small pan, then add the crumbs and a pinch of salt and mix well.

2. Spread the crumbs over the base of a 20cm cake tin, 6cm tall (springform if you have one), and press down firmly with a glass until you have a firm, flat base. Put the tin into the hot oven for 20 minutes while you make the topping.

3. Put the cheese into a large bowl and beat with a whisk to soften it and get rid of any lumps. Mix in the soured cream, cornflour, sugar, lemon zest and vanilla extract. Beat the whole eggs together, and then add them to the mixture, little by little, beating until smooth.

4. Take the tin out of the oven and brush the surface of the base lightly with egg white. Turn the oven down to 130°C/fan 110°C/gas ½, and keep the door open for a couple of minutes to help it to cool.

5. Leave the base for a few minutes while the oven cools, then pour the mixture into the tin, and shake gently to level it. You can run your finger gently over the top to get rid of any air bubbles. Put on the hot baking sheet and bake for 1½ hours, until set, but still slightly wobbly. Run a thin spatula around the edge to separate the cake from the tin, then turn the oven off and allow the cheesecake to cool completely inside before taking it out, removing from the tin and refrigerating.

Cheat: if your cheesecake cracks on top, cover it with fresh fruit, or fruit compote or coulis (see page 407), just before serving and no one will ever know the difference.

Puddings

And I mean puddings, rather than desserts. If you want to end the meal elegantly, turn to the tarte au citron on page 383. If, however, you're craving something sticky, or oozy, or even wobbly, then read on.

That's not to say none of the recipes in this chapter are suitable for what's still rather quaintly known as 'entertaining': a simple panna cotta or a magnificent trifle can both be dressed to impress, but, like the humbler bread and butter pudding, or rhubarb fool, they're both fundamentally satisfying desserts.

In other words, they encourage you to make a bit of a pig of yourself – much as I love tarte au citron, a single rich, citrussy sliver is enough. With trifle, however, I could happily eat the entire bowl, and one day, I fully intend to.

Many of these are dishes that must be prepared ahead of time, which makes them absolutely perfect candidates for guests, when you're loath to leave the conversation and start faffing about in the kitchen. Panna cotta, rhubarb fool, trifle all fit the bill – even the crèmes brûlées just need finishing off with a blowtorch.

But you don't need a tableful of people to make any of them: a homemade pudding once a week is an easy way to lift the spirits, because who could fail to be cheered by the sight of a sticky toffee pudding and a jug of yellow custard, or even a simple lemon sorbet in front of the Saturday film? This is the kind of food that makes me happy, and I hope it does the same for you.

Perfect
Crumble

Crumble is the ultimate childhood pudding: hot, sweet, and incredibly comforting. It took me nearly two decades to make something that matched up to the stuff we scoffed at school. Dot the dinner lady, I salute you – how I wish I'd asked for the recipe, instead of just seconds.

Interestingly, *The Oxford Companion to Food* suggests that crumble probably originated in the Second World War, as a quicker, easier alternative to pastry, and would have originally used whatever fat was available at the time. These days, butter is de rigueur, but sprinkling over a little water, as suggested by Nigel Slater in his *Real Fast Puddings*, helps to bind the mixture together – Nigella Lawson cleverly freezes the topping before cooking it, which slows down the melting of the butter, and gives the baked crumble a more satisfyingly craggy texture.

To boost the flavour, Mary Norwak, author of *English Puddings*, suggests using light brown sugar. This imparts a rather sandy texture, so I compromise with a mixture of this and crunchy demerara, and also substitute some of the flour with ground almonds, although not quite so much as Jane Grigson recommends, as I find this makes it a bit spongy, like a cobbler. You can also add a few handfuls of oats on top, and a little ground ginger or cinnamon if you like.

Serves 4

100g plain flour
50g ground almonds
125g chilled, unsalted butter, cut
    into cubes
35g demerara sugar
35g caster sugar, plus extra for the fruit as required
About 900g fresh fruit, stoned or cored as necessary and cut
    into chunks – cooking apples should be softened in a pan
    with a tablespoon of water and a little sugar first
Handful of porridge oats/chopped nuts (optional)

1. Preheat the oven to 220°C/fan 200°F/gas 7. Combine the
   flour, ground almonds and butter in a food processor or large
   bowl, and pulse briefly, or rub with your fingertips, until the
   mixture resembles very coarse breadcrumbs, with a few larger
   lumps. Add the sugars and stir through.

2. Sprinkle with a little cold water and rake through with a fork
   until you have a lumpy, crumbly mixture. Put this into the
   freezer for 10 minutes, or, if making ahead, into the fridge until
   you're ready to bake.

3. Meanwhile, put your prepared fruit in a lightly greased, shallow
   baking dish, and sprinkle with sugar – taste it first to see how
   much you think it needs. You can also add any spices at this
   point (½ teaspoon of ground cinnamon or ginger, for example,
   for apples or plums).

4. Arrange the crumble over the top of the fruit – don't press
   it down. Now is the time to sprinkle with oats or nuts if you
   are inclined. Bake for about 30 minutes, until golden and
   bubbling, and cool slightly before serving.

Perfect
Custard

*Y*ou really can't beat a jug of rich yellow custard. The perfect partner for an apple crumble, the only topping for a trifle, and, at its simplest, utterly divine poured over a sliced banana, it's a recipe to master. I must confess to undimmed affection for lumpy Bird's, but if you're after the proper stuff, this beats the gloopy ready-made supermarket versions hands down.

Delia's Proper Custard Sauce uses cornflour to help stabilize the mixture, and, as it starts off with double cream, only takes a couple of minutes to thicken in the pan – it's absurdly easy, and great for knocking up on a custard whim, but although luxuriously creamy, is too bland to go with anything special. Upping the egg content, and using whole milk instead, lets you in for a whole lot more stirring, but the result has a delicious silky richness that makes it worthwhile.

The important thing when making custard is to keep it cool – it will curdle if it gets too hot – so I've tried making it in a bowl suspended above a pan of simmering water, as suggested by Tom Norrington-Davies in *Just Like Mother Used to Make*, but as long as it's made in a thick-bottomed pan, and over a very low heat, it's an unnecessary precaution. I've included the instructions below, though, for the faint of heart.

Serves 6 (makes 600ml)

568ml whole milk
1 vanilla pod, slit in half and
    seeds scraped out
6 egg yolks
2 tablespoons caster sugar
1 tablespoon cornflour

1. Put the milk into a thick-bottomed pan with the vanilla pod and seeds on a gentle heat. Stir, then bring the milk to just below a simmer; do not allow it to boil.

2. Meanwhile, beat the egg yolks, sugar and cornflour together in a large bowl.

3. Remove the vanilla pod from the hot milk and pour the milk on to the yolk and sugar mixture, stirring all the time.

4. Turn the heat down as low as it will go, and pour the custard back into the pan. Stirring slowly and continuously, cook until it coats the back of a wooden spoon – the longer you cook it, the thicker it will be. Alternatively, if you're not feeling terribly brave, suspend a heatproof bowl over a pan of simmering water, pour the yolk and milk mixture into that, and proceed as above. Bear in mind you'll be tied to the stove for about 15 minutes, so put some good music on.

5. Decant into a jug and, if you're not using it immediately and dislike custard skin, press some clingfilm on to the surface to prevent one forming.

Custard know-how

To see whether custard is cooked,
lift the wooden spoon out of the
pan and run your finger down the
back — if it leaves a clear line in the
custard, it's thick enough to serve.

To rescue curdled custard, take it
off the heat immediately and strain it through a
fine sieve, then whiz in a blender until smooth —
depending on how bad the situation is, you may
then be able to add it to a milk and cornflour paste
and reheat it as normal. Or you may have to start
again. Sorry.

Custards aren't just for pudding — one of Rowley
Leigh's signature dishes at Café Anglais is a baked
Parmesan custard, served with anchovy toast. Find
the recipe online.

Vanilla is just one flavour of custard: try infusing yours
with nutmeg, star anise or a cinnamon stick instead.

Bird's custard was invented by a Birmingham
chemist in 1837 to please his wife, who was allergic
to eggs. Now that's love.

Baked custards, such as crème brûlée, crème caramel
and the classic British custard tart, use the same
basic recipe (although crème brûlée is generally
enriched with double cream rather than milk) but
the custard thickens in the oven rather than in the
pan. It's advisable to cook them in a bain-marie,
or water bath, for a really silky texture — the same
applies to bread and butter pudding.

Perfect
Apple Pie

More proof, if it were needed, that the simplest dishes are often the tastiest, this never fails to disappoint. The Americans seem to have stolen the rights somewhere along the line, only to restyle it as some sort of national fetish, but we all know that only one country makes a decent pie — although we can't blame them for trying. Interestingly, since those first brave settlers crossed the ocean with a pocketful of pips, our recipes have diverged — the American version retains the pastry shell of medieval pies (much like our own pork pie in form, if not flavour), while over here, the fashion since the seventeenth century has been a simple pastry topping. The French, meanwhile, saucy as ever, favour a topless *tarte aux pommes*, garnished with rows of fussily sliced apple and glazed with jelly, but then they're content to leave the hard work to the local pâtisserie.

A sweet, crisp shortcrust is perfect here — using a puff pastry, as bearded celebrity chef Antony Worrall Thompson recommends, seems overly fancy somehow. Nigella cooks her apples briefly in butter and sugar before adding them to the pie dish, which gives a very sweet, caramelized finish more suited to a tarte Tatin than an honest British apple pie — instead, coat them with butter in the dish itself, for a gorgeously rich, but defiantly appley filling.

The mixture of dessert and cooking apples is, like the butter, an idea borrowed from Jane Grigson's *English Food*, and gives a more interesting flavour to the filling. This way I don't think it needs cinnamon, or ginger, or any of the other adornments suggested by Delia, Jamie and all the rest, but if you do, by all means add them along with the sugar.

Serves 6

1 quantity of shortcrust pastry
  (see page 359)
600g cooking apples (about
  2 medium Bramleys)
300g dessert apples – Cox's Orange
  Pippins are ideal here
125g butter
125g golden caster sugar, plus extra to dust
1 egg, beaten with 1 teaspoon water

1. Preheat the oven to 200°C/fan 180°C/gas 6 and put a baking tray on the middle shelf. While the pastry is chilling, peel and core the apples and cut into 2–3cm chunks. Put them into a 20cm pie dish. (Don't do this too far in advance or they will discolour.)
2. Melt the butter in the microwave, or a small pan, and stir in the sugar. Pour over the apples and mix well. Brush the rim of the pie dish with beaten egg.
3. Roll out the pastry on a floured surface until about 5mm thick. Roll it around your pin, and then unroll it on top of the pie, pressing it around the rim and cutting off any excess. Brush the

top with egg, sprinkle with sugar, then cut a small hole in the centre to allow the steam to escape.

4. Put on the baking tray and bake for about 45 minutes, until golden. Serve with ice cream or custard (see page 399).

Tarting up your pie

Use any extra pastry to make an apple shape (or anything else you might fancy seeing on the top of your pie) and fix to the pastry using the egg wash. Alternatively, if you're feeling particularly ambitious, you can make a lattice top for your pie. Cut the rolled pastry into strips about 1cm wide. Brush the rim of the dish with egg wash, and cover it with pastry strips, laid end to end all the way round, cutting off any excess. Brush again with egg wash, and then arrange pastry strips in parallel across the width of the dish, leaving a gap between each so you can see the filling, and pressing them firmly down on the pastry rim at each end to secure. Brush with egg wash, then arrange a second layer of strips across the dish at an approximate 45° angle to the first to give a criss-cross effect. Trim off any excess, then put a second layer of pastry strips all the way round the rim and brush the whole lot with egg wash.

Perfect
Rice Pudding

A bowl of homemade rice pudding, golden and caramelized on top, warm and milky beneath, is one of the most wonderfully comforting sights on earth – it's a whole different dish to the starkly white and astonishingly bland stuff of school dinners, so often served with a mean little dollop of chewy red jam slopped carelessly into the middle.

Short-grain pudding rice is the best choice; basmati is too stodgy, and Angela Hartnett may use Arborio, but she's part Italian, which excuses her mistake – I think it makes it too chalky. It should be lubricated with a mixture of milk and cream – Marcus Wareing cooks a kind of vanilla custard for his, but I think this makes it far too rich to serve in anything but teeny-tiny restaurant portions – and baked slowly in the oven, rather than cooked on the hob, or it won't develop the delicately speckled skin which connoisseurs fight over.

Although the Romans used a vaguely similar dish to treat upset stomachs, rice puddings as we know them first appeared on the scene in medieval times, when they were made with almond milk and served as a luxurious Lenten dish for the piously fasting rich, rice being a pricey import in fourteenth-century Britain. To take the rice pudding back to its roots, I've eschewed the vanilla pod used in the otherwise exemplary recipe in Simon Hopkinson and Lindsey Bareham's *The Prawn Cocktail Years*, in favour of more traditional sweet spices. Inspired by the nineteenth-century recipe recommended by Delia Smith, taken from Eliza Acton's hugely popular 1845 book *Modern Cookery for Private Families*, which stayed in print for over fifty years, I've added some syrupy sweet Pedro Ximénez sherry to give the pudding a rich raisiny edge – you can substitute brandy or dark rum if you like, or leave it out altogether if you must. Like most milk puddings, it's best left to cool for a while before serving.

Serves 4

50g butter
50g soft light brown sugar
100g pudding rice
1 litre whole milk
Zest of ½ a lemon, finely grated
1 bay leaf
½ teaspoon freshly grated nutmeg
¼ teaspoon cinnamon
A pinch of salt
150ml double cream
2 tablespoons sweet sherry,
    preferably Pedro Ximénez

1. Preheat the oven to 160°C/fan 140°C/gas 3. Put the butter into a flameproof pie dish over a gentle heat, and, when melted, add the sugar. Stir and cook for a few minutes, then tip in the rice and stir to coat. Cook until the rice has swelled slightly (2–3 minutes), stirring continuously, then add the

milk and stir well to dislodge any clumps of rice and sugar on the bottom of the pan.

2. Add the lemon zest, bay leaf, spices and a pinch of salt, then pour in the cream and sherry and bring to a simmer.

3. Bake the pudding for about 2 hours, until it has set, but is still slightly wobbly; it may need a little longer than this, but check on it regularly. Serve warm, but not piping hot.

Simple fruit coulis

Take 500g of soft fruit (peaches, strawberries, apricots, blackcurrants — whatever happens to be in season) and remove any stems or stones. Chop larger fruit roughly, and then put into a blender with 300g of caster sugar and whiz to a purée. Taste and add more sugar if the fruit needs it, then keep refrigerated until ready to use.

Perfect
Bread and Butter Pudding

*T*he British equivalent of the Italian panzanella salad, or the Arabic fattoush, this is a way of using up stale bread that's good enough to merit letting bread stale for. Blandly milky, comfortingly stodgy and modestly spiced, it's a childhood favourite that still delivers.

It does, however, require patience: there's no point making it with fresh bread, it just goes soggy, which is not the idea at all. Otherwise, you can use just about any plain or sweet loaf you happen to have hanging around — potato and thyme might be a bad idea, but white bloomers, panettone or even chewy sourdough all yield pleasing, if very different results.

You also need to give the ingredients time to get to know one another — leaving the bread to soak in the custard gives a softer, more yielding texture, although I like to add a second layer of bread and custard just before baking to give the pudding a crisp top, like Delia's version.

Thankfully there's no need to spend hours caressing the custard as it infinitesimally thickens over a candle flame — the thinner the sauce, the better it will be absorbed by the bread, so you can just mix the ingredients together and pour them on without further ado. Baking the pudding in a bain-marie, as suggested by *Leiths Cookery Bible*, moderates the temperature, giving the finished dish a smoother, silkier texture which contrasts beautifully with the crunchy, caramelized top.

Because this is such a plain pudding, I don't think soaking the dried fruit in booze first is gilding the lily – it's an idea I nicked from the nineteenth-century cookery writer Eliza Acton, and she doesn't seem to have been a woman given to needless extravagance. Hot toddy and hot-ish pudding in one quivering, creamy mouthful; come on, 3 tablespoons of brandy is hardly going to break the bank. Hopefully.

Do heed the instruction to leave it to cool slightly before tucking in – like many milk-and-egg-based dishes, the flavour develops as the temperature drops.

Serves 4

50g currants, raisins or sultanas,
    or a mixture (optional)
3 tablespoons brandy (optional)
200ml whole milk
100ml double cream
1 vanilla pod, halved
Zest of ½ a lemon
75g slightly salted butter
8 slices of slightly stale good white bread,
    fruit bread or panettone
3 eggs
2 tablespoons caster sugar
1 tablespoon demerara sugar
Nutmeg, to grate

1. If using panettone or any other sort of fruit bread, feel free to skip this step. Otherwise, put the dried fruit into a small cup or jar, pour over the brandy, cover tightly and leave to plump up overnight.

2. When you're ready to start making the pudding, pour the milk and cream into a small pan and add the vanilla pod. Bring gently to a simmer, then turn off the heat, add the lemon zest and leave to cool.

3. Meanwhile, butter both the bread and your baking dish and cut the bread into triangles. Arrange half these triangles in overlapping rows inside. Beat the eggs together with the caster sugar until well combined, then remove the vanilla pod from the pan before beating the milk and the cream into the egg mixture. Pour a little more than half this custard over the bread, scatter with the soaked fruit if using, and leave to sit for 20 minutes.

4. Preheat the oven to 200°C/fan 180°C/gas 6. Use the remaining bread to make a top layer in the baking dish and drizzle over the rest of the custard. Dot the top with the rest of the butter, scatter with demerara sugar and grate a little nutmeg over the top.

5. Place the baking dish in a slightly larger roasting tin, and fill this up to halfway with cold water, to make a bain-marie.

6. Bake for 35–45 minutes, until golden brown on top. Allow to stand for 10 minutes before serving.

Perfect
Sticky Toffee Pudding

*S*TP, as us aficionados know it (or maybe that's just me), sounds like the ultimate school dinner staple; heavy, gooey and unapologetically sweet, it's just the thing to set you up for a game of lacrosse, a page of trig, and assorted other jolly wheezes. But you won't find Enid Blyton's schoolgirls tucking into sticky toffee pud after lights out, or Billy Bunter scoffing the stuff from his tuckbox, because, as every food nerd knows, it was invented in the 1970s by Francis Coulson of the Lake District's Sharrow Bay Hotel.

Mr Coulson may well have been even better at publicity than he was at puddings, however, because according to Simon Hopkinson, the late and 'legendary' chef once admitted to him that he'd adapted the idea from one Mrs Martin of Lancashire. Some years later, this good lady's son contacted Hopkinson to tell him she'd been given the recipe by a Canadian friend, which makes sticky toffee pudding about as British as flipper pie. No matter, wherever it comes from, I'm glad it made the trip.

Coulson's recipe, as recorded by Gary Rhodes (who, in an audacious attempt at thickening the plot, bills it as 'a good old English pudding which is made all over the country'), uses chopped dates, softened in boiling water, and folded into creamed butter and sugar, along with eggs, self-raising flour and vanilla essence. Stolen or not, I prefer it to Hopkinson's updated version, which blends the dates to a purée, and mixes everything together in one go — whatever Simon says about all that careful creaming being destroyed by the hot water, Coulson's recipe still rises higher than his, and boasts a more interesting texture.

Ever modish, young Jamie Oliver makes his STP with yoghurt, which keeps it moist, but weighs the batter down — and his cornucopia of sweet spices gives the whole thing a gingerbread flavour. I've restricted myself to a sober pinch of cloves, to complement the dates without overpowering them, and added walnuts, instead of Delia's pecans, to give the dish a bit of crunch: this is one dish sweet enough to stand up to their bitterness.

I like Jamie's simple toffee sauce better than all the creamy, butterscotchy varieties which appear to have been inspired by Francis Coulson's 'original' version, but it strikes me that I'm missing a trick by simply drizzling it on top of the pudding. Lining the dish with a layer of sauce, and then putting it into the freezer to firm it up while making the batter (a trick I must confess to have stolen myself, from the internet), yields sticky deliciousness all the way through — this is one transatlantic migrant which will have no problem getting its visa renewed.

Serves 6

175g medjool dates, stoned and roughly chopped
1 teaspoon bicarbonate of soda
300ml boiling water
50g unsalted butter, softened

80g golden caster sugar
80g dark muscovado sugar
2 large free-range eggs, beaten
175g plain flour
1 teaspoon baking powder
A pinch of ground cloves
A pinch of salt
75g walnut halves, roughly chopped

For the sauce
115g unsalted butter
75g golden caster sugar
40g dark muscovado sugar
140ml double cream
A pinch of salt

1. Preheat the oven to 200°C/fan 180°C/gas 6. Butter a deep baking dish approximately 24 x 24cm.
2. Make the sauce by putting all the ingredients into a pan and heating slowly until the butter has melted, then turn up the heat and bring to the boil. Boil for about 4 minutes, until the sauce has thickened enough to coat the back of a spoon. Pour half the sauce into the base of the dish and put it into the freezer.
3. Put the dates and bicarbonate of soda into a heatproof dish and cover with the boiling water. Leave to soften while you prepare the rest of the pudding.
4. Beat together the butter and both sugars until fluffy, and then beat in the eggs, a little at a time. Sift in the flour, baking powder, cloves and a pinch of salt until well combined, then add the dates and their soaking water, and the walnuts, and mix well.
5. Take the baking dish out of the freezer and pour the batter on

top of the toffee sauce. Put into the oven for 30 minutes, until firm to the touch, then take out of the oven and heat the grill to medium.

6. Poke a few small holes evenly over the surface of the pudding with a skewer or fork, and pour over the rest of the sauce. Put briefly under the grill, keeping an eye on it as it burns easily. Serve with vanilla ice cream.

Perfect
Chocolate Fondants

*T*he downfall of many a *Masterchef* hopeful, this little pudding has developed a fearsome, and quite undeserved, reputation in recent years. The issue is the fondant aspect, here indicating a melting middle rather than anything to do with French fancies or violet creams. To achieve that perfect gooey interior, concealed within a fluffy shell, you need to get your timing dead on. Crack that, and you've cracked the secret of the fondant.

That said, this is a pudding with an air of dark sophistication about it; you don't want it to smack too much of the childish chocolate cake, so starting with a sponge mixture, as Nigella Lawson does for her saucy-sounding molten chocolate babycakes, is a mistake.

Getting too fancy is equally dangerous: Raymond Blanc's meringue-like version ends up tough and dry, and John Torode's complicated recipe has me more stressed than a finalist on his television show.

This is a recipe where the best method is the simplest: beat together the eggs and yolks (for extra richness) with sugar to make the fondant light and fluffy, as suggested by Tamasin Day-Lewis, then fold in melted butter and chocolate, along with a little cocoa powder to give it a more intense flavour, and a negligible amount of flour.

The difficult part comes in the cooking – so, if you're relying on these to impress (and the recipe is easily scaled up), please, please check the timings in your oven first. A dry run of a chocolate pudding is never unwelcome, and that way, if your oven thermometer runs slightly hotter or colder than mine, you won't end up with a molten brown disaster on your hands on the night. (If that does happen, spoon them into bowls and top with ice cream – I guarantee no one will complain.)

Lining the moulds with cocoa powder, as Gordon Ramsay suggests, not only looks pretty but will help you turn the fondants out if you're feeling brave – if you have a crisis of confidence, serve them in the moulds with a blob of crème fraîche on top instead.

Makes 2

> 60g unsalted butter, cut into dice,
>   plus extra to grease
> 1 tablespoon cocoa powder
> 60g dark chocolate, broken into pieces
> 1 egg and 1 egg yolk
> 60g caster sugar
> A pinch of salt
> 1 tablespoon plain flour

1. Preheat the oven to 200°C/fan 180°C/gas 6 if baking the fondants immediately, and put a baking tray on the middle shelf. Boil the kettle for your bain-marie. Grease the inside of two small ramekins or pudding moulds with butter, then put the

cocoa into one and turn it until the inside is well coated, holding it over the second mould to catch any escaping powder. Once coated, tip the remaining cocoa into the second mould and repeat.

2. Pour the boiling water into a small pan and put the butter and chocolate pieces in a heatproof bowl set over, but not touching, the simmering water. Stir occasionally until both butter and chocolate have melted. Allow to cool slightly.

3. Whisk together the egg, yolk, sugar and a pinch of salt until pale and fluffy. Gently and slowly fold in the melted chocolate and butter, followed by the flour.

4. Spoon the mixture into the prepared moulds, stopping just short of the top – at this point the moulds can be refrigerated until needed, or even frozen for up to a month, as the puddings need to be served straight from the oven.

5. Put the fondants on the hot baking tray and bake for 12 minutes (14 if from cold, 16 if frozen), until the tops are set and beginning to come away from the sides of the moulds. Leave to rest for 30 seconds, then serve in the ramekins or loosen the edges and turn out on to plates if you're feeling confident – they're great with clotted cream or plain ice cream.

Perfect
Chocolate Mousse

*C*rêpes suzettes and rhum baba may have come and gone, and profiteroles long outstayed their welcome (or is that just me?), but chocolate mousse is one 60s favourite that's immune to the vagaries of fashion. Richly flavoured, yet light as air, there are few more perfect ways to end a meal.

The classic recipe comes from Elizabeth David. Her simple chocolate mousse, in *French Provincial Cooking*, is just that — an egg, and an ounce of chocolate (or, less neatly, 30g), per person, turned into something quite, quite magical. You don't need to add butter, like Julia Child, or double cream, like Gordon Ramsay — they'll weigh down the mixture and dilute its flavour, and fiddling around with an Italian meringue, like Franco-American chef Daniel Boulud, is just a waste of time. The reluctantly health-conscious might be interested to hear that Raymond Blanc's egg-white-only version is surprisingly good, although it does inevitably lack the richness of the whole-egg recipes.

But David's mousse, brought up to date for modern tastes with a little sugar, is unbeatably simple and delicious. The beauty of it is that you can play around with flavourings to suit your own taste — add more sugar, or leave it out completely, pop in a teaspoon of coffee, or booze (whisky, rum, Grand Marnier — whatever you fancy), a sprinkle of chilli flakes or a few cardamom seeds – just make sure you work quickly, and with a light hand, and you have one of the easiest, and most fashionably retro puddings around.

Makes 2

**60g plain chocolate
   (at least 70% cocoa)
2 medium free-range eggs
2 teaspoons caster sugar (or to taste)**

1. Break the chocolate into pieces and put it into a bowl over, but not touching, a pan of simmering water. When the chocolate begins to melt, turn the heat off. Separate the eggs.
2. Whisk the egg whites into soft peaks, then add the sugar, and whisk briefly.
3. Mix the egg yolks quickly into the melted chocolate and then whisk in a third of the egg white. Fold the rest very gently into the mixture until just combined (be careful not to over-mix), then put into two serving bowls and refrigerate for at least 4 hours, until set.

TIP

Chocolate-only chocolate mousse
Vegans, or the inquisitive of mind, might be interested in the 'Chocolate Chantilly' recipe of French culinary chemist Hervé This, which calls for chocolate to be melted with water over a low heat, then whisked up into an intensely rich,

dairy-free cream while the mixture is cooling in a bowl of iced water. It's amazing stuff. His book *Molecular Gastronomy* is a useful adjunct to *McGee on Food and Cooking*, a masterpiece which anyone seriously interested in cookery would do well to invest in — although, at 883 pages, it's perhaps not one you should feel too guilty about dipping in and out of.

Perfect
Panna Cotta

As I once heard someone say to the half-Italian chef Angela
Hartnett on television, panna cotta is just blancmange with a
fancy accent. As is so often the case, however, it's smoother,
richer, more elegant than its British counterpart — infinitely less
suitable for pouring into a bunny mould and serving at a
children's party perhaps, but rather more likely to impress at a
dinner party.

Like blancmange, however, it's child's play to make:
despite the name, there's next to no cooking
involved. But, with a recipe this simple, there's
also no room for error.

The most important ingredient, of course, is the
cream — but using just double cream, as recommended by Ursula
Ferrigno in her *Complete Italian Cookery Course*, makes the panna cotta so
rich it's almost impossible to finish. Although the dish should be
luxuriously creamy, this is too much.

Likewise, Giorgio Locatelli's milk-only recipe feels just a little bit
frugal and clean, like an Asian milk jelly. Yoghurt, as used by Nigel
Slater and Irish chef Denis Cotter, makes the panna cotta taste, well,
like yoghurt, and Angela Hartnett's long-life cream, intended to
'stabilize' the mixture, renders it sadly bland.

The Silver Spoon hedges its bets with a combination of milk and cream, which I think produces the best results – definitely creamy, but stopping just short of sickly. However, to make the flavour a little more interesting, I've added tangy buttermilk to the mixture as well, to help balance the sweetness of the cream and sugar.

The other important issue is the set: a florid Las Vegas chef once told me a good panna cotta should jiggle 'like the breast of a beautiful lady': in other words, it should be wobbly, rather than rock hard, and (and here the analogy breaks down) melt in the mouth, rather than chewy. I think I've got the balance just right here.

These are plain panna cottas, which make a beautifully simple pudding with some sharp fresh fruit, or a compote, but I've listed some alternative flavouring ideas below. If you choose an alcohol-based one like rose water, however, wait until the mixture has cooled slightly, or it'll evaporate into the ether.

Serves 4

2 x 2g leaves of gelatine
300ml double cream
115g caster sugar
100ml whole milk
50ml buttermilk
Vegetable oil, to grease

1. Soak the gelatine leaves in cold water. While they're soaking, pour the cream into a small pan, add the sugar and heat gently,

stirring until the sugar has dissolved. Bring to a simmer, then take off the heat. Allow to cool slightly.

2. Squeeze out the gelatine thoroughly and stir it into the warm cream mixture until dissolved. Pour the mixture through a sieve into a clean bowl and stir in the milk and buttermilk. Taste for sweetness and add more sugar if necessary.

3. Grease the inside of four espresso cups or small ramekins and divide the mixture between them. Allow to cool, then cover and refrigerate for at least 4 hours, or overnight, until set.

4. To turn out, dip the dishes very briefly into boiling water and invert on to plates, thumping the bottom to encourage them. Serve with berries or fruit compote.

Panna cotta flavour suggestions
- 2 teaspoons rose or orange blossom water (taste and add more if necessary – brands vary in strength) added at the end of step 2, once the mixture has cooled slightly
- 50ml neat elderflower cordial, added in step 1
- Seeds from ½ a vanilla pod, added to the cream and sugar in step 1
- A strip of unwaxed lemon zest, added to the cream in step 1, heated, then left to infuse off the heat for 15 minutes before removing. Bring the cream back to a simmer before step 2
- Crushed seeds of 2 cardamom pods, added as for lemon zest
- 1 cinnamon stick, added as for lemon zest
- 1 stalk of lemongrass, split, and 2 slices of ginger, added as for lemon zest

Perfect
Rhubarb Fool

*L*ike trifle, the very name of this wonderfully British pudding is a joy, almost a whimsy worthy of Carroll himself — Elizabeth David puts it very nicely when she writes that 'soft, pale, creamy, untroubled, the English fruit fool is the most frail and insubstantial of English summer dishes'. Although, that said, the name probably comes from the French word to press.

We're better at the kind of fruit that really shines in a fool, however: sweet-sour berries and currants, and, of course, bitter rhubarb.

The recipe here is for rhubarb, because its natural astringency makes it the most difficult fool to get right, but it's simple enough to adapt to more easygoing fruits: just simmer them gently, with sugar to taste, until they collapse, then use as below.

The important thing with rhubarb is not to add any liquid when cooking it (shame on you, Antony Worrall Thompson), or you'll dilute the flavour and make your fool runny. I don't think there's any need to waste power by baking it, as Simon Hopkinson does, when softening in a pan works just as well. Rowley Leigh suggests turning the heat up at the end to burn off any excess liquid, then draining the rhubarb before adding it to the fool — both excellent ideas that will help stop the syrup splitting the cream.

Neither do you need to purée it before use – once broken down, the strands will be easy to fold through the cream (the Nigel Slater school of half-hearted mixing, 'so the fruit forms pale pink streaks', is not for me; it may look pretty, but the distribution is very haphazard).

Nigel uses an almost 50:50 mix of cream and custard, which smacks too much of a compromise with that other great pudding, rhubarb and custard, for my liking – I prefer a blander base, for maximum contrast with the bittersweet fruit. Yoghurt is too sour on its own, but combined with cream, it lends the dish a delicate tanginess which feels appropriately summery.

Vanilla, ginger and orange are all popular flavourings for rhubarb fool, but I don't think it needs any extras. All I'm going to top it with, however, is fresh mint, to remind me of my grandmother's garden in midsummer – which is exactly where I'd like to be eating this fool.

Serves 4

450g rhubarb, roughly chopped
5 tablespoons golden caster sugar
300ml double cream
100ml Greek yoghurt
A small bunch of mint, leaves only

1. Put the chopped rhubarb into a pan with 4 tablespoons of sugar, put the lid on and heat gently until tender. Take the lid off and turn up the heat slightly to let some of the juice evaporate. Taste

and add more sugar if necessary, then drain the rhubarb well, reserving the juice. Leave to cool.

2. Pour the cream into a large bowl and whip until it forms soft peaks. Stir in the yoghurt, fold in the cooled rhubarb, making sure it's well distributed, and chill for at least an hour.

3. Serve the fool, preferably in glasses, with the reserved juice for people to pour over the top, and a few torn mint leaves atop each portion.

Perfect
Summer Pudding

*B*ritain is a land of two seasons: the short dark days of bread and butter pudding, and the lazy, light evenings of the summer variety. The latter is brief, but glorious – a solid bread pudding doesn't sound particularly suited to warmer weather, but, well chilled and sodden with sharp, fruity juices, it's remarkably refreshing stuff, especially when served with a dollop of cold, ivory cream.

I have no time for bad bread, and summer pudding is no exception – Tom Norrington-Davies may believe it's best made 'with the most plastic sliced bread you can get your mitts on' but I can't put it better than Nigel Slater: cheap bread 'turns slimy rather than moist . . . it's like eating a soggy J-cloth'.

That said, you do need thin, homogeneous slices, rather than something full of artisanal holes – go for a good soft white bloomer or similar, and ask the baker or supermarket to slice it for you.

I've always considered blackcurrants the life and soul of summer pudding, so I'm surprised by Elizabeth David's haughty claim that the authentic recipe includes only redcurrants and raspberries. Nigel Slater doesn't care – he adds blackcurrants for 'their glorious colour and for the extra snap of tartness that they bring', but I find myself won over by the gentler flavour of David's pudding, unadulterated by the aggressive tang of Ribena. Somehow, blackcurrants seem too intense and in your face for such an old-fashioned pudding.

There doesn't seem to be much need to macerate the fruit overnight with sugar, as Jane Grigson suggests: they're not noticeably more juicy the next morning, but a couple of tablespoons of water helps the situation, despite David's insistence that no further lubrication is needed.

I also find the bread soaks up more juice if the fruit is added hot, as Ballymaloe recommends, while buttering the basin makes it much easier to unmould.

The flavours of summer pudding are so modest, so subtle that to add any other ingredients seems like a mistake. That said, a delicate hint of rose water, the scent of a British garden in summer, seems pleasingly apt; but if you don't have any in the house, feel free to leave it out. Serve with thick, cold cream.

Serves 6

Butter, to grease
½ a loaf of slightly stale, good-quality
    white bread, crusts removed
225g redcurrants
675g raspberries
2–3 tablespoons caster sugar
1 teaspoon rose water

1. Grease a pudding basin or a deep, narrow bowl (about 1 litre capacity) with butter, then line it with bread, cutting the bread so it fits the basin snugly with no gaps. Cut a lid and set aside.
2. Put the fruit into a small pan with the sugar, 2 tablespoons of water and the rose water and heat very gently until just simmering – don't stir it unless absolutely necessary to avoid crushing the fruit. Taste and add more sugar, or indeed rose water, if you think it needs it.
3. Pour the hot fruit and most of the syrup into the bread-lined basin and top with the lid of bread, keeping any excess syrup (or fruit) to serve it with. Put a small plate on top of the basin, pressing it into the bread lid, and weigh it down with a tin or similar.
4. When the pudding is cool, refrigerate overnight before turning out on to a serving dish and dousing with extra syrup (useful for covering any pale patches). Serve with plenty of cream.

Perfect
Winter Trifle

*I*n my experience, people don't tend to be tepid for trifle. Either they love it — just the way their mum or their granny always made it — or they loathe it, and nothing will persuade them to give the dish a second chance. For me, it's the obvious choice to end my fantasy last meal: the other courses may change according to whim, but the trifle is not for turning. As you may have guessed, I adore the stuff.

There do seem to be as many variations on the theme as there are hundreds and thousands in a tub: this one is specifically designed for the winter, which means it doesn't contain the classic tinned raspberries which always put in an appearance in my ancestral version. The summer variation would use berries (these days, probably fresh, but macerated with a couple of spoonfuls of sugar for half an hour before use, to make them nice and juicy) instead of compote, sitting on top of boudoir biscuits soaked in medium-dry sherry, and topped with custard and cream as below, with crystallized rose petals replacing the pomegranate if I'm feeling fancy.

A successful trifle needs a solid foundation. Sarah Raven bakes a Madeira cake specifically for the occasion, and Nigella uses the same thing, but I find both disintegrate too quickly; although you want the base to soak up a goodly amount of booze and fruit juice, it should retain some texture of its own. In a summer trifle, this means sugar-coated boudoir biscuits alone, but here I've added almond-scented amaretti too: their sweet nuttiness works brilliantly with the winter fruit compote, and I like the defiant crunch they add to the base.

Sherry is an absolute must: no deviations on the theme allowed. I will generously allow you to use any fruit you like, however — frozen berries or jarred summer fruits are better than the fresh or tinned sort in winter — while gently suggesting that the compote below, full of warming spice, feels like by far the most satisfying choice for cold weather. Dried fruit always has a rather festive feel for me, and, even after soaking, retains a chewiness which ensures it won't dissolve into the background.

As I'm not using jelly (my mum never puts it into a trifle, and I won't countenance it either), a robust custard is required to take the strain of the upper layers. Bird's would be the nostalgic choice, but for a special occasion, Nigella's more luxurious cream and milk version seems appropriate; Helen Saberi's all-cream recipe is too rich for my taste (I like to eat trifle in quantity, as I may have mentioned), and Rose Prince's milk custard too thin.

On top, I've gone for a thick layer of whipped cream. A syllabub, frothy with wine and cream, is the more impressive and traditional choice, but, though delicious in its own right, I think the flavours are lost here.

Flaked almonds add a little crunch, and pomegranate seeds a flash of seasonal colour; indeed, the jewel-like sparkle is entirely appropriate for such a regal dish.

Serves 6–8 (depending on enthusiasm for trifle)

For the fruit compote

**4 handfuls of dried fruit – I like a mix of figs,
prunes and apricots**

½ a cinnamon stick

3 cloves

Zest and juice of 2 oranges

For the custard

300ml whole milk

300ml double cream

I vanilla pod, slit in half and seeds scraped out

6 egg yolks

I tablespoon cornflour

3 tablespoons caster sugar

Also

**I packet of boudoir biscuits (also sold as
lady fingers or savoiardi)**

I packet of ratafia or amaretti biscuits

100ml sweet sherry

300ml whipping cream

15g flaked almonds, toasted

Seeds of ¼ of a pomegranate

1. Begin by making the compote. Put all the ingredients into a small pan and just cover with cold water. Heat gently until it comes to the boil, then simmer for about 15 minutes, until the fruit is plump and the surrounding liquid has become slightly syrupy. Allow to cool.

2. Meanwhile, make the custard. Stir together the milk and cream

in a thick-bottomed pan and add the vanilla pod and seeds. Heat gently until the mixture is just below a simmer, but do not allow it to boil. While it heats, beat the egg yolks and cornflour together in a large heatproof bowl and stir in the sugar.

3. Remove the vanilla pod from the hot milk mixture and pour this on to the yolks and sugar, stirring all the time.

4. Turn the heat down to medium-low, and pour the custard back into the same pan. Stirring steadily, cook the mixture until it coats the back of a wooden spoon – the longer you cook it, the thicker it will get. If it doesn't appear to be thickening at all after 10 minutes, you may have the heat slightly too low, but only turn it up a notch, or you'll spoil all your hard work. (Alternatively, if you're not feeling terribly brave, suspend a heatproof bowl over, but not touching, a pan of simmering water, pour the yolk and milk mixture into that, pour the hot milk on to them, and proceed as above.) Bear in mind you'll be tied to the stove for at least 20 minutes, so put some good music on to keep yourself entertained. Once the custard has thickened, decant into a jug to cool, pressing some clingfilm on to the top to stop a skin forming.

5. Line the base of a glass trifle bowl with boudoir biscuits and, after picking out all the spices (3 cloves, remember!), spoon the cooled compote and its juices over the top. Scatter with amaretti and pour over the sherry with a liberal hand. Dollop the cooled custard on top, then cover with clingfilm and refrigerate until set.

6. Whip the cream in a large bowl to soft peaks, then spoon on top of the trifle and chill for at least 2 hours before serving.

7. Just before serving, arrange the almonds and pomegranate seeds on top of the cream – if you leave them there too long the seeds will bleed into the cream, and the nuts will go soggy. Take to the table with all due fanfare.

Perfect
Lemon Sorbet

*H*aving spurned sorbets for years as the poor man's knickerbocker glory, one hot Italian summer I suddenly realized the value of their clean, sharply refreshing qualities: double chocolate gelato doesn't quite cut the mustard above 30°C.

In their aptly-titled volume, *Ice Creams, Sorbets and Gelati*, Caroline and Robin Weir divide ices into creams (ice cream and gelati), water ices (sorbets and granitas) and hybrids, with a foot in both camps (parfaits and sherbets). Water ices are based on a flavoured sugar syrup rather than a custard — and are thus much quicker and easier to make. In fact, sorbets are the easiest ice of the lot: granitas must be beaten at regular intervals during the freezing process in order to develop their characteristic crystalline texture. Sorbets should, in theory, be smooth — which is less labour-intensive, particularly if you're lucky enough to own a machine to take care of the churning side of things.

My recipe, which borrows heavily from the Weirs' version, starts with a sugar syrup, which is easy to adjust to the tartness, or otherwise, of your fruit — lemons are such capricious creatures that it's important to sweeten to taste, even if you make the recipe a lot. It should be as sharp and zingy as a sea breeze, with flecks of aromatic zest for a double lemon hit. Some recipes add egg white, or even vodka, to improve the consistency, but it's easier, and nicer, to keep the recipe simple, and simply remember to get it out of the freezer in good time before scooping. If you want to pour vodka over the top to serve, however, I certainly won't stop you.

Serves 6–8

350g caster sugar
14 lemons, at least 5 unwaxed or well scrubbed

1. Put 250g of the sugar into a pan with 250ml of boiling water and heat until the sugar has dissolved, stirring occasionally to help it along. Bring to the boil and allow the mixture to simmer for a few minutes until slightly thickened, then allow to cool completely.
2. Finely zest the unwaxed or scrubbed lemons and juice all the fruit, then strain to remove any pulp and stray pips. Add the zest and stir in the rest of the sugar to dissolve. Chill for a couple of hours.
3. Add equal amounts of syrup and cold water to the mixture, 25ml at a time, and taste, until the flavour is to your liking – remember that freezing will mute it, so it should be quite intense at this point.
4. Put into an ice cream maker and churn according to instructions. Alternatively pour into a strong plastic box and put in the coldest part of the freezer. After 1 hour 30 minutes it should have frozen round the edges – take it out and beat it vigorously with a fork, electric whisk or in a food processor until you have a uniformly textured icy slush. Put back into the freezer and repeat at least twice more every hour and a half, then freeze for at least another hour.
5. Transfer the sorbet to the fridge for 20 minutes before serving.

Bibliography

Acton, Eliza, *Modern Cookery for Private Families* (Southover Press, 1993; first published 1845)

Acton, Johnny, and Sandler, Nick, *Preserved* (Kyle Cathie, 2009)

Aikens, Tom, *Fish* (Ebury, 2008)

Allen, Darina, *Darina Allen's Ballymaloe Cookery Course* (Kyle Cathie, 2007)

Allen, Rachel, *Bake* (Collins, 2008)

Anand, Anjum, *I Love Curry* (Quadrille, 2010)

Andrews, Colman, *Catalan Cuisine* (Grub Street, 1997)

Bareham, Lindsey, *The Big Red Book of Tomatoes* (Grub Street, 2011)

Bareham, Lindsey, *A Celebration of Soup* (Penguin, 2001)

Bayless, Rick, *Mexican Kitchen* (Absolute Press, 2007)

Beard, James, *New Fish Cookery* (Little, Brown, 1994)

Beeton, Isabella, *Mrs Beeton's Book of Household Management* (Oxford University Press, 2000; first published 1861)

Bell, Annie, *Baking Bible* (Kyle Books, 2012)

Bell, Annie, *Gorgeous Christmas* (Kyle Cathie, 2009)

Berry, Mary, *Mary Berry's Christmas Collection* (Headline, 2006)

Bertinet, Richard, *Crust: Bread to Get Your Teeth Into* (Kyle Cathie, 2007)

Bertinet, Richard, *Dough: Simple Contemporary Bread* (Kyle Cathie, 2008)

Bertinet, Richard, *Pastry* (Ebury Press, 2012)

Blanc, Raymond, *Foolproof French Cookery* (BBC Books, 2002)

Bloomfield, April, *A Girl and Her Pig* (Canongate, 2012)

Blumenthal, Heston, *In Search of Total Perfection* (Bloomsbury, 2009)

Boggiano, Angela, *Pie* (Mitchell Beazley, 2009)

Bompas, Sam, and Parr, Harry, *Feasting with Bompas and Parr* (Pavilion, 2012)

Boulestin, Marcel, *What Shall We Have Today?* (Heinemann, 1931)

Bourdain, Anthony, *Anthony Bourdain's Les Halles Cookbook* (Bloomsbury, 2004)

Brissenden, Rosemary, *South East Asian Food* (Penguin, 1996)

Butcher, Sally, *Veggiestan* (Pavilion, 2011)

Campion, Charles, *Fifty Recipes to Stake Your Life On* (Timewell Press, 2004)

Campion, Charles, *Food from Fire: The Real Barbecue Book* (Mitchell Beazley, 2006)

Child, Julia, Bertholle, Louisette, and Beck, Simone, *Mastering the Art of French Cooking* (Penguin, 2009)

Clark, Claire, *Indulge* (Absolute Press, 2010)

Clark, Max, and Spaull, Susan, *Leiths Meat Bible* (Bloomsbury, 2010)

Clark, Samuel, and Clark, Samantha, *Moro* (Ebury Press, 2001)

The Cook's Illustrated Cookbook (Cook's Illustrated, 2011)

Colwin, Laurie, *Home Cooking: A Writer in the Kitchen* (Fig Tree, 2012)

Corbin, Pam, *Preserves: River Cottage Handbook No. 2* (Bloomsbury, 2008)

Cornwall Federation of Women's Institutes, *Cornish Recipes: Ancient and Modern* (A. W. Jordan, Truro, 1930)

Costa, Margaret, *Four Seasons Cookery Book* (Grub Street, 2008)

Cotter, Denis, *Wild Garlic, Gooseberries and Me* (Collins, 2007)

David, Elizabeth, *A Book of Mediterranean Food* (Penguin, 1998)

David, Elizabeth, *An Omelette and a Glass of Wine* (Penguin, 1986)

David, Elizabeth, *English Bread and Yeast Cookery* (Grub Street, 2010)

David, Elizabeth, *French Country Cooking* (Penguin, 1996)

David, Elizabeth, *French Provincial Cooking* (Grub Street, 2007)

David, Elizabeth, *Italian Food* (Penguin, 1998)

David, Elizabeth, *Summer Cooking* (Grub Street, 1999)

Davidson, Alan (ed.), *The Oxford Companion to Food* (Oxford University Press, 1999)

Day-Lewis, Tamasin, *All You Can Eat* (Weidenfeld & Nicolson, 2008)

DeGroff, Dale, *The Craft of the Cocktail* (Proof Publishing, 2003)

Deighton, Len, *Len Deighton's French Cooking for Men* (HarperCollins, 2010)

Del Conte, Anna, *Amaretto, Apple Cake and Artichokes: The Best of Anna Del Conte* (Vintage, 2006)

Del Conte, Anna, *Risotto with Nettles* (Vintage, 2010)

Dickson Wright, Clarissa, *Clarissa's Comfort Food* (Kyle Cathie, 2008)

Dods, Meg, *The Cook and Housewife's Manual* (Rosters, 1988; originally published 1829)

Eastwood, Harry, *Carneval* (Bantam Press, 2010)

Elliot, Rose, *30-Minute Vegetarian* (Collins, 2012)

Elliot, Rose, *Vegetarian Christmas* (Thorsons, 2000)

Fearnley-Whittingstall, Hugh, *The River Cottage Meat Book* (Hodder & Stoughton, 2004)

Fearnley-Whittingstall, Hugh, and Fisher, Nick, *The River Cottage Fish Book* (Bloomsbury, 2007)

Ferrigno, Ursula, *Complete Italian Cookery Course* (Mitchell Beazley, 2006)

Francatelli, Charles E., *A Plain Cookery Book for the Working Classes* (History Press, 2010)

Gedda, Gui, and Moine, Marie-Pierre, *Cooking School Provence: Shop, Cook, and Eat Like a Local* (Dorling Kindersley, 2007)

Goldstein, Darra, *A Taste of Russia* (Sphere, 1987)

Good Housekeeping Cookery Book: The Cook's Classic Companion (Collins & Brown, 2004)

Gott, Huw, Beckett, Will, Turner, Richard, and Lepard, Dan,
  Hawksmoor at Home (Preface, 2011)
Granger, Bill, *Every Day* (Murdoch, 2006)
Gray, Rose, and Rogers, Ruth, *The River Café Classic Italian Cookbook*
  (Michael Joseph, 2009)
Grigson, Jane, *Jane Grigson's English Food* (Penguin, 1998)
Grigson, Jane, *Jane Grigson's Fruit Book* (Penguin, 2000)
Grigson, Jane, *Jane Grigson's Vegetable Book* (Penguin, 1998)
Hart, Alice, *Friends at My Table* (Quadrille, 2012)
Hartley, Dorothy, *Food in England* (Piatkus, 2009)
Hartnett, Angela, *Angela Hartnett's Cucina: Three Generations of Italian Family
  Cooking* (Ebury Press, 2007)
Hazan, Marcella, *The Essentials of Classic Italian Cooking* (Macmillan, 1980)
Helou, Anissa, *Lebanese Cuisine* (Grub Street, 1994)
Helou, Anissa, *Modern Mezze* (Quadrille, 2007)
Henderson, Margot, *You're All Invited* (Fig Tree, 2012)
Herbert, Henry and Tom, *The Fabulous Baker Brothers* (Headline, 2013)
Hermé, Pierre, *Macarons* (Grub Street, 2011)
Herráiz, Alberto, *Paella* (Phaidon, 2011)
Hilferty, Trish, *Lobster & Chips* (Absolute Press, 2005)
Hix, Mark, *British Regional Food* (Quadrille, 2008)
Holt, Geraldene, *Geraldene Holt's Cake Stall* (Prospect Books, 2011)
Hom, Ken, *Complete Chinese Cookbook* (BBC Books, 2011)
Hopkinson, Simon, *The Good Cook* (BBC Books, 2011)
Hopkinson, Simon, and Bareham, Lindsey, *The Prawn Cocktail Years*
  (Michael Joseph, 2006)
Hopkinson, Simon, and Bareham, Lindsey, *Roast Chicken and Other
  Stories* (Ebury Press, 1999)
Huang, Ching-He, *Chinese Food Made Easy* (HarperCollins, 2008)
Jackson, C. J., and Waldegrave, Caroline, *Leiths Fish Bible*
  (Bloomsbury, 2005)

Jaffrey, Madhur, *Madhur Jaffrey's Ultimate Curry Bible* (Ebury, 2003)

Johansen, Signe, *Scandilicious* (Saltyard, 2011)

Jones, Lily, *Lily Vanilli's Sweet Tooth* (Canongate, 2012)

Keller, Thomas, *Bouchon* (Artisan Division of Workman Publishing, 2004)

Keller, Thomas, and Rouxel, Sebastien, *Bouchon Bakery* (Artisan, 2012)

King, Si, and Myers, Dave, *The Hairy Bikers' Food Tour of Britain* (Weidenfeld & Nicolson, 2009)

Kiros, Tessa, *Falling Cloudberries* (Murdoch, 2004)

Lambert Ortiz, Elisabeth, *The Complete Book of Mexican Cooking* (Grub Street, 1998)

Larousse Gastronomique (Hamlyn, 2009)

Lawrence, Sue, *A Cook's Tour of Scotland* (Headline, 2006)

Lawrence, Sue, *Scots Cooking* (Headline, 2000)

Lawrence, Sue, *Scottish Baking* (Birlinn, 2016)

Lawson, Nigella, *Feast* (Chatto & Windus, 2004)

Lawson, Nigella, *How to be a Domestic Goddess* (Chatto & Windus, 2003)

Lawson, Nigella, *How to Eat: The Pleasures and Principles of Good Food* (Chatto & Windus, 1999)

Leith, Prue, and Waldegrave, Caroline, *Leiths Cookery Bible* (Bloomsbury, 2003)

Lepard, Dan, *The Handmade Loaf* (Mitchell Beazley, 2008)

Locatelli, Giorgio, *Made in Italy* (Fourth Estate, 2008)

McGee, Harold, *The Curious Cook* (HarperCollins, 1992)

McGee, Harold, *McGee on Food and Cooking* (Hodder & Stoughton, 2004)

McKee, Gwen, and Davidson, Tupper, *The Little Gumbo Book* (Quail Ridge Press, 1986)

McLagan, Jennifer, *Cooking on the Bone* (Grub Street, 2008)

McNeill, F. Marian, *The Scots Kitchen* (Birlinn, 2015)

Malouf, Tarek, *The Hummingbird Bakery Cookbook* (Ryland, Peters & Small, 2009)

Mariani, John, *The Dictionary of American Food and Drink* (Ticknor & Fields, 1983)

Menezes, Maria Teresa, *The Essential Goa Cookbook* (Penguin, 2000)

Miers, Thomasina, *Mexican Food Made Simple* (Hodder & Stoughton, 2010)

Mitcham, Howard, *Creole Gumbo and All That Jazz* (Addison-Wesley, 1978)

Moore, Victoria, *How to Drink* (Granta, 2009)

Morales, Martin, *Ceviche: Peruvian Kitchen* (Weidenfeld & Nicolson, 2013)

Nairn, Nick, *Nick Nairn Cook School* (Cassell Illustrated, 2008)

Nilsen, Angela, *Good Food: The Ultimate Recipe Book* (BBC Books, 2007)

Norrington-Davies, Tom, *Just Like Mother Used to Make* (Cassell Illustrated, 2004)

Norwak, Mary, *English Puddings: Sweet and Savoury* (Grub Street, 2009)

Oliver, Jamie, *Jamie's America* (Michael Joseph, 2009)

Oliver, Jamie, *Jamie's Dinners* (Penguin, 2004)

Oliver, Jamie, *Jamie's Italy* (Michael Joseph, 2005)

Olney, Richard, *The French Menu Cookbook* (Collins, 2010)

Ortega, Simone and Inés, *1080 Recipes* (Phaidon, 2007)

Ottolenghi, Yotam, and Tamimi, Sami, *Ottolenghi: The Cookbook* (Ebury Press, 2008)

Ottolenghi, Yotam, and Tamimi, Sami, *Plenty* (Ebury Press, 2010)

Owen, Sri, *The Rice Book* (Frances Lincoln, 2003)

Paltrow, Gwyneth, *My Father's Daughter* (Grand Central Publishing, 2011)

Paston-Williams, Sara, *Good Old-Fashioned Puddings* (National Trust Books, 2007)

Patel, Kaushy, *Prashad* (Headline Home, 2012)

Pettigrew, Jane, *Traditional Teatime Recipes* (National Trust Books, 2007)

Pizarro, José, *José Pizarro's Spanish Flavours* (Kyle Books, 2012)

Powell, Julie, *Cleaving* (Fig Tree, 2009)

Prince, Rose, *The New English Kitchen* (Fourth Estate, 2005)

Prince, Rose, *The Pocket Bakery* (Weidenfeld & Nicolson, 2013)

Prince, Thane, *Jams and Chutneys: Preserving the Harvest* (Dorling Kindersley, 2008)

Raven, Sarah, *Sarah Raven's Garden Cookbook* (Bloomsbury, 2007)

Rhodes, Gary, *New British Classics* (BBC Books, 1999)

Rhodes, Gary, *Rhodes Around Britain* (BBC Books, 1994)

Richards, Morfudd, *Lola's Ice Creams and Sundaes* (Ebury, 2009)

Roahen, Sara, *Gumbo Tales: Finding My Place at the New Orleans Table* (Norton, 2008)

Roden, Claudia, *Arabesque* (Michael Joseph, 2005)

Roden, Claudia, *The Book of Jewish Food* (Viking, 1997)

Rombauer, Irma S., *Joy of Cooking* (Simon & Schuster, 1999)

Roux, Michel, *Pastry: Savoury and Sweet* (Quadrille, 2008)

Roux, Michel, *Sauces: Savoury and Sweet* (Quadrille, 2009)

Roux, Michel Jr, *A Life in the Kitchen* (Weidenfeld & Nicolson, 2009)

Roux, Michel Jr, *The French Kitchen* (Weidenfeld & Nicolson, 2013)

Roux, Michel Jr, and Cazals, Jean, *Le Gavroche Cookbook* (Cassell, 2001)

Saberi, Helen, and Davidson, Alan, *Trifle* (Prospect Books, 2009)

Sampson, Susan, *12,167 Kitchen and Cooking Secrets* (Robert Rose, 2009)

Segnit, Niki, *The Flavour Thesaurus* (Bloomsbury, 2010)

The Silver Spoon (Phaidon, 2005)

Singh, Vivek, *The Cinnamon Club Seafood Cookbook* (Absolute Press, 2006)

Singh, Vivek, *Curry: Classic and Contemporary* (Absolute Press, 2008)

Slater, Nigel, *Appetite* (Fourth Estate, 2000)

Slater, Nigel, *Real Cooking* (Michael Joseph, 1997)

Slater, Nigel, *Real Fast Puddings* (Penguin, 2006)

Slater, Nigel, *Real Food* (Fourth Estate, 2009)

Slater, Nigel, *Tender, Vols. I & II* (Fourth Estate, 2009–10)

Smith, Delia, *Delia's Complete Cookery Course* (BBC Books, 1992)

Spaull, Susan, and Burrell, Fiona, *Leiths Baking Bible* (Bloomsbury, 2006)

Spry, Constance, and Hume, Rosemary, *The Constance Spry Cookery Book* (Grub Street, 2004)

Stein, Rick, *English Seafood Cookery* (Penguin, 1988)

Stein, Rick, *Rick Stein's India* (BBC Books, 2013)

Steingarten, Jeffrey, *It Must've Been Something I Ate* (Headline, 2003)

Stevens, Daniel, *Bread: River Cottage Handbook No. 3* (Bloomsbury, 2009)

This, Hervé, *Kitchen Mysteries: Revealing the Science of Cooking* (Columbia University Press, 2007)

Thompson, David, *Thai Street Food* (Conran, 2010)

Tonks, Mitch, *Fish Easy* (Pavilion, 2012)

Toombs, Dan, *How to Make British Indian Restaurant Style Meals* (The Curry Guy Publishing, 2012)

Torode, John, *John Torode's Beef* (Quadrille, 2008)

Usmani, Sumayya, *Summers Under the Tamarind Tree* (Frances Lincoln, 2016)

Wareing, Marcus, *How to Cook the Perfect . . .* (Dorling Kindersley, 2007)

Warner, Valentine, *The Good Table* (Mitchell Beazley, 2011)

Watson, Guy, and Baxter, Jane, *Riverford Farm Cook Book* (Fourth Estate, 2008)

Weir, Caroline and Robin, *Ice Creams, Sorbets and Gelati* (Grub Street, 2010)

White, Florence, *Good Things in England* (Persephone Books, 1999)

Willinsky, Helen, *Jerk: Barbecue from Jamaica* (Ten Speed Press, 2007)

Wilson, Bee, *Consider the Fork: A History of How We Cook and Eat* (Penguin, 2013)

Wilson, C. Anne, *Food and Drink in Britain: From the Stone Age to Recent Times* (Penguin, 1976)

Wilson, Tim and Warde, Fran, *Ginger Pig Meat Book* (Mitchell Beazley, 2011)

Wolfert, Paula, *Mediterranean Cooking* (HarperCollins, 1996)

<u>Websites</u>
bbc.co.uk/food
bbcgoodfood.com
theboywhobakes.co.uk
britishlarder.co.uk
chezpim.com
chowhound.com
dailymail.co.uk
davidlebovitz.com
deliaonline.com
deliciousmagazine.co.uk
foodnetwork.com
ft.com
theguardian.com
independent.co.uk
jamesbeard.org
jamieoliver.com
mamtaskitchen.com
marthastewart.com
meemalee.com
nigella.com
nytimes.com
oldmarkethousebrixham.co.uk
thepioneerwoman.com
porridgelady.com
racheleats.wordpress.com
saveur.com
shesimmers.com
smittenkitchen.com
telegraph.co.uk
waitrose.com

Acknowledgements

*T*hanks, as ever, to my *Guardian* editor turned watery hobo Susan Smillie — one of the bravest women I know, and not just for publishing me: *Perfect* would be rubbish without you. Also to Suzie Worroll, Malik Meer, Tim Lusher, Will Dean and everyone else on *G2* who gave so generously of their stomach space every week for a good cause. Equally huge thanks to another great woman, Juliet Annan at Fig Tree, for making all my childhood dreams come true and putting my name on a book in the first place, and to my excellent editors Jenny Lord and Sophie Missing, and the ever eagle-eyed Annie Lee, as well as Sarah Ballard and Lara, Zoe and Eli at UA for doing all the hard stuff for me. Gratitude is also due to all the many people who came round for dinner during the eight years this book has been in the making, and found themselves at a taste test instead: housemates, friends, relatives, boyfriend, even dog — thanks everyone; I promise one day we'll just get a pizza. Lastly, thanks to the column's original readers for your enthusiasm, advice and almost all of your comments: you're still wrong about the carbonara thing though.

Index

(Perfect recipes in bold)

trifle 430–33, **432**
Turner, Mich: fairy cakes 338–9

Usmani, Summayya: aloo gobi
231–2

Vanilli, Lily: Bakewell tart 376, 377
chocolate cake 354
vegetables: cooking 219–21
stock **171**
see also individual vegetables
Vianello, Toni: risotto 260
Victoria sandwich 341–3, **342**
vinaigrette 284–7, **287**
potato salad 51–3, **52**

Wareing, Marcus: chocolate chip cookies 328
meringues 387
omelette 15
pesto 300
poached eggs 8

rice pudding 405
scones 322
Weir, Caroline and Robin: lemon
sorbet 434
Welch, Tristan: cheese soufflé 68
Welsh rarebit 61–3, **62**
White, Florence: chocolate cake 353, 354
White, Marco Pierre: fish pie 176
mash 205
tarte au citron 383
Wilson, Bee: on non-stick cookware xx
wine: boeuf bourguignon 146–9, **148**
cooking with 149–50
winter trifle 430–33, **432**
Wolfert, Paula: hummus 55
Worrall Thompson, Antony:
apple pie 402
rhubarb fool 424

yeast 39
Yorkshire puddings 239–42, **240**